THE STRATEGY OF SOCIAL CHOICE

ADVANCED TEXTBOOKS IN ECONOMICS

VOLUME 18

Editors:

C.J. BLISS

M.D. INTRILIGATOR

Advisory Editors:

L. JOHANSEN

D.W. JORGENSON

M.C. KEMP

J.-J. LAFFONT

J.-F. RICHARD

NORTH-HOLLAND PUBLISHING COMPANY
AMSTERDAM · NEW YORK · OXFORD

THE STRATEGY
OF SOCIAL CHOICE

H. MOULIN
Université Paris IX – Dauphine and
Laboratoire d'Econométrie de l'Ecole Polytechnique

1983

NORTH-HOLLAND PUBLISHING COMPANY
AMSTERDAM · NEW YORK · OXFORD

© NORTH-HOLLAND PUBLISHING COMPANY – 1983

All rights reserved. No part of this publication may be reproduced, stored in a retrieval system, or transmitted, in any form or by any means, electronic, mechanical, photocopying, recording or otherwise, without the prior permission of the copyright owner.

ISBN: 0444 86371 0

Publishers

NORTH-HOLLAND PUBLISHING COMPANY
AMSTERDAM · NEW YORK · OXFORD

Sole distributors for the U.S.A. and Canada

ELSEVIER SCIENCE PUBLISHING COMPANY, INC.
52 VANDERBILT AVENUE
NEW YORK, N.Y. 10017

PRINTED IN THE NETHERLANDS

INTRODUCTION TO THE SERIES

The aim of the series is to cover topics in economics, mathematical economics and econometrics, at a level suitable for graduate students or final year undergraduates specializing in economics. There is at any time much material that has become well established in journal papers and discussion series which still awaits a clear, self-contained treatment that can easily be mastered by students without considerable preparation or extra reading. Leading specialists will be invited to contribute volumes to fill such gaps. Primary emphasis will be placed on clarity, comprehensive coverage of sensibly defined areas, and insight into fundamentals, but original ideas will not be excluded. Certain volumes will therefore add to existing knowledge, while others will serve as a means of communicating both known and new ideas in a way that will inspire and attract students not already familiar with the subject matter concerned.

The Editors

To my parents

CONTENTS

Introduction to the series   v

Preface   xi

1. Introduction   1

   1. Prescriptive judgements or descriptive analysis   1
   2. Normative versus positive approach to voting   2
   3. The implementation problem   3
   4. Classifying voting methods   4
   5. Voting and the non-strategic theory of social choice   6
   6. Development of the strategic theory of voting   7
   7. Relation to the economics of incentives   11
   References   13

2. Social choice functions and correspondences   17

   1. Summary of the results   17
   2. Basic definitions and notation   18
   3. Efficiency   20
   4. Anonymity and neutrality   22
   5. The Condorcet winner and related s.c.c.   25
   References   32

3. Monotonicity and the Arrow theorem   33

   1. Summary of the results   33
   2. Monotonic s.c.c.   34
   3. Strongly monotonic s.c.c.   39

	4. Examples of a strongly monotonic s.c.c.	43
	5. Strongly monotonic s.c.f.: Impossibility result	48
	6. Social welfare functions: Arrow's theorem	52
	References	57

4. Strategy-proofness and monotonicity 59

　1. Summary of the results 59
　2. Strategy-proof social choice functions and game forms 59
　3. The case of a binary choice 62
　4. The Gibbard–Satterthwaite theorem 65
　5. Restricted domains 68
　References 75

5. Sophisticated voting 77

　1. Summary of the results 77
　2. Sophisticated implementation 78
　3. Voting by binary choices 87
　4. A necessary condition 102
　References 115

6. Voting by veto 117

　1. Summary of the results 117
　2. The minority principle 118
　3. The proportional veto core 122
　4. Proof of theorem 1 126
　5. Voting by integer veto 135
　6. General voting by veto 148
　References 153

7. Cooperative voting 155

　1. Summary of the results 155
　2. Effectivity functions 156

3. Maximal effectivity functions	171
4. Stable effectivity functions	176
5. Implementation by strong equilibrium	188
6. Implementation by Nash equilibrium	200
References	211

Index   213

PREFACE

The theory of voting attempts to classify actual voting methods with respect to their ethical and strategical features. It provides theoretical foundations to the neoclassical approach to democracy, a rapidly developing field which we refer to as "public choice" and to welfare economics in general. It is intimately related to the incentive problem, a main issue in current economic theory.

While textbooks on social choice (Sen, Fishburn) on the one hand, or game theory (Owen, Case) on the other hand are available, only the pioneering book of Farquharson addresses the conceptual problem of strategic voting by itself. Most of the fundamental mathematical results (e.g. the Gibbard–Satterthwaite theorem) emerged only in the seventies, some of them in the late seventies (e.g. Maskin's implementation concept). At that time a technical unification took place: through the concepts of strong monotonicity and effectivity functions most of the statements that the theory had produced were rearranged consistently from Arrow's impossibility to implementation by strong equilibrium.

This volume is entirely self-contained and uses only elementary mathematical techniques: there are finitely many candidates and voters, and only ordinal preferences enter the picture. However, the conceptual difficulty of some of the definitions, and the mathematical complexity of some of the proofs, is fairly high. The economically oriented reader will find a long introduction relating the proposed results to the literature, especially to welfare economics and the economics of incentives. The mathematically minded reader will find nearly 30 problems, some of them difficult, to check his or her understanding of the theorems.

The book seems most appropriate for use in a course on social choice theory and/or public choice for first- or second-year graduate students. It could also be used in any course on game theory.

CHAPTER 1

INTRODUCTION

1. Prescriptive judgements or descriptive analysis

Social choice theory provides theoretical foundations to the neoclassical approach to democracy, a rapidly developing field which we refer to as "public choice" (see Mueller, 1979), and to welfare economics in general. Its major concern, pioneered by the eighteenth-century political philosophers, is normative decision-taking: several agents have to decide on some issue of collective interest whereas their opinions (preferences) about the issue might differ. Despite their conflicting interests, they must agree on one particular "final" decision. A "social" choice is any proposed solution of this problem, where society is taken to be the group of agents concerned by the issue, no matter how small.

To solve the possibly very sharp opposition of contradictory opinions, social choice theory takes an axiomatic route: it explores systematically all conceivable rules by which all potential conflicts are each given one particular resolution. Such rules are called social choice functions (or correspondences). They are the basic ingredient of the theory and their mathematical study its main activity.

The relevance of this approach to collective decision crucially depends on the agents' willingness and ability to bargain. Let us take an archetypical example. Given a committee, i.e. a fixed set of agents, who must together elect one among a well-defined set of candidates (these candidates being physical persons or any political or economic issue), we may think of two opposite patterns of collective behaviour. At one extreme the committee will go to an omniscient godfather, someone that every agent sees as wise and just, tell him in full detail how the various interests conflict and let him decide sovereignly. This is the ideal context where pure social choice theory operates: accordingly, it has much to say on virtually every prescriptive judgement arising in a political (e.g. what apportionment method is more fair, more faithful to the "one man one vote" doctrine?) or economic context (what is the just consumption level of a given public good? what compensatory side-payments are just among heirs sharing indivisible goods?).

At the other extreme no consensus exists on a supra authority that could settle the matter and the agents will bargain until some issue is agreed upon. Whereas in the social choice approach the decision power was indivisible into the hands of some legal or moral emanation from the collectivity (a central planner, a judge, or a referee), here the power flows pervasively and changingly among agents and coalitions of agents. Under this jungle-style decision process, the only rule is no rule and very little "social" behaviour is likely to emerge. Game theory at large addresses itself to the formalization of patterns of behaviour arising in such environments. There it provides powerful descriptive tools to analyse the subtle mixture of struggle and cooperation inherent in any social interaction.

These two approaches possess similar defects: a host of different possibly inconsistent, prescriptive judgements make it difficult for a well-meaning referee to arbitrate among arbitration methods, just as the great many game-theoretic equilibrium concepts kill any hope of making predictive use of the theory.

2. Normative versus positive approach to voting

Modern modelization of collective decision-making always involves both normative features (prescriptive value judgements as represented by social choice mappings) and positive features (strategic behaviour as represented by game-theoretic equilibrium concepts). This point is perhaps best illustrated by the literature on voting methods, since the corresponding formalization entails a minimum of a priori assumptions (as opposed to, say, the prerequisites of microeconomics) and the conceptual added value is therefore more transparent.

A voting method is a constitution attached to a given set of agents and a given set of candidates (or outcomes, or issues). Viewed as a social choice mapping this constitution scrutinizes every conceivable opinion by every individual agent over the set of candidates and selects for each particular profile (i.e. every particular choice of an opinion for each agent) a subset of "good" candidates (ideally a singleton). Viewed as a "game form" it allocates the decision power among individual agents by assigning to each agent a message space (a strategy space) from which he or she sovereignly selects one. Then, for every particular choice of one message by each agent, the game form determines the "winning" candidate.

The key observation is that every democratic voting method must simultaneously be thought of as a social choice mapping and as a game form.

Democracy, in its neoclassical acceptation, means that the goals of collective action must rely on the opinion of individuals and depend on these opinions only. Accordingly, the only relevant information for collective decision is the profile itself: as soon as an agent realizes that through his or her message he or she influences the final decision, he or she will use it strategically, i.e. manipulate the decision-making mechanism for the sake of his or her own interest. At this point freedom of speech means a right to lie, and taking into account the quoted manipulations amounts to recognizing that the agent will send a sincere message only if it is selfishly rational to do so.

3. The implementation problem

To say that the agents involved in any voting method realize that they actually face a game, the strategies of which are their own messages, induces a genuine complexity of the analysis. This is the same as saying that when firms realize that they do influence the price we switch from a perfect competition framework to oligopoly analysis. In both cases the conceptual difficulty results from the potential variety of strategic behaviour by the agents: if anything, game theory tells us that no straightforward equilibrium concept exists to describe this behaviour.

The concept of implementation proves to be central for describing the relationship between the normative (in terms of equity or efficiency axioms) and the positive (in terms of how utility-maximizing agents can be expected to distort their messages) properties of voting methods. The feasibility problem is to ask whether or not a particular ethic (represented by a social choice mapping) can be materialized in a world of selfish individual agents (i.e. the decision power can be decentralized via a particular game form) according to some pattern of behaviour (i.e. some equilibrium concept). At this level of generality the implementation problem bears upon the essence of social decision-making: given that society views as desirable certain ethics of collective decision, is it possible, and if so how, to decentralize the decision power among individual agents in such a way that by freely exercising this decision power the agents eventually select the very outcome(s) recommended as a priori desirable? Only a limited number of economic and political issues have been explored so far along this line (see section 7 below). However, the relevance of this approach to economic and political decision-making is self-evident.

Each game-theoretical equilibrium concept gives rise to a different implementation notion. Specifically, we explore the implementation problem for two non-cooperative concepts: i.e. dominant strategy equilibrium and sophisticated perfect equilibrium, and two cooperative concepts: i.e. strong equilibrium and Nash equilibrium (which in our context involve a fair amount of coalitional agreement). Non-cooperative behaviour allows us to implement social choice functions (i.e. a deterministic single candidate is chosen for all profiles) whereas cooperative behaviour implements only social choice correspondences (i.e. the choice set contains several outcomes for one profile).

4. Classifying voting methods

As the main output of the implementation technology, we will prove many theorems, some of them difficult. Altogether we classify, with respect to their main strategic features, familiar (Condorcet, Borda) and less familiar (voting by veto) voting methods. Although one can conceive infinitely many, three main families clearly emerge.

First, the scoring methods translate the utilitarian view into a voting method. Assume that every agent has a fixed scale utility, and the various utility levels (which might differ from one agent to the other) are common knowledge. Then an agent's message is simply an ordering of the various candidates and those candidates which score best on total (collective) utility are elected. Two typical examples are the Borda voting method, where the utility levels are common to each agent and in arithmetical progression, and plurality voting, where each agent casts a vote for his or her (supposedly) top candidate and the candidate(s) with the maximal number of votes are elected. These methods are characterized by a very appealing ethical property: Young's consistency property (see section 5 below). On the other hand, they give rise to wild strategic manipulations, both by non-cooperative and cooperative agents.

A second family of voting methods follows from the Condorcet majority principle: if a candidate happens to beat every other candidate in pairwise contests, in which case we call it a Condorcet winner, then it should be unconditionally elected. If a Condorcet winner exists, then the social choice that it defines is robust against any (individual and/or coalitional) manipulations. If no Condorcet winner exists (a situation often quoted as the Condorcet paradox), then cooperative instability occurs. The family of voting by binary choices does implement the Condorcet majority principle: the final outcome is reached by a predetermined sequence of binary votes, each one taken by majority vote. These methods implement a well-defined social choice function when players behave non-cooperatively (and this social choice function picks the Condorcet winner if there is one) but are highly vulnerable to coalition formation when the Condorcet paradox occurs.

The third family is the voting by veto method: the agents are endowed with a certain number of veto tokens (say one token per agent when the number of candidates exceeds the number of voters by exactly one) and they successively exercise their veto rights, ultimately leaving just one candidate on the floor, which is then elected.

These voting rules illustrate the minority principle, which claims that any minority should be given the right to veto as many candidates as is compatible with the feasibility of the decision process. This principle prevents any minority from being crushed by the opposing majority, as should indeed be the case according to the majority principle. The voting by veto methods are the natural constitutions that overcome the cooperative instability following from the Condorcet paradox. They yield a non-empty core for every possible profile and the outcome of non-cooperative voting behaviour always belongs to this core. The consistency of the cooperative and non-cooperative voting behaviour is a unique feature of voting by veto methods. Therefore the social choice correspondences that these methods implement can be justified both on normative and positive grounds as a reasonable answer to the social choice problem, especially when the electorate is small and cooperation among the voters plausible.

The most remarkable feature of the game-oriented attack of the social choice problem is the positive character of the analysis: our important results are not impossibility theorems (stating that such a list of strategic and ethical properties are inconsistent – see Arrow's famous impossibility result as well as the Gibbard–Satterthwaite theorem). On the contrary, we associate to each behavioural scenario (formalized as a specific equilibrium concept) several families of voting methods where this scenario is likely to yield a socially satisfactory outcome. These voting methods allow an egalitarian distribution of decision power among the individual agents, thus ruling out dictatorial trivialities.

The next three sections provide the historical and bibliographical information necessary to relate this course with the social choice and economics literature.

5. Voting and the non-strategic theory of social choice

During the nineteenth century various authors, including C.L. Dodgson, alias Lewis Carroll, proposed and discussed the ethical properties of several voting methods. There strategical considerations are virtually absent, except as a moral pollution of the decision process: "principles of voting make an election more of a game of skill than a real test of the wishes of the electors. My own opinion is that it is better for elections to be decided according to the wish of the majority than of those who happen to have most skill at the game" (C.L. Dodgson quoted by Farquharson, 1969).

Contemporary voting theory brought to an end the controversy first opened during the late eighteenth century by Condorcet (1785) and Borda (1781). For that purpose an axiomatic characterization of both the Condorcet majority principle and the (utilitarianist) scoring functions was built up.

May (1952) proposed a set of conditions that characterize the binary majority relation, namely aRb, iff a is preferred to b by at least as many agents as b is preferred to a. Since the binary majority relation is not in general transitive (owing to the Condorcet paradox), two routes are open to convert it to a decision rule. The first route is to pick a social choice function or correspondence that always selects a Condorcet winner if there is one, and some natural ersatz if there isn't one. Several methods were suggested, which we review in Chapter 2, section 5. Another route is to approximate the binary majority relation by a "close" ordering, thus achieving a social welfare function that aggregates a profile into a collective preference ordering. This route was taken by Kemeny (1959), Kemeny and Snell (1960), and later systematically explored by Young and Levenglick (1978). For a comprehensive survey of this approach see Barthelemy and Monjardet (1980).

A fairly simple characterization of the scoring functions was obtained by Young (1974, 1975) by considering a variable sized electorate body and using a generalized unanimity property: "if two committees meeting separately arrive at the same consensus ordering, then meeting together this should still be their consensus". Then a social choice correspondence is a scoring function if and only if it is anonymous, neutral and consistent.

The growing concern of economists for the social choice problem was initiated by Arrow's seminal book (Arrow, 1963) who formalized first the Benthamite approach to collective welfare as an aggregation of preference operators. Arrow's famous impossibility theorem points out the logical inconsistency of the Benthamite approach with the ordinalist requirement that only preference ordering should matter. In our framework we shall derive Arrow's theorem from the (technically more profound) strong monotonicity of social choice correspondences: no (deterministic) social choice function exists which is strongly monotonic and non-dictatorial (theorem 1, Chapter 3). Since the inclusion of minimal strongly monotonic s.c.c. (i.e. the more deterministic strongly monotonic s.c.c.) play a central role in cooperative voting (see Chapter 7) we regard implementation theory as the synthetic viewpoint that embodies a large number of possibility results and incorporates the traditional impossibility results as interesting particular cases, not as disturbing mathematical dead-ends. This is how Arrow himself invites us to deal with his result: "The philosophical and distributive implications of the paradox of social choice are still not clear. Certainly there is no simple way out. I hope that others will take this paradox as a challenge rather than a discouraging barrier" (Arrow, 1972).

Most of the developments of non-strategic social choice theory are to be found in the books by Sen (1970), Fishburn (1973), Pattanaik (1971) and Kelly (1979).

6. Development of the strategic theory of voting

It is self-evident that voting methods are relevant to virtually every issue within the field of public choice: taxes, public services, as well as policy orientations can be decided by vote. The economic viewpoint at these non-marketed decision problems is to regard them as games where individuals pursue their own interest within the mutual dependency pattern imposed by the decision rule.

Immediately following the massively influential book by Von Neumann and Morgenstern (1944), the pioneers of social choice theory were quite aware of the conflicting implications of any collective decision rule. Most clearly, Black (1958) and Guilbaud (1952) took into account the strategic behaviour of the electoral body. Their formal analysis of this phenomenon remains elementary, however, just as game theory at the time did not provide the necessary equilibrium concepts to analyse the subtle mixture of conflictual and cooperative behaviour generated by most decision mechanisms. Not surprisingly, then, Arrow's seminal axiomatization of the social choice problem does not include any explicit game-theoretic considerations. Next, from the early fifties to the late sixties the whole development and diversification of social choice theory ignores the manipulation problem.

Farquharson's book (1969) can be approximately taken as the starting point of the game-oriented social choice literature (see also Dummett and Farquharson, 1961) and the Gibbard–Satterthwaite theorem (see Gibbard, 1973; Satterthwaite, 1973, 1975) as its seminal result. The theorem states that when at least three candidates are to be compared, the only strategy-proof social choice functions are the dictatorial ones. In other words, no non-dictatorial voting method exists where the secret ballot paradigm applies: a voter's sincere message cannot be his or her optimal strategy no matter how the other agents vote. If the vote is actually taken by secret ballot, an incentive does exist for some agents in some profiles to acquire the information about other agents' opinions: polls are a strategical necessity.

To escape the Gibbard–Satterthwaite impossibility result, two lines of research have been investigated: one restricts the domain of feasible preferences, the other changes the equilibrium concept.

6.1. Restricted domains of preferences

Black (1958) had already noticed that when the candidates are linearly ordered and the agents' preferences are single-peaked with respect to that ordering, then a Condorcet winner exists and yields a strategy-proof voting rule.

Next Inada (1969) and Sen and Pattanaik (1969) characterized the restricted domains guaranteeing a transitive majority relation for any number of agents. By seeking restricted domains that guarantee only the existence of a Condorcet winner (the underlying majority relation being not necessarily transitive over the whole set of outcomes), many more satisfactory domains obtain. Typically the outcomes (candidates) form a tree configuration and the preferences are single-peaked with respect to that tree (Demange, 1980). This context is applicable to the location of public service problems (Hansen and Thisse, 1980).

Another generalization of Black's result consists of characterizing all non-manipulable voting rules when the preferences are single-peaked (see Moulin, 1980a, for the real line case, and Chichilnisky and Heal, 1981, for the multi-dimensional case). Chapter 4, section 5, is devoted to these various results.

Another typical restriction of the domain of preferences considers voting rules that allow some randomness in the final decision. Thus, the game form aggregates individual messages into a lottery over the candidates. Next the agents are endowed with a cardinal utility over (deterministic) candidates and compare lotteries by means of their expected utility (which amounts to restricting the domain of feasible preferences). The social choice problem was first attacked within that framework by Intriligator (1973). In that context a random dictator mechanism, where an agent is chosen to be the dictator according to a fixed probability distribution, is a fairly trivial strategy-proof decision rule. Gibbard (1977, 1978), and then Hylland (1980) proved conversely that every strategy-proof voting method is essentially a random dictator mechanism under a mild attainability assumption (when all agents agree on the top candidate a, then a should be elected with probability one). This negative result severely narrows the interest of random voting mechanisms. Another approach to this result is proposed in Barbera and Sonnenschein (1977) and McLennan (1980). Without the attainability condition, Barbera (1977, 1979) derives nice strategy-proof probabilistic voting rules.

Assuming that the preferences of individual agents are dichotomous, i.e. each agent can partition the candidates in one subset of equally good candidates and one subset of equally bad candidates, Brams and Fishburn (1978) and Weber (1978) observe that approval voting is a strategy-proof voting method. An agent casts a subset of candidates – presumably the set of his or her "good" candidates – and those candidates with a maximal number of votes are elected. The strategy-proofness feature of approval voting – although only true on a highly restricted domain of preferences – makes it an appealing alternative to plurality voting.

A general, although hardly applicable, characterization of the restricted domains on which strategy-proof social choice functions as well as Arrow's social welfare function can be constructed, is proposed in Kalai and Muller (1977). See also Kalai and Ritz (1980).

Other restrictions of preferences allow us to overcome the Gibbard–Satterthwaite impossibility result: they derive from the microeconomic theory of preferences. Typically the set A of outcomes must be endowed with some additional structure – usually A is a subset of some euclidean space – and assumptions like separability, linearity and concavity can be made on preferences. We review the main results in that direction in section 7 below.

6.2. Changing the equilibrium concept

Since the strategy-proofness requirement is too demanding, the obvious way out of the impossibility is to weaken the equilibrium notion. This is what Farquharson (1969) actually did when he originally introduced the idea of sophisticated voting. The sophisticated voters mutually anticipate their respective behaviour by successively deleting dominated strategies. Thus, if at some particular profile a dominating strategy equilibrium exists (i.e. the voting method is strategy proof at that particular profile) then it will be the sophisticated equilibrium. Farquharson observed that the family of voting by (majority) binary choices led to an unambiguous sophisticated equilibrium for all profiles.

This means that non-cooperative and completely informed agents have a fully predictable voting behaviour. A game form sharing this property is called dominance-solvable (a terminology introduced in Moulin, 1979). Voting by veto methods are another example of dominance-solvable voting methods (this was originally proved by Mueller (1978) and later generalized by Moulin (1980b)). The systematic study of dominance-solvable game forms is the subject of Chapter 5. A more detailed bibliography will be found there.

Another route, initiated by Pattanaik (1976a, 1976b) and Peleg (1978a, 1978b), investigates the consequences of cooperative voting. This is conceptually different from the non-cooperative notions of strategy-proof and sophisticated voting. The main problem there is to avoid cooperative instability. Within the framework of (cooperative) simple games, Nakamura (1975, 1979) gives first the necessary and sufficient conditions that guarantee a non-empty core for all profiles. Next, in the context of game forms Peleg uses the concept of strong equilibrium to propose an "elimination procedure" (in our terminology a social choice function) which is robust against coalitional manipulations.

This voting rule is essentially a voting by veto method. The fact that voting by veto are well-behaved procedures, both with respect to non-cooperative and cooperative behaviour of the agents, was next recognized through a series of papers by Polishuk (1978), Oren (1981), Moulin (1980c) and Dutta (1980). The whole of Chapter 6 is devoted to these results.

The last decisive step in the construction of the theory is due to Maskin who introduced the concept of implementation and derived some necessary and sufficient conditions for implementation by Nash and/or strong equilibrium (see Maskin, 1977, 1979). The main benefit derived from the implementation viewpoint is emphatically to distinguish the social choice function or correspondence summarizing one's ethical view of the collective decision problem from the game form of which the equilibrium outcomes coincide with the prescribed social choice function or correspondence. This allows us also to compare various equilibrium concepts and the related implementability conditions, as suggested in the Dasgupta–Hammond–Maskin survey paper (1979).

Two technical definitions play a central role in our theory of strategic voting. One is the notion of a strongly monotonic social choice correspondence originally introduced by Muller and Satterthwaite (1977) and Maskin (1977), in slightly different but equivalent formulations: the Muller–Satterthwaite theorem (theorem 1, Chapter 3), stating that a strongly monotonic social choice function must be dictatorial, is indeed the shortest way to derive both the Arrow and Gibbard–Satterthwaite negative results; next the strongly monotonic social choice correspondences which are inclusion minimal are implementable by Nash and (essentially) by strong equilibrium (see Chapter 7, sections 5 and 6). The second crucial device is that of an effectivity function, a generalization of cooperative simple games introduced by Moulin and Peleg (1980): it leads to the main results on cooperative voting (see Chapter 7, sections 2–5). These two concepts are the mathematical output of the strategical theory of social choice.

Closely related to the analysis developed in the subsequent chapters are the book by Pattanaik (1978) and Peleg's (1980) lecture notes.

For the sake of completeness, we mention now many works that do not seek strategically well-behaved voting methods but, on the contrary, insist on the "pathological" instability of the majority voting methods and some related other methods (which are typically derived from a cooperative simple game). For that purpose the resulting space is supposed to be a euclidean space and individual preferences are single-peaked (e.g. concave with a unique maximum point). It turns out that extremely stringent conditions must be satisfied for a Condorcet winner to exist (Plott, 1967) and that in general cycling of the binary majority relation is likely to be wild (see Cohen, 1979, and Schofield, 1977, 1978). Although this approach yields poor theoretical insight, it seems appropriate to conduct experimental studies.

7. Relation to the economics of incentives

Microeconomics has only recently addressed the issue of demand revelation in a systematic way: the problem is to design a mechanism, i.e. a specification for each individual agent, of a set of messages and a system of (positive or negative) rewards in such a way that the information conveyed by the messages is reliable, thus allowing the decision-maker to reach an efficient decision. The methodology here parallels that of the strategy of social choice, although the results are technically different and conceptually narrower.

The demand revealing mechanisms have been completely characterized in one particular context that deserves to be mentioned here: there is one public good and one private good and each agent utility is additively separable and linear with respect to money. The problem is to produce the public good at an efficient level. The difficulty is to share the cost of production among the agents concerned without inducing them to undermine their willingness to pay. Clarke (1971) and Groves and Ledyard (1977) discovered strategy-proof mechanisms that implement the efficient level of public good. Next, Green and Laffont (1979) characterized all such mechanisms by asking each agent to reveal his willingness to pay and then charging him the external effect caused by his message. This generalizes Vickrey's second bid auction (the highest bidder wins the object at the second highest bid). One negative result, however, restricts the interest of these mechanisms: it is impossible to ensure both strategy-proofness and budget-balancedness. In other words, the total price charged to individual agents cannot exactly cover the production cost for all feasible profiles (this result is due to Green and Laffont, 1979).

Other families of strategy-proof mechanisms have been proposed in several contexts: see Groves and Ledyard (1980) and Laffont and Maskin (1980). Impossibility results are also available: Hurwicz (1972) proves, in the context of pure exchange economics, that no non-dictatorial strategy-proof mechanisms exist that implement an individually rational and Pareto-optimal allocation, a result later generalized by Satterthwaite and Sonnenschein (1979).

Another approach that produces a rich family of strategy-proof decision-making mechanisms is to state the decision problem in the incomplete information framework: every agent is endowed with a "subjective" probability distribution over other agents' type and the equilibrium concept is Harsanyi's Bayesian equilibrium. D'Aspremont and Gérard-Varet (1979) remark that strategy-proof mechanisms – within the context of Bayesian Incentive Compatible (BIC) mechanisms – exist that moreover achieve an efficient outcome. Since any decision-maker must be endowed with complete information, these decision rules are of little applicability to the decentralization problem. See also Myerson (1979, 1980) for some applications of the BIC mechanisms to bargaining and the "principal agent" problem.

The sophisticated equilibrium has been little used in the context of exchange economies. Exceptions are the study of the divide and choose method (see Kolm, 1972; Crawford and Heller, 1979) and more generally the "auctioning the leadership" methods. In these mechanisms the agents bid to become the leader and the winner proposes an allocation that can only be opposed by the status quo outcome. Crawford (1979) proves that these game forms sophisticatedly implement a quasi-egalitarian allocation. When one public good is present, Moulin (1981) proposes a similar game form to implement an efficient version of the Clarke–Groves mechanism.

When cooperation of the agent is in order (which in fact can be axiomatized by either the strong equilibrium or the Nash equilibrium – see Chapter 7) the main concern has been to study mechanisms that implement the competitive equilibrium. This can be done in many ways. These results can be viewed as deepening the Debreu–Scarf equivalence result of the core and the competitive equilibrium because a game in normal form embodies more strategic information than one in characteristic form. Since the literature of the strategic approach to economic equilibrium is already vast and rapidly growing, we simply refer the reader to the book edited by Laffont (1979), the special issues of the *Review of Economic Studies* (1979, vol. XLVI, 143) and of the *Journal of Economic Theory* (1980, vol. 22, 2).

The cost allocation problem can also be given fruitful insights from the implementation viewpoint: Young (1979, 1980) proposes a non-cooperative auction mechanism to implement, by strong equilibrium, an efficient allocation of costs that is equitable in the sense of the core.

References

Arrow, K.J., 1963, Social choice and individual values, John Wiley, New York.
Arrow, K.J., 1972, Nobel Memorial Lecture.
d'Aspremont, C. and L.A. Gérard-Varet, 1979, "Incentives and incomplete information", Journal of Public Economics 11, 25–45.
Barbera, S., 1977, "The manipulation of social choice mechanisms that do not leave too much to chance", Econometrica 45, 1573–1588.
Barbera, S., 1979, "Majority and positional voting in a probabilistic framework", Review of Economic Studies 46, 397–389.
Barbera, S. and H. Sonnenschein, 1977, "Mixture social welfare functions", Research memo no. 215, Princeton University.
Barthelemy, J.P. and B. Monjardet, 1981, "The median procedure in cluster analysis and social choice theory", Mathematical Social Sciences 1, 235–267.
Black, D., 1958, The theory of committees and elections, Cambridge University Press, Cambridge.
Borda, J.C. de, 1781, Mémoires sur les élections au scrutin, Histoire de l'Académie Royale des Sciences, Paris.
Brams, S.J., 1975, Game theory and politics, Free Press, New York.
Brams, S.J. and P. Fishburn, 1978, "Approval voting", The American Political Science Review 72, 831–847.

Chichilnisky, G. and G. Heal, 1981, Incentive compatibility and local simplicity, University of Essex, mimeo.
Clarke, E., 1971, "Multipart pricing of public goods", Public Choice 11, 17–33.
Cohen, L., 1979, "Cyclic sets in multidimensional voting models", Journal of Economic Theory 20, 1–12.
Condorcet, Marquis de, 1785, Essai sur l'application de l'analyse à la probabilité des décisions rendues à la pluralité des voix, Paris.
Crawford, V., 1979, "A procedure for generating pareto efficient egalitarian equivalent allocations", Econometrica 47, 49–61.
Crawford, V. and W. Heller, 1979, "Fair division with indivisible commodities", Journal of Economic Theory 21, 10–27.
Dasgupta, P., P. Hammond and E. Maskin, 1979, "The implementation of social choice rules: Some general results on incentive compatibility", The Review of Economic Studies 46, 185–216.
Demange, G., 1980, "Single peaked orders on a tree", Cahier du Laboratoire d'Econométrie de l'Ecole Polytechnique, Paris.
Dummett, M. and R. Farquharson, 1961, "Stability in voting", Econometrica 29, 33–43.
Dutta, B., 1980, Further results on voting by veto, in: P. Pattanaik and M. Salles, eds., Proceedings of the Conference on Collective Choice, Caen, September 1980, North-Holland Publishing Company, Amsterdam.
Farquharson, R., 1969, Theory of voting, Yale University Press.
Fishburn, P.C., 1973, The theory of social choice, Princeton University Press, Princeton.
Gibbard, A., 1973, "Manipulation of voting schemes: A general result", Econometrica 41, 587–601.
Gibbard, A., 1977, "Manipulation of schemes that mix voting with chance", Econometrica 45, 665–681.
Gibbard, A., 1978, "Straightforwardness of game forms with lotteries as outcomes", Econometrica 46, 595–614.
Green, J. and J.J. Laffont, 1979, Incentives in public decision making, Studies in public economics, vol. 1, North-Holland Publishing Company.
Groves, T. and J. Ledyard, 1977, "Optimal allocations of public goods: A solution to the free-rider problem", Econometrica 45, 783–809.
Groves, T. and J. Ledyard, 1980, "The existence of efficient and incentive compatible equilibria with public goods", Econometrica 48, 6, 1487–1506.
Guilbaud, G.T., 1952, Les theories de l'intérêt général et le problème logique de l'agrégation, Economie Appliquée, Paris.
Hansen, P. and J.F. Thisse, 1980, Condorcet, Weber and Rawls locations, S.P.U.R. Université Catholique de Louvain, Belgique.
Hurwicz, L., 1972, On informationally decentralized systems, in: C.B. McGuire and R. Radner, eds., Decision and Organization, North-Holland Publishing Company, Amsterdam.
Hylland, A., 1980, Strategy-proofness of voting procedures with lotteries as outcomes and infinite sets of strategies, mimeo, Oslo, Norway.
Inada, K.I., 1969, "A note on the simple majority rule", Econometrica 37, 490–506.
Intriligator, M., 1973, "A probabilistic model of social choice", The Review of Economic Studies 40, 553–560.
Journal of Economic Theory, 1980, Special issue on non-cooperative approaches to the theory of perfect competition, 22, 2.
Kalai, E. and E. Muller, 1977, "Characterizations of domains admitting non-dictatorial social welfare functions and non-manipulable voting procedures", Journal of Economic Theory 16, 456–469.
Kalai, E. and Z. Ritz, 1980, "Characterization of the private alternatives domains admitting Arrow social welfare functions, Journal of Economic Theory 22, 12–22.

Kelly, J.S., 1979, Arrow impossibility theorems, Academic Press, New York.
Kemeny, J., 1959, "Mathematics without numbers", Daedalus 88, 571–591.
Kemeny, J. and L. Snell, 1960, Mathematical models in the Social Sciences, Ginn, Boston.
Kolm, S.C., 1972, Justice et Equité, Monographie du Séminaire d'Econométrie no. 8, C.N.R.S., Paris.
Laffond, G., 1980, Révélation des préférences et utilités unimodales, Thèse, CEREMADE, Université Paris IX.
Laffont, J.J., editor, 1979, Aggregation and revelation of preferences, Studies in Public Economics, vol. 2, North-Holland Publishing Company, Amsterdam.
Laffont, J.J. and E. Maskin, 1980, "A differential approach to dominant strategy mechanism", Econometrica 48, 6, 1507–1520.
Maskin, E., 1977, "Nash equilibrium and welfare optimality", forthcoming in Mathematics of Operations Research.
Maskin, E., 1979, "Implementation and strong Nash equilibrium", in: J.J. Laffont, ed., Aggregation and revelation of preferences, North-Holland Publishing Company, Amsterdam.
May, K.O., 1952, "A set of independent necessary and sufficient conditions for simple majority decision", Econometrica 20, 680–684.
McLennan, A., 1980, "Randomized preference aggregation: Additivity of power and strategy proofness", Journal of Economic Theory 22, 1–11.
Moulin, H., 1979, "Dominance-solvable voting schemes", Econometrica 47, 1337–1351.
Moulin, H., 1980a, "On strategy-proofness and single peakedness", Public Choice 35, 437–455.
Moulin, H., 1980b, "Implementing efficient, anonymous and neutral social choice functions", Journal of Mathematical Economics 7, 249–269.
Moulin, H., 1981, "Implementing just and efficient decision making", Journal of Public Economics 16, 193–213.
Moulin, H., 1982, "Voting with proportional veto power", Econometrica 50, 145–162.
Moulin, H. and B. Peleg, 1982, "Core of effectivity functions and implementation theory", Journal of Mathematical Economics 10, 115–145.
Mueller, D., 1978, "Voting by veto", Journal of Public Economics 10, 57–75.
Mueller, D., 1979, Public choice, Cambridge Surveys of Economic Literature, Cambridge University Press, Cambridge.
Mueller, E. and M. Satterthwaite, 1977, "The equivalence of strong positive association and strategy proofness", Journal of Economic Theory 14, 412–418.
Myerson, R., 1979, "Incentive compatibility and the bargaining problem", Econometrica 47, 61–73.
Myerson, R., 1980, "Optimal coordination mechanisms in generalized principal agent problems", D.P. 429 Kellog G.S.M., Northwestern University.
Nakamura, K., 1975, "The core of a simple game with ordinal preferences", International Journal of Game Theory 4, 95–104.
Nakamura, K., 1979, "The vetoers in a simple game with ordinal preferences", International Journal of Game Theory 8, 55–61.
Neumann, J. von and O. Morgenstern, 1944, Theory of games and economic behaviour, Princeton University Press, Princeton, New Jersey.
Oren, I., 1981, "The structure of exactly strongly consistent social choice functions", Journal of Mathematical Economics 8, 207–221.
Pattanaik, P., 1971, Voting and collective choice, Cambridge University Press, Cambridge.
Pattanaik, P., 1976a, "Threats, counter-threats and strategic voting", Econometrica 44, 91–104.
Pattanaik, P., 1976b, "Counter-threats and strategic manipulations under voting schemes", Review of Economic Studies 43, 11–18.
Pattanaik, P., 1978, Strategy and group choice, North-Holland Publishing Company, Amsterdam.

Peleg, B., 1978a, "Consistent voting systems", Econometrica 46, 153–161.
Peleg, B., 1978b, "Representation of simple games by social choice functions", International Journal of Game Theory 7, 81–94.
Peleg, B., 1980, Game theoretic analysis of voting in committees, The Institute of Mathematics, The Hebrew University of Jerusalem.
Plott, C., 1967, "A notion of equilibrium and its possibility under majority rule", American Economic Review 57.
Polishuk, I., 1978, "Monotonicity and uniqueness of consistent voting systems", forthcoming in Journal of Mathematical Economics.
Review of Economic Studies, 1979, vol. XLVI, no. 143.
Satterthwaite, M.A., 1973, The existence of strategy-proof voting procedures, a topic in social choice theory, Ph.D. Dissertation, University of Wisconsin, Madison.
Satterthwaite, M.A., 1975, "Strategy-proofness and Arrow's conditions: Existence and correspondence theorems for voting procedures and social welfare functions", Journal of Economic Theory 10, 187–217.
Satterthwaite, M.A. and H. Sonnenschein, 1979, Strategy-proof allocation mechanisms, D.P. no. 395, Kellog's G.M.S., Northwestern University.
Schofield, N., 1977, "Transitivity of preferences on a smooth manifold of alternatives", Journal of Economic Theory 14, 149–171.
Schofield, N., 1978, "Instability of simple dynamic games", Review of Economic Studies 45, 575–594.
Sen, A., 1970, Collective choice and social welfare, North-Holland Publishing Company, Amsterdam.
Sen, A. and P.K. Pattanaik, 1969, "Necessary and sufficient conditions for rational choice under majority decision", Journal of Economic Theory 1, 178–202.
Weber, R., 1978, Comparison of Public Choice Systems, Cowles Foundation Discussion Paper no. 498, New Haven.
Young, H.P., 1974, "An axiomatization of Borda's rule", Journal of Economic Theory 9, 43–52.
Young, H.P., 1975, "Social choice scoring functions", SIAM Journal of Applied Mathematics 28, 824–838.
Young, H.P., 1979, "Exploitable surplus in n-person games", in: Brams, Schotter and Schwödiauer, eds., Applied game theory, Physica-Verlag, Wien.
Young, H.P., 1980, "Cost allocation and demand revelation in public enterprises", I.I.A.S.A. working paper, 80–130, Laxenburg, Austria.
Young, H.P. and A. Levenglick, 1978, "A consistent extension of Condorcet's election principle", SIAM Journal of Applied Mathematics 35, 285–300.

CHAPTER 2

SOCIAL CHOICE FUNCTIONS AND CORRESPONDENCES

1. Summary of the results

We assume a world of innocence and frankness where everybody's preferences are publicly known or revealed without bias and the only question is to compare various notions of "good" decisions.

We formalize the collective decision problem by a mapping that selects for any given profile of preferences (i.e. the data of one preference for each individual agent) a subset of outcomes, called the choice set, and interpreted as the set of collectively desirable outcomes for that profile. This mapping is a social choice correspondence: it summarizes a particular ethic of collective decisions, a compromising rule applicable to every possible configuration of individual preferences.

All familiar voting methods satisfy three basic properties: efficiency (the outcome should be Pareto optimal), anonymity (every agent's opinion should influence equally the final decision) and neutrality (no outcome should be a priori favoured by the social choice correspondence). We show that these three requirements together are in general inconsistent with the choice set being a singleton for every profile (theorem 1).

The examples of social choice correspondences proposed here are of two types: the scoring correspondences assign a score (real number) to every possible rank of an outcome; then for every outcome the total of its score over all individual preferences is computed and the choice set is made up of those outcomes with maximal total score. On the other hand, the Condorcet-type correspondences regard as desirable any outcome that is preferred to every other outcome by a majority of agents.

Throughout we adhere to the assumption that the outcomes are finitely many and that indifferences are ruled out. Therefore every agent can linearly order the feasible outcomes. Moreover, every linear ordering of the outcomes is a feasible ordering: the domain of profiles is "unrestricted".

2. Basic definitions and notation

A collective decision problem arises when a given set of individual agents must collectively select one among a given set of outcomes, whereas the respective opinions of these agents might conflict.

We denote by N, with current element i, the set of *agents*, and by A, with current element a, the set of *outcomes* (or alternatives). In the typical examples that we shall consider below agents will be voters involved in a particular ballot, of which the candidates are viewed as outcomes; or agents are individual consumers and outcomes are vectors of resource allocations.

The opinion of an agent i over the set A of outcomes is described by a preference ordering u_i.

We assume that u_i is a *linear order*, namely a complete binary relation that is transitive and antisymmetric: any two outcomes are comparable and indifferences are ruled out. The notation

$$u_i(a) < u_i(b)$$

means that agent i with preference u_i prefers b to a. Similarly we write

$$u_i(a) \leq u_i(b)$$

for (agent i prefers b to a) or ($a = b$).

Notice that the materialization of a preference as a utility level is mathematically irrelevant: we use it to make the formulas easier to read.

We denote by $L(A)$ the set of linear orders over A.

Definition 1. Given A and N, *a preference profile* $\boldsymbol{u}$ is the data for each agent of a particular linear ordering of A:

$$\boldsymbol{u} = (u_i)_{i \in N}, \quad \text{where } u_i \in L(A) \text{ for every } i.$$

Thus, $L(A)^N$ is the set of all possible preference profiles for given A and N.

Each particular preference profile determines a collective decision problem: given $\boldsymbol{u}$, what outcome(s) should be considered as socially desirable? Any systematic answer to this vague question is a social choice function (correspondence).

Definition 2. Given A and N, *a social choice function (correspondence)* is a single-valued (multi-valued) mapping from the set $L(A)^N$ of preference profiles into the set A of outcomes

$$L(A)^N \ni u \to S(u) \in A \quad \text{or} \quad \emptyset \ne S(u) \subset A.$$

We say that $S(u)$ is the *choice set* associated with profile u.

We shall use the abbreviations s.c.f. and s.c.c. for social choice functions and social choice correspondences, respectively.

Remark 1. The very concept of social choice correspondence might seem useless. That is to say, given a profile u, if the associated choice set $S(u)$ is not a singleton, then to reach an unambiguous decision, society must pick one outcome a within $S(u)$. Denoting $a = T(u)$ we are left finally with a social choice function!

However, social choice correspondences are important for two reasons: in order to meet certain elementary equity requirements (anonymity, neutrality – see definition 4 below) it is very often necessary to allow ties (see theorem 1 below). Secondly, the strong monotonicity requirement, a crucial property as far as implementation is concerned, can only be met by s.c.c. In fact, if we want the strategic behaviour of the agents to be described by Nash or strong equilibria, then some indeterminacy must result in the actual choice set. (See theorem 1, Chapter 3 and theorem 9, Chapter 7.)

Example 1: Scoring correspondences. Suppose that A, the set of alternatives, is finite with cardinality p and let $s = (s_1, \ldots, s_p)$ be a vector of $\mathbf{R}^p$ such that

$$s_1 \geqslant s_2 \geqslant \cdots \geqslant s_p \quad \text{and} \quad s_1 > s_p.$$

Given N and a profile $u \in L(A)^N$, assign a score of s_k to each voter's k most preferred alternative, and let the choice set $S_s(u)$ consist of the alternative(s) with highest total score. We call S_s the *scoring correspondence* associated with s. Formally, if u is an element of $L(A)$ and a an alternative, denote $\varphi(u, a) \in \{1, \ldots, p\}$ the rank of alternative a in u (where $\varphi(u, a) = 1$ stands for: a is the top alternative of u). Then $\sigma(a; u) = \sum_{i \in N} s_{\varphi(u_i, a)}$ is the total score of a associated to profile u and $S_s(u)$ is made up of those outcomes that maximize $\sigma(\cdot; u)$ over A.

A typical example of a scoring correspondence is the *plurality correspondence*, one of the most commonly used s.c.c. It corresponds to $s_1 = 1$ and

$s_2 = s_3 = \cdots = s_p = 0$. There each voter casts one vote for his or her most preferred alternative(s) and the alternative with the largest total number of votes wins.

Another example is the widely used *Borda* scoring method where $s_1 = p$, $s_2 = p - 1,\ldots$, and $s_p = 1$.

3. Efficiency

Among several ethical criteria that we shall discuss below (see sections 4 and 5) efficiency is the least debatable: it amounts to saying that common interest should not be violated.

Given A, N and a preference profile $u \in L(A)^N$ we shall say that outcome a is *Pareto superior* to outcome b if a is unanimously preferred to b:

$$\forall i \in N, \quad u_i(b) < u_i(a).$$

Efficiency simply means that whenever a is Pareto superior to b, outcome b should not belong to the choice set.

Definition 3. Given A, N and a preference profile $u \in L(A)^N$ we say that an outcome is a *Pareto optimum* if it is not Pareto inferior to any other outcome of A. We denote by Par(u) the set of Pareto optimal outcomes for profile u. We call it the Pareto set of profile u.

We say that an s.c.c. (s.c.f.) S is *efficient* if for all profiles it selects only Pareto-optimal outcomes:

$$\forall u \in L(A)^N; \quad S(u) \subset \text{Par}(u); \quad S(u) \in \text{Par}(u).$$

As an example any scoring correspondence such that $s_2 < s_1$ is efficient (see example 1) and is not efficient whenever $s_2 = s_1$.

Remark 2. Since in $L(A)$ indifferences are ruled out, we do not distinguish strong versus weak Pareto optimality.

The mathematical properties of the set Par(u) of Pareto optima have been extensively studied in the last two decades. Here we work in the technically limpid context where A and N are both finite, indifferences are ruled out and every linear ordering is feasible. We simply state two facts about the Pareto set.

Lemma 1. When A and N are both finite and u is a preference profile where indifferences are ruled out ($u \in L(A)^N$), then:

(a) the Pareto set is non-empty; and

(b) it is a singleton if and only if the top outcomes of the various agents coincide:

$$\text{Par}(u) = \{a\} \Leftrightarrow \forall i \in N, \quad \forall b \in A : u_i(b) \leq u_i(a).$$

Proof. Obvious.

The second property above implies that all efficient s.c.c. are known on all profiles such that the top outcomes of the various agents coincide: a property often quoted as *unanimity* of the s.c.c.

In general the Pareto set is not a singleton. It can be even very large relative to A. This is actually the major drawback of the Pareto set viewed as a s.c.c. For instance, if there are (at least) two agents whose interests are opposite, then the Pareto set is the whole set A, so that the efficiency criterion does not discriminate *at all* among A:

$$\forall u \in L(A)^N, \left[\exists i, j \in N, \forall a, b \in A : u_i(a) < u_i(b) \Leftrightarrow u_j(b) < u_j(a)\right]$$

$$\Rightarrow \left[\text{Par}(u) = A\right].$$

We now give a rough estimate of the size of the Pareto set. It measures the extent to which the efficiency criterion expectedly reduces the number of admissible outcomes. For that purpose we assume that for all i, u_i is a random variable with uniform probability over $L(A)$ (thus every particular linear ordering is drawn with probability $1/p!$, where $p = |A|$ is the cardinality of A) and that all u_i, $i \in N$, are independent variables. Given $n = |N|$, the number of agents, one can compute the expected cardinality of the Pareto set $\text{Par}(u)$: it has been done by O'Neill (1981). Table 2.1 gives the result for low n and p.

For fixed n the number of Pareto optima increases slowly with p: for $n = 2$ one expects less than 3 Pareto optima among 10 feasible outcomes, only 4.5 Pareto optima among 50 outcomes, and less than 10 among 10^4 outcomes!

On the other hand, for fixed p the Pareto set develops rapidly when n increases. For $p = 100$ and $n = 10$ not less than 93 outcomes are, on the average, Pareto optimal!

Table 2.1
Expected cardinality of the Pareto set (from O'Neill, 1981)

p \ n	1	2	3	4	5	10	15
1	1	1	1	1	1	1	1
2	1	1.50	1.75	1.89	1.94	1.998	1.9999
3	1	1.83	2.36	2.66	2.82	2.994	2.9998
4	1	2.08	2.88	3.38	3.67	3.988	3.9996
5	1	2.28	3.34	4.05	4.48	4.981	4.9994
6	1	2.45	3.75	4.67	5.26	5.972	5.9091
7	1	2.59	4.12	5.26	6.01	6.961	6.999
8	1	2.72	4.46	5.82	6.74	7.948	7.998
9	1	2.83	4.77	6.35	7.44	8.933	8.998
10	1	2.93	5.06	6.86	8.13	9.918	9.997
20	1	3.60	7.27	11.03	14.12	19.67	19.99
50	1	4.50	10.93	19.2	27.7	48.18	49.93
100	1	5.19	14.3	27.9	43.9	93.8	99.72
1000	1	7.49	28.8	76.5	157.	765.	980.2
10^4	1	9.79	48.7	164.	426.	4947.	9116.5

n = number of agents; p = number of outcomes.

Notice, finally, that ruling out indifferences is a crucial assumption for the above computation: but the larger is A, the less realistic it is to assume that every agent can rank all outcomes along a linear order.

4. Anonymity and neutrality

When the agents involved in a collective decision problem must be treated equally (as is the case in most voting procedures), then an axiomatic solution of this problem, as s.c.c. and s.c.f. typically are, must ensure that every individual opinion influences equally the collective decision. This is what the anonymity criterion formalizes.

Definition 4. Given A, N and an s.c.c. (s.c.f.) S we say that S is *anonymous* if it is a symmetrical correspondence (function) of its variables u_i, $i \in N$.

For all permutations τ from N into itself, and every profile u, denote by u_τ the profile $u_\tau = (u_{i,\tau})_{i \in N}$, where $u_{i,\tau} = u_{\tau(i)}$, all $i \in N$. Then S is anonymous if and only if for all τ and all u, $S(u_\tau) = S(u)$.

A similar equity requirement concerns outcomes viewed as candidates among which we do not want the s.c.c. (s.c.f.) to discriminate: we call it the neutrality requirement.

Definition 5. Given A, N and s.c.c. (s.c.f.) S we say that S is *neutral* if the following holds true.

For every permutation σ of A into itself, denote by $\boldsymbol{u}^\sigma$ the profile

$$\boldsymbol{u}^\sigma = (u_i^\sigma)_{i \in N}, \quad \text{where } u_i^\sigma(a) = u_i(\sigma(a)), \quad \text{all } i \in N \text{ and all } a \in A.$$

Then for all $\boldsymbol{u}$ and all σ, $S(\boldsymbol{u})^\sigma = \sigma^{-1}[S(\boldsymbol{u})]$.

An example of an s.c.c. that is simultaneously efficient, anonymous and neutral is any scoring correspondence (see section 2) and all familiar voting methods listed in section 5. In voting theory these three requirements are primary. However, it is not in general possible to meet them without leaving some indeterminacy in the social choice.

Theorem 1. Let A and N be both finite with respective cardinality p and n. The two following statements are equivalent:
 (i) n has at least one prime factor less than or equal to p; and
 (ii) there exists no social choice function which is simultaneously efficient, anonymous and neutral.

Thus, except for some configurations of (n, p) no social choice function is simultaneously efficient, anonymous and neutral. To make intuitive the result, let us consider the following profile when $p = n = 2$:

$$u_1(a) < u_1(b); \quad u_2(b) < u_2(a).$$

Since the two agents conflict on the (unique) binary choice, a or b, there is no way to solve the dilemma in favour of one alternative without actually favouring one agent and/or one alternative (in fact here not even an anonymous and neutral s.c.f. exists! See problem 1) so that the choice set must contain both a and b.

This in turn justifies why very sensible social choice correspondences are actually multi-valued for some profiles: the presence of ties cannot be avoided without violating one among the three quoted requirements.

Proof of theorem 1.

(α) We prove (i) $\Rightarrow$ (ii) per absurdum.

Suppose $n = \ell \cdot m$, where ℓ and m are integers with $2 \leq \ell \leq p$, and let S be an efficient anonymous and neutral s.c.f.

We pick a subset A_0 of A with cardinality ℓ and a permutation σ of A into itself such that
 (i) the restriction of σ to $A \setminus A_0$ is the identity; and
 (ii) the restriction of σ to A_0 is a circular permutation (i.e. $\sigma^\ell = $ identity and $\sigma^\ell \neq \sigma^{\ell-1}, \ldots, \sigma^1$).

Finally, we pick a linear order $u \in L(A)$ such that

$$\forall a \in A_0, \quad \forall b \in A \setminus A_0 : u(b) < u(a). \tag{1}$$

Now consider a profile v where for all $k = 0, 1, \ldots, (\ell - 1)$ exactly m agents have the preferences u^{σ^k}. We will show that $S(v)$ must be empty – a contradiction.

Let a_0 be the top outcome of u. For any element a in A_0 there exists $k \in \{0, 1, \ldots, (\ell - 1)\}$ such that $\sigma^k(a) = a_0$, implying that a is the top outcome of u^{σ^k}. Therefore a belongs to the Pareto set $\text{Par}(v)$. Conversely, every preference u^{σ^k}, $k = 0, 1, \ldots, (\ell - 1)$, still satisfies (1) so that any outcome in $A \setminus A_0$ is Pareto inferior to any outcome in A_0. Hence, $A_0 = \text{Par}(v)$ and by the efficiency assumption, $S(v) \in A_0$.

We observe now that the preference profile v^σ consists also of m agents with preferences u^{σ^k}, all $k = 0, 1, \ldots, (\ell - 1)$ (remember that σ^ℓ = identity). Thus, for some permutation of N we have $v^\sigma = v_\tau$. Simultaneously applying anonymity and neutrality yields:

$$\begin{aligned} S(v^\sigma) &= \sigma^{-1}[S(v)] \\ S(v_\tau) &= S(v) \end{aligned} \Rightarrow \sigma(S(v)) = S(v).$$

Therefore $S(v)$ must be a fixed point of σ, i.e. an element of $A \setminus A_0$. This is the desired contradiction.

(β) To prove the converse implication we select n and p such that every prime factor of n is strictly above p and displays an efficient anonymous and neutral social choice function.

The Coombs social choice function

This s.c.f. results from a successive elimination algorithm. First we eliminate those alternatives which are ranked last most often, and then we repeat this elimination argument among the remaining alternatives, and so on. Formally, let A and N be given with cardinality p and n. For any profile $u \in L(A)^N$ and any subset B of A we define the set $\text{PL}(u, B)$ of the *plurality losers over* B as follows: $a \in \text{PL}(u, B) \leftrightarrow \{a \in B$ and the number $\gamma(a)$ of agents that rank a last among B is maximal over B at $a\}$.

We remark that $\text{PL}(u, B)$ can be viewed as the plurality correspondence of the opposite profile $\tilde{u}$ over B (where $\tilde{u}_i$ is the opposite order of u_i over B for all i).

To construct now the successive elimination s.c.f. we observe that for all subsets B of A with cardinality $q \leq p$, the set $\text{PL}(u, B)$ of plurality losers over B cannot be B itself unless B is a singleton. Otherwise the function γ should be constant over B; in view of the identity $\sum_{a \in B} \gamma(a) = n$ this would yield $q \cdot \gamma = n$ – a contradiction of our assumption that every prime factor of n strictly exceeds p. Thus, we have

$$\emptyset \neq \text{PL}(u, B) \subsetneq B, \quad \text{all } \emptyset \neq B \subset A.$$

This shows that the decreasing sequence

$$B_0 = A, B_1 = A \setminus \text{PL}(u, A);$$
$$B_2 = B_1 \setminus \text{PL}(u, B_1); \ldots; B_t = B_{t-1} \setminus \text{PL}(u, B_{t-1})$$
(2)

shrinks to a singleton for some t.

This is how we define the Coombs s.c.f. Its anonymity and neutrality are self-evident. To see that it is efficient suppose a, $\{a\} = \cap_t B_t$ is Pareto inferior to b. There exists t such that $b \in B_t \setminus B_{t+1} = \text{PL}(u, B_t)$. Since a belongs to B_t this contradicts the obvious fact that an element in B cannot be Pareto inferior to an element in $\text{PL}(u, B)$.

In problem 1 we explore the existence of an anonymous and neutral social choice function.

Problem 1: Anonymous and neutral s.c.f.

(1) Given two integers, n and p, show the following implications: (i): $\{n$ and p are not relatively prime$\} \Rightarrow$ (ii): $\{p$ can be written as the sum of (non-trivial) divisors of $n\} \Rightarrow$ (iii): $\{n$ has at least one prime factor less than or equal to $p\}$.

Show that the converse implications do not hold.

(2) Given A and N with cardinalities p and n, respectively, such that (ii) holds true, show that there exist no anonymous and neutral social choice function on $L(A)^N$.

(3) Conversely, assuming that (ii) fails, show the existence of some anonymous and neutral s.c.f.

5. The Condorcet winner and related s.c.c.

The Condorcet approach to the social choice problem is crucial to the strategic analysis developed in subsequent chapters. A Condorcet winner is an outcome defeating every other outcome in binary contest where a majority decides: for instance, an alternative which is ranked first by a strict majority of agents is the Condorcet winner in every associated profile. The normative consequences are clear: the opinion of a strict majority overcomes any contradictory opinion by the opposing minority. This *majority principle* was introduced by Condorcet as early as 1785. Since then it has been of fundamental relevance in the development of modern democratic theory. We shall discuss the majority principle at length in Chapters 4 and 5 when investigating its striking strategical implications.

Here we concentrate on the primitive difficulty toward actual realization of the Condorcet proposal: for some profiles the Condorcet winner fails to exist, a situation well known as the "Condorcet paradox". To overcome this difficulty we define several social choice correspondences that we call Condorcet-type s.c.c. since they select the Condorcet winner(s) when one exists and suggest a meaningful subset of quasi-Condorcet winners when a Condorcet paradox arises.

Let us define first the Condorcet winner associated with a given preference profile.

Definition 6. Given A and N, a profile $\boldsymbol{u} \in L(A)^N$ and any two distinct outcomes $a, b \in A$, we denote by $N(a, b, \boldsymbol{u})$ the number of agents i such that $u_i(a) > u_i(b)$.

We say that a is a *Condorcet winner* of profile $\boldsymbol{u}$ if

$$N(a, b, \boldsymbol{u}) \geq \frac{n}{2}, \quad \text{all } b \in A, \quad b \neq a.$$

We denote by $CW(\boldsymbol{u})$ the (possibly empty) subset of Condorcet winner(s) of profile $\boldsymbol{u}$.

The very notion of a Condorcet winner relies on the *majority principle*: if outcome b is viewed as less desirable than outcome a by a majority (in fact a non-minority) of agents, then b should not be taken as a socially desirable outcome. In other words, the only admissible outcomes are those which defeat every other in a binary majority contest.

A basic observation, due to Condorcet himself, is that CW is *not* a social choice correspondence with variable $\boldsymbol{u}$ since for some profile the Condorcet winner may fail to exist.

Lemma 2. Given A and N, with cardinalities p and n, respectively, let us suppose

$$p \geq 3 \quad \text{and} \quad (n = 3 \text{ or } n \geq 5). \tag{3}$$

Then there exists at least one profile $u \in L(A)^N$ such that CW(u) is the empty set.

Proof. Given a positive integer n we can easily check that the two following statements are equivalent.

(i) There exist three positive integers n_i, $i = 1,2,3$, such that $n = n_1 + n_2 + n_3$ and, moreover,

$$n_i + n_j > \frac{n}{2}, \quad \text{all } i, j \in \{1,2,3\}, \quad i \neq j.$$

(ii) $n = 3$ or $n \geqslant 5$.

Now we fix A and N with cardinalities p and n, respectively, satisfying (3). We pick three different outcomes, a, b and c, and three integers n_i, $i = 1,2,3$ such that (i) holds. Let N_1, N_2 and N_3 be a partition of N, where N_i has cardinality n_i. Then consider a profile u such that:

for all $i \in N_1$: $u_i(a) > u_i(b) > u_i(c) > u_i(d)$,

for all $i \in N_2$: $u_i(c) > u_i(a) > u_i(b) > u_i(d)$, for all $d \neq a,b,c$. (4)

for all $i \in N_3$: $u_i(b) > u_i(c) > u_i(a) > u_i(d)$,

We can easily check that no Condorcet winner is associated with u.

The fact that for some profiles Condorcet winner(s) may fail to exist is known in the literature as the Condorcet paradox.

Given that the u_i, $i \in N$, are independent uniformly distributed random variables over $L(A)$ one can compute probabilistic estimates for the occurrence of the Condorcet paradox (similar to the estimated size of the Pareto set presented in section 3). We refer the reader to Sen (1970), especially the table on p. 164.

We present now two social choice correspondences of which the choice set is the set of Condorcet winner(s) when the latter is non-empty. When the Condorcet paradox arises, these s.c.c. arbitrate among A in the same spirit.

Definition 7. Given A and N, both finite, a profile $u \in L(A)^N$ and an outcome $a \in A$ we define $c_u(a)$, the *Copeland score* of a at u, as

$$c_u(a) = \text{cardinality}\{b \in A/N(a,b,u) \geqslant n/2\}.$$

Any outcome maximizing c_u over A is called a Copeland winner and the subset of those winners defines *the Copeland* social choice correspondence

$$C(u) = \{a \in A / c_u(a) \geq c_u(b), \text{ all } b \in A\}.$$

Similarly, we define $k_u(a)$, the *Kramer score* of a at u, as

$$k_u(a) = \inf_{b \in A, b \neq a} N(a, b, u).$$

An outcome maximizing k_u over A is called a Kramer winner and the subset of those winners defines the *Kramer social choice correspondence*

$$K(u) = \{a \in A / k_u(a) \geq k_u(b), \text{ all } b \in A\}.$$

By the finiteness of A, both $C(u)$ and $K(u)$ are never empty. We let the reader check that both C and K are efficient anonymous and neutral s.c.c. Moreover, they coincide with the set of Condorcet winners when the latter is non-empty.

Lemma 3. Whenever $CW(u)$ is non-empty we have

$$C(u) = K(u) = CW(u).$$

Proof. Since an outcome is a Condorcet winner if and only if its Copeland score is p, equality $C(u) = CW(u)$ when the latter is non-empty is obvious. To prove that $K(u) = CW(u)$ under the same assumption we observe similarly that an outcome a is a Condorcet winner if and only if its Kramer score is at least $n/2$. Moreover, the inequality system

$$\frac{n}{2} \leq k_u(a) < k_u(b)$$

is absurd since it would imply $N(a, b, u) \geq n/2$ and $N(b, a, u) > n/2$. Therefore, if at least one Condorcet winner exists, it maximizes k_u over A (it belongs to $K(u)$) and conversely the score of any b in $K(u)$ must be at least $n/2$ (implying $K(u) \subset CW(u)$). ∎

The two generalizations of the Condorcet winner proposed by Copeland and Kramer differ. The former simply retains in the choice set those outcomes that defeat no fewer outcomes in binary majority contest than any other outcome, whereas the latter selects the Condorcet winner(s), if any, and otherwise those outcomes for which the size of an objecting coalition (i.e. a majority coalition preferring some other outcome) is as small as possible. To illustrate this difference we give an example where no Condorcet winner exists, whereas the two choice sets $C(u)$ and $K(u)$ are disjoint:

$A = \{a, b, c, d\}$, N consists of seven agents,

three of them with preference: $u_1(a) > u_1(b) > u_1(c) > u_1(d)$,

two of them with preference: $u_2(b) > u_2(d) > u_2(c) > u_2(a)$,

two of them with preference: $u_3(d) > u_3(c) > u_3(a) > u_3(b)$.

Here we have

$$c_u(b) = c_u(d) = 2 > 1 = c_u(a) = c_u(c),$$

henceforth $C(u) = \{b, d\}$.
Also:

$$k_u(a) = 3 > 2 = k_u(b) = k_u(c) = k_u(d),$$

so that $K(u) = \{a\}$.

The Copeland s.c.c. recommends $\{b, d\}$ since each of them defeats two among the other outcomes whereas, a, c only defeats one other outcome in a binary contest. On the other hand, the Kramer s.c.c. recommends a since only a tight majority can object against a (in favour of c and/or in favour of d) whereas some five agents majority have objections against b (namely a), c (namely b) and d (namely b).

As a final remark we emphasize a major defect of the Copeland and Kramer s.c.c. Contrary to the Condorcet winner set which in general can be expected to be a singleton (exercise: if n is odd there is at most one Condorcet winner) the Copeland and Kramer choice sets usually contain several outcomes. Thus, if $p \geq 3$ and $n \geq 2$ the Copeland and Kramer s.c.c. are not social choice functions.

More results on the Copeland and Kramer s.c.c. can be found in Kramer (1977), Sraffin (1978) and Demange (1982). Other generalizations of the

Condorcet winner set are proposed by Miller (1977, 1980) (see problem 4) and Nansen (see problem 5).

The next problem compares the Condorcet winner set with some familiar scoring correspondences

Problem 2: Condorcet winner and scoring correspondences. The scoring correspondences are defined in example 1, section 2. For every profile $u \in L(A)^N$ we shall denote by $B(u)$ the corresponding Borda choice set, and by $P(u)$ the plurality choice set.

(a) Give an example where $B(u)$ and $CW(u)$ are both singletons and disjoint. Give an example where an outcome is ranked first by a strict majority of agents and yet is not a Borda winner.

(b) Give an example where $P(u)$ and $CW(u)$ are both singletons; $P(u) = \{a\}$, $CW(u) = \{b\}$, whereas:
- b gets the lowest plurality score, and
- a is a Condorcet loser: every other outcome defeats it in a pairwise contest.

(c) Show that a Borda winner cannot be a Condorcet loser.

Problem 3: The Condorcet cycle. We fix A and N both finite and we suppose that n, the cardinality of N, is *odd*.

For fixed profile u we say that outcome a *dominates* outcome b if $N(a, b, u) > n/2$, i.e. if a defeats b in a majority binary contest. Since n is odd the dominance relation is complete and asymmetric.

A *Condorcet set* is a subset $A_c \subset A$ such that:

(i) no outcome in A_c is dominated by an outcome outside A_c; and

(ii) no proper subset of A_c meets condition (i).

(a) Show that for all profiles u there is exactly one Condorcet set, denoted $A_c(u)$.

Show that an outcome a belongs to the Condorcet set $A_c(u)$ if and only if every other outcome b can be reached from a along a *domination path*: there exists a path $\{a = \alpha_1, \alpha_2, \ldots, \alpha_K = b\}$ such that α_k dominates α_{k+1}, for every $k = 1, \ldots, K-1$.

(b) Show that if a Condorcet winner exists (necessarily unique) then it coincides with the Condorcet set

$$A_c(u) = CW(u), \quad \text{whenever } CW(u) \neq \emptyset.$$

If no Condorcet winner exists, show that $A_c(u)$ contains at least three outcomes and is a *domination cycle*:

$$A_c(u) = \{a_1, \ldots, a_K\},$$

where a_k dominates a_{k+1}, $k = 1, \ldots, (K-1)$, and a_K dominates a_1.

(c) Give an example where the Condorcet set includes inefficient outcomes:

$$\exists u \text{ No}\{A_c(u) \subset \text{Par}(u)\}.$$

Problem 4: Miller's uncovered set (Miller, 1977, 1980). We use the assumptions and notations of problem 3.

For a given profile u we say that outcome a *covers* outcome b if every outcome dominated by b is dominated by a as well:

$$a \text{ covers } b \Leftrightarrow \forall c \in A \ (b \text{ dominates } c) \Rightarrow (a \text{ dominates } c).$$

We denote by $D(a)$ the *dominion* of a, i.e. the set of outcomes dominated by a.

(a) Show that a covers b if and only if $D(b)$ is a *proper* subset of $D(a)$; show that a covers b only if a dominates b.

(b) Define the *uncovered set* associated with profile u as the set of outcomes that are not covered by any other outcome. It is denoted $A_c^*(u)$.

Show that outcome a is uncovered if and only if every other outcome in A is reachable from a via a domination path of no more than two steps. Deduce the inclusion $A_c^*(u) \subset A_c(u)$.

(c) Show that a Copeland winner is an uncovered outcome:

$$C(u) \subset A_c^*(u).$$

Deduce that the uncovered set is never empty and that A_c^* is a Condorcet-type s.c.c.

(d) Show that the uncovered set is made of efficient outcomes only:

$$A_c^*(u) \subset \text{Par}(u), \quad \text{all } u \in L(A)^N.$$

Another useful reference on the uncovered set is Bordes (1976).

In this chapter examples of s.c.c. and s.c.f. were of two types: the scoring correspondences, definitely utilitarian in spirit, of which the most typical example is the Borda correspondence; the second family was the Condorcet-type correspondence (Copeland, Kramer and some others introduced in problems 3 and 4) that all comply with the majority principle.

References

Bordes, G., 1976, "Consistency, rationality and collective choice", Review of Economic Studies 43, 451–458.
Demange, G., 1982, "A limit theorem on the minimax set", Journal of Mathematical Economics 9, 145–164.
Kramer, G., 1977, "A dynamical model of political equilibrium", Journal of Economic Theory 16, 310–334.
Miller, N., 1977, "Graph-theoretical approaches to the theory of voting", American Journal of Political Science 21, 769–803.
Miller, N., 1980, "A new solution set for tournaments and majority voting: Further graph-theoretical approaches to the theory of voting", American Journal of Political Science 24, 68–96.
Moulin, H., 1980, "La stratagie du vote", Monographie du Séminaire d'Econométrie no. 14, C.N.R.S., Paris.
O'Neill, B., 1981, "The number of outcomes in the Pareto optimal set of discrete bargaining games", Mathematics of Operations Research 6, 571–578.
Sen, A., 1970, Collective choice and social welfare, in: Advanced textbooks in economics, North-Holland Publishing Company, Amsterdam.
Sraffin, P., 1978, Introduction to the social choice theory for environmental decision making, Dept. of Mathematics, Beloit College, Beloit, Wisconsin.

CHAPTER 3

MONOTONICITY AND THE ARROW THEOREM

1. Summary of the results

A social choice correspondence is monotonic if, whenever the position of an outcome in the choice set improves upon every agent's preferences, then it remains in the choice set afterwards. It is strongly monotonic if, whenever the position of an outcome improves upon every agent's preferences, then only this outcome can enter the choice set. These two properties are defined and exemplified in sections 2–4. Theorem 1 states that for strongly monotonic social choice correspondences the choice set cannot be a singleton for all profiles. Thus, strong monotonicity yields some indeterminacy of the social choice. This result is very profound: it implies Arrow's theorem (theorem 3) as well as the Gibbard–Satterthwaite theorem (Chapter 4). However, non-trivial strongly monotonic social choice correspondences do exist (theorem 2): they play a central role in implementation by strong equilibria and by Nash equilibria (Chapter 7).

In the final section of this chapter Arrow's concept of social welfare function is proposed as a seemingly more satisfactory solution to our normative problem: a social welfare function actually aggregates every profile of preferences into a "collective" preference ordering. The famous impossibility result proves that this formalism, however appealing it looks, does not in general yield any meaningful decision rule.

This chapter attacks some technical results of primary importance for the strategic analysis developed subsequently. The two increasingly demanding properties of monotonicity that we shall define here turn out to be crucial to implementability by game forms. A basic reference for the results presented in this chapter is Peleg (1980).

2. Monotonic s.c.c.

We show first an example of a non-monotonic s.c.c.

Example 1: Plurality with run-off. This voting method is widely used in various political issues: the first step is a plurality voting, where a candidate winning a strict majority of votes is elected. If no such outcome emerges, the two best-scoring candidates compete in a run-off, i.e. a binary majority contest.

The inclusion maximal s.c.c. compatible with the above method is defined as follows.

Given a profile u let $p(a, u)$ be the plurality score of a w.r.t. u (i.e. the number of agents who rank a first). Say that a couple $\{a, b\}$ is a top couple of u if $p(a, u) \geqslant p(c, u)$ and $p(b, u) \geqslant p(c, u)$ for any outcome c different from a and b.

Now the plurality with run-off s.c.c. is denoted PR and defined by:

$$a \in \mathrm{PR}(u), \quad \mathrm{iff} \begin{cases} \text{There exists an outcome } b \text{ such that } \{a, b\} \text{ is a} \\ \text{top couple and } b \text{ does not defeat } a \text{ in the majority} \\ \text{contest: } N(a, b, u) \geqslant n/2. \end{cases}$$

Notice that PR is an efficient anonymous and neutral s.c.c.

Now consider a situation where three candidates compete among 17 voters and the profile is:

- 6 agents $u(a) > u(b) > u(c)$,
- 5 agents $u(c) > u(a) > u(b)$,
- 4 agents $u(b) > u(c) > u(a)$,
- 2 agents $u(b) > u(a) > u(c)$.

After the first round a and b (with plurality scoring 6 each above scoring 5 by c) go for a run-off where a passes b by 11 to 6.

Suppose now that the two agents with preferences $u(b) > u(a) > u(c)$ change their minds. They estimate that a is after all a better candidate than b and their new preference is therefore $u(a) > u(b) > u(c)$.

Although this change of opinion strictly improves upon the position of a, it actually prevents the election of a. That is to say, in the new profile a and c pass the first round (with plurality scoring 8 and 5, respectively) but a is knocked down by c 8 to 9 in the run-off.

This example shows a major drawback of any plurality with run-off social choice function: it can respond negatively to an improvement in the position of the previously elected outcome. A monotonic s.c.c. is one that does not suffer this defect.

Definition 1. Given A and N, two profiles $u, v \in L(A)^N$ and an outcome a we say that v *is obtained from* u *by an improvement of* a if

$$\forall i \in N, \qquad u_i(b) < u_i(c) \Leftrightarrow v_i(b) < v_i(c),$$

$$\forall b, c \in A \setminus \{a\}, \qquad u_i(a) > u_i(b) \Rightarrow v_i(a) > v_i(b).$$

Definition 2. We say that a s.c.c. S is *monotonic* if for all $u, v \in L(A)^N$ and all outcomes a we have:

$$\left. \begin{array}{l} a \in S(u) \text{ and } \begin{array}{l} v \text{ is obtained from } u \\ \text{by an improvement of } a \end{array} \end{array} \right\} \Rightarrow \begin{cases} a \in S(v), \\ S(v) \subset S(u). \end{cases} \qquad (1)$$

Thus, a s.c.c. is monotonic if, whenever the position of a desirable outcome (an outcome in the choice set) improves, whereas the relative position of other outcomes is fixed, then this outcome remains in the choice set and the choice set does not expand.

Most familiar s.c.c. are monotonic.

Lemma 1. In any scoring correspondence, all four Condorcet-type s.c.c. (Copeland, Kramer, the Condorcet cycle and the uncovered set – problems 3 and 4, Chapter 2) are monotonic.

Proof. To prove that a scoring correspondence is monotonic, observe that when v is obtained from u by an improvement of a the score of a does not decrease, whereas the score of any other outcome does not increase: this implies (1). To prove that the above-mentioned four Condorcet-type s.c.c. are monotonic, observe that when v is obtained from u by an improvement of a, then the Copeland and Kramer scores of a do not decrease, whereas the Copeland and Kramer scores of any other outcome do not increase. The proof that the Condorcet cycle and the uncovered set are monotonic s.c.c. is left as an exercise for the reader.

An example of a non-monotonic s.c.c. is the plurality run-off s.c.c. presented above, or any part of it (see the counter-example profile).

In general s.c.c. defined by successive rounds of voting tend to be non-monotonic; see the Coombs and Nansen methods (problem 6 below).

In problem 5 we propose some monotonic social choice *functions*, thus proving that monotonicity is compatible with the determinacy of the social choice (the choice set being always a singleton). We also explore the existence of a monotonic, as well as efficient anonymous and neutral s.c.f.

Problem 5: Monotonic social choice functions. We fix A and N with respective cardinalities p and n throughout the problem.

The dictatorial s.c.f. is the following:

$$S_i(u) = \text{top outcome of } u_i, \quad \text{all } u \in L(A)^N.$$

It is trivially efficient, neutral and monotonic, together with an extreme lack of anonymity.

We propose now an anonymous and monotonic s.c.f.:

(a) Given a profile u we denote by m_u the binary majority relation:

$$\forall a, b \in A \quad m_u(a, b) = a, \quad \text{if } N(a, b, u) \geq n/2,$$
$$= b, \quad \text{if } N(a, b, u) < n/2.$$

Notice that ties are broken in favour of the left-hand candidate.

Suppose now that $\{a_1, \ldots, a_p\}$ is a fixed ordering of A (not depending on u) and consider the following sequence:

$$b_1 = m(a_1, a_2),$$

$$b_k = m(b_{k-1}, a_{k+1}), \quad \text{all } k, \quad 2 \leq k \leq p-1.$$

Defining $S(u) = b_{p-1}$, show that S is an anonymous and monotonic s.c.f. and that S is a Condorcet-type s.c.f.

Show that if $p \geq 4$ or ($p = 3$ and n even), then S is not efficient.

Monotonicity and the Arrow theorem

(b) For any given u we define now inductively a sequence $\{\varphi^1, \ldots, \varphi^{p-1}\}$, where for all k, $1 \leq k \leq p-1$, φ^k is a mapping from $\{a_{k+1}, \ldots, a_p\}$ into A:

$$\varphi^1(a_t) = m_u(a_1, a_t), \qquad \text{all } t, \quad 2 \leq t \leq p,$$

$$\varphi^k(a_t) = m_u(\varphi^{k-1}(a_k), \varphi^{k-1}(a_t)), \quad \text{all } t, \quad k+1 \leq t \leq p.$$

Show that the s.c.f. $S(u) = \varphi^{p-1}(a_p)$ is a monotonic anonymous s.c.f. and is, furthermore, a Condorcet-type s.c.f.

Show that this s.c.f. is efficient as well.

(c) Borrowed from Moulin (1980).

We suppose now that n is prime and strictly superior to p.

For any given profile u, any subset C of A (possibly empty) and any outcome a outside C we denote by n_a^C the cardinality of the following (possibly empty) subset of N:

$$\{i \in N / u_i(a) \leq u_i(b), \quad \text{for all } b \in A \setminus C\}.$$

Given any ordering $\{a_1, \ldots, a_p\}$ of A we consider the following property:

$$\exists (t_1, \ldots, t_p) \in \mathbf{R}_+^p \text{ s.t.} \begin{cases} 1 = n_{a_1} \cdot t_1, \\ 1 = n_{a_2} \cdot t_1 + n_{a_2}^{a_1} \cdot t_2, \\ \vdots \\ 1 = n_{a_k} \cdot t_1 + n_{a_k}^{a_1} \cdot t_2 + \cdots + n_{a_k}^{a_1 \cdots a_{k-1}} \cdot t_k, \\ \vdots \\ 1 = n_{a_p} \cdot t_1 + n_{a_p}^{a_1} \cdot t_2 + \cdots \cdots + n \cdot t_p. \end{cases}$$

(Notice that $n_{a_p}^{a_1 \cdots a_{p-1}} = n$.)

Prove the existence of at least one ordering $\{a_1, \ldots, a_p\}$ satisfying this property.

Prove that any two orderings of A satisfying the above property have the same terminal element a_p.

Defining $S(u) = a_p$, prove that S is an efficient anonymous, neutral and monotonic s.c.f.

In the next problem we introduce the Nansen voting method, a variant of Borda scoring that generalizes the Condorcet winner as well.

Problem 6: The Nansen method – a non-monotonic Condorcet-type s.c.c. (borrowed from Sraffin, 1978). For some cardinalities of A and N we have defined above (proof of theorem 1) the Coombs social choice function. For any cardinalities of A and N the same definition yields the Coombs social choice correspondence.

That is to say, for a fixed profile u, the sequence $B_0 = A, B_1, \ldots, B_t, \ldots$ given by (2) (Chapter 2) is strictly decreasing, and therefore vanishes after finitely many iterations. The last non-empty subset B_t is taken to be $CO(u)$ thus defining the Coombs s.c.c. CO.

The definition of the Nansen s.c.c., denoted NA, is similar. For any profile u and any subset B of A we denote by $BL(u, B)$ the set of *Borda losers* over B for profile u defined as the subset of those elements of B with minimal Borda scoring for the restriction of u over B. Then the last non-empty subset C_t of the following sequence:

$$C_0 = A; \quad C_{t+1} = C_t \backslash BL(u, C_t),$$

is taken to be $NA(u)$.

The definition of the *Black* s.c.c. is quite different:

$$BLA(u) = CW(u), \quad \text{if } CW(u) \text{ is non-empty}$$

$$= B(u) \quad \text{(the Borda correspondence) otherwise.}$$

(a) Show that CO, NA and BLA are efficient, anonymous and neutral.

(b) Show that both NA and BLA are Condorcet-type s.c.c. whereas CO is not.

(c) Show that BLA is monotonic whereas NA and CO are not.

(d) Show that NA satisfies the following property (expressing a strong consistency of this s.c.c. with the majority principle):

Suppose u is such that A can be partitioned as $A = A_1 \cup A_2$ where:

$$\forall a \in A_1, \quad \forall b \in A_2: N(a, b, u) > n/2. \tag{2}$$

Then $NA(u) \subset A_1$.

In words, if every outcome in A_1 is preferred by a strict majority to every outcome in A_2, then all socially desirable outcomes should belong to A_1.

Show that the Copeland s.c.c. satisfies (2) as well but neither the Kramer s.c.c., nor CO nor BLA do.

(e) Give an example where $NA(u)$ and $C(u)$ are disjoint.

3. Strongly monotonic s.c.c.

Strong monotonicity is a seemingly innocuous strengthening of monotonicity.

Definition 3. Given A and N, a s.c.c. S is *strongly monotonic* if for all u, $v \in L(A)^N$ and all outcomes a we have:

$$\left.\begin{array}{l} v \text{ is obtained from } u \text{ by} \\ \text{an improvement of } a \end{array}\right\} \Rightarrow S(v) \subset \{a\} \cup S(u). \tag{3}$$

Thus, S is strongly monotonic if improving upon the position of an outcome a cannot add to the choice set any outcome but a. Contrary to property (1) of definition 1, we do not assume that a belongs to the original choice set. In fact, lemma 1 below shows that (3) can be interpreted as:

Suppose v is obtained from u by an improvement of a, then:

if $a \in S(u)$, then $a \in S(v) \subset S(u)$

if $a \notin S(u)$, then $S(v) \subset \{a\} \cup S(u)$:

only a is a possible new outcome.

Lemma 2. If S is strongly monotonic, then it is monotonic.

Proof. Say that v is obtained from u by an *elementary* improvement of a for agent i, if all agents but i have the same preference in u and v and in agent i's preferences the rank of a has been increased by one:

$$u_i: \cdots < u_i(b) < u_i(a) < u_i(c) < u_i(d) < \cdots, \tag{4}$$
$$v_i: \cdots < v_i(b) < v_i(c) < v_i(a) < v_i(d) < \cdots .$$

Clearly, every improvement of a can be decomposed in a sequence of elementary improvements.

We must prove that if a belongs to $S(u)$ and v is obtained from u by an improvement of a, then a belongs to $S(v)$ as well. Without loss of generality we may assume that v is obtained from u by an elementary improvement of a for agent i.

In view of (4), u is obtained from v by an (elementary) improvement of c. Thus, by strong monotonicity:

$$S(u) \subset \{c\} \cup S(v).$$

Since $S(u)$ contains $a \neq c$ this inclusion shows that $S(v)$ contains a as well.

To prove that strong monotonicity is a much stronger requirement than monotonicity we give an equivalent more striking formulation of it called a strong positive association.

Definition 3. Given A and N, two profiles u and v, and an outcome a we shall say that the position of a is preserved from u to v if the following implication holds:

$$\forall i \in N, \quad \forall b \in A: u_i(b) < u_i(a) \Rightarrow v_i(b) < v_i(a). \tag{5}$$

In other words, the position of a is preserved if no outcome has passed a in the preference of any agent.

One consequence of implication (5) is that the rank of a in the preference of any agent has not decreased (and possibly increased). But the converse is not true, as the following example shows:

$u_i: b > c > a > d > e > f,$

$v_i: c > b > a > e > f > d.$

From u_i to v_i, a preserves its position.

$w_i: d > a > b > c > e > f.$

From u_i to w_i a does not preserve its position (although its rank increases).

Comparing definitions 1 and 3 we find that if profile v is obtained from profile u by an improvement of a, then the position of a is preserved from u to v.

Let us illustrate further that the shift from one profile to another can be much deeper when only the position of a is preserved. When profile v is obtained from u by an improvement of a, v and u are very close: i.e. the relative ordering of all outcomes in $A \setminus \{a\}$ coincide in v_i and u_i for all $i \in N$.

On the other hand, when the position of a is preserved from u to v these two profiles may differ sharply on $A\setminus\{a\}$: see the example above. As an exercise the reader can check that given u, a and a pair $\{b, c\} \subset A\setminus\{a\}$ a profile v can be found such that:

- the position of a is preserved from u to v; and
- all agents changed their minds about b and c from u to v:

$$[u_i(b) < u_i(c)] \Leftrightarrow [v_i(c) < v_i(b)], \quad \text{all } i.$$

Lemma 3 (Peleg, 1980). A s.c.c. S is strongly monotonic if and only if it satisfies the following property of "strong positive association" (SPA):

$$\begin{aligned}\forall u\, v \in L(A)^N \\ \forall a \in A\end{aligned} \left\{\begin{aligned}a \in S(u) \text{ and the position of} \\ a \text{ is preserved from } u \text{ to } v\end{aligned}\right\} \Rightarrow a \in S(v). \tag{6}$$

Proof.

Step 1. Strong positive association $\Rightarrow$ strong monotonicity.

Fix a s.c.c. S satisfying SPA, two profiles u and v, and an outcome a. We suppose that v is obtained from u by an elementary improvement of a for agent i (see proof of lemma 2). Say that the outcome b is ranked immediately above a in u_i and immediately below it in v_i, everything else being unchanged. Choosing any outcome $c \in S(v)$ we distinguish three cases:

(α) $c \neq b, a$: then $v_i(b) > v_i(c)$ or $v_i(b) < v_i(a) < v_i(c)$. In each case the position of c is preserved from v to u so that by SPA $c \in S(u)$.

(β) $c = b$: then again the position of c is preserved from v to u, hence $c \in S(u)$.

(γ) $c = a$.

In each case the inclusion $S(v) \subset \{a\} \cup S(u)$ is established, thus proving (3) for elementary improvements. Since every improvement of a can be decomposed into a sequence of elementary improvements, we conclude that S is strongly monotonic.

Step 2. Strong monotonicity $\Rightarrow$ strong positive association.

Fix a strongly monotonic s.c.c. S, one profile u and an outcome $a \in S(u)$. We will prove that $a \in S(v)$ for two types of profile v.

Type 1. v is obtained from u by an elementary improvement of a.

Say that from u to v, outcome a has passed b in agent i's preference ordering. Then u is obtained from v by an elementary improvement of b so that by strong monotonicity:

$$S(u) \subset \{b\} \cup S(v).$$

Therefore $a \in S(u)$ implies $a \in S(v)$ (since $b \neq a$).

Type 2. v is obtained from u by an elementary improvement of outcome b for agent i, where $b \neq a$ and b is not ranked immediately below a in u_i.
   Thus, we have:

$$u_i(a) < \cdots < u_i(b) < u_i(c)$$

or

$$u_i(b) < u_i(c) < \cdots < u_i(a).$$

In both cases we have that u is obtained from v by an elementary improvement of c. Thus, by strong monotonicity:

$$S(u) \subset \{c\} \cup S(v).$$

By assumption $c \neq a$ therefore the above inclusion, together with $a \in S(u)$, implies $a \in S(v)$.

To complete the proof of lemma 3 it remains to check that if v is any profile such that the position of a is preserved from u to v, then there exists a finite sequence of profiles

$$u = w_0, \ldots, w_t, \ldots, w_T = v$$

such that the shift from w_t to w_{t+1} is of type 1 or type 2 only.

To make this point clear we concentrate on the preferences of one particular agent, say agent 1. Fix u_1 and v_1 and set

$$U_1 = \{b/u_1(b) < u_1(a)\}; \qquad U^1 = \{b/u_1(b) > u_1(a)\},$$

$$V_1 = \{b/v_1(b) < v_1(a)\}; \qquad V^1 = \{b/v_1(b) > v_1(a)\}.$$

By assumption $U_1 \subset V_1$. We set $\tilde{U} = V_1 \setminus U_1$. Thus, $\tilde{U} \subset U^1$. The shift from u_1 to v_1 is now decomposed into three sequences.
   (1) A sequence of elementary shifts of type 2 from u_1 to u'_1, where:
   (a) u'_1 ranks U^1, $\{a\}$, U_1 in that order;
   (b) on U_1 it coincides with u_1; and
   (c) on U^1 it ranks $U^1 \setminus \tilde{U}$, $\tilde{U}$ in that order.

(2) A sequence of elementary improvements of a (type 1 shifts) from u'_1 to u''_1, where:
  (a) u''_1 ranks $U^1\setminus\tilde{U}$, a, $\tilde{U}$, U_1 in that order; and
  (b) it coincides with u'_1 on $A\setminus\{a\}$.
(3) A sequence of elementary shifts of type 2 from u''_1 to v_1, where independently $U^1\setminus\tilde{U}$ next $\tilde{U}\cup U_1$ are reordered as in v_1. This completes the proof of lemma 3.

4. Examples of a strongly monotonic s.c.c.

Seeking meaningful examples of a strongly monotonic s.c.c. is not an easy task.

One obvious example is the Pareto s.c.c. of which the choice set is the Pareto set for all profiles (we let the reader check that it satisfies SPA). Surely efficiency of the social choice is a fundamental requirement that virtually all s.c.c. to be considered here meet. However, the Pareto set can be a very large subset of A (especially when some individual preferences conflict – see Chapter 2, section 3). Thus, we think of the Pareto s.c.c. as a trivial solution of our collective decision problem. The very aim of social choice is to explore more deterministic solutions of the collective decision problem by imposing additional criteria on the arbitration method: one single outcome has to be selected anyway.

Ideally, one would like the social choice to be perfectly deterministic for all profiles, i.e. a social choice function. Unfortunately, a fundamental result (theorem 1, section 5) states that a strongly monotonic social choice function necessarily is a dictatorial one under the mild assumption that S can elect at least three different outcomes (the case where the set A contains only two outcomes will be studied in section 3, Chapter 4: there a rich family of s.c. *functions* are strongly monotonic).

Dictatorial s.c.f. are, again, trivial solutions of the social choice problem, that overcome the difficulty of having to compromise among possibly conflicting opinions of individual agents by not compromising at all and saying that all opinions but one are irrelevant. They do not meet the most primitive requirement that an individual should not be a dummy: he or she should have some influence on the choice set for some possible profile.

Interpreting optimistically theorem 1 we would say that strong monotonicity is a too demanding property since it forces some indeterminacy in the final choice set; therefore we should not show obstinacy in imposing a property that somehow lacks intuitive appeal. What objections should we raise after all against a monotonic if not strongly monotonic s.c.f.?

The weakness of the above argument cannot be demonstrated yet. Below (in Chapters 6 and 7) we will disclose the profound justification of strong monotonicity. From Chapter 4 we find that a s.c.f. is strategy proof (i.e. telling the truth is a dominating strategy) if and only if it is strongly monotonic. When the outcome space contains at least three elements, this yields the Gibbard-Satterthwaite impossibility result (theorem 2, Chapter 4). When the outcome space is a doubleton, this allows a complete characterization of strategy-proof voting methods.

Going to more cooperative equilibrium concepts (like Nash or strong equilibrium), strong monotonic s.c.c. (especially those which are inclusion minimal with this property) again play a central role. See Chapter 7, sections 5 and 6.

The next lemma establishes that the two families of s.c.c. proposed so far, namely scoring correspondences and Condorcet-type s.c.c., are not strongly monotonic.

Lemma 4 (Peleg, 1980). Suppose that A and N are given such that $p \geqslant 3$ and ($n = 3$ or $n \geqslant 5$).

Let S_s be a scoring correspondence with an associated scoring vector s such that

$$s_1 > s_2 \geqslant s_3 \geqslant \cdots \geqslant s_p.$$

Then S_s is *not* strongly monotonic.

Proof. By lemma 3 it suffices to prove that S_s violates SPA. Without loss of generality we can assume

$$s_1 = 1; \qquad s_2 = 0.$$

We pick a triple $\{a, b, c\}$ within A and two integers, n_1 and n_2, such that

$$1 \leqslant n_1 \leqslant n_2; \qquad 2n_2 + n_1 = n. \tag{7}$$

Clearly, the above system has a solution if and only if $n = 3$ or $n \geqslant 5$ (for n odd take $n_1 = 1$, for n even take $n_1 = 2$).

We order N arbitrarily and consider a profile u such that:

for $1 \leq i \leq n_1$: $\quad u_i(c) > u_i(b) > u_i(a)$,
for $n_1 + 1 \leq i \leq n_1 + n_2$: $u_i(a) > u_i(c) > u_i(b)$,
for $n_1 + n_2 + 1 \leq i \leq n$: $u_i(b) > u_i(a) > u_i(c)$;

all other outcomes being Pareto inferior to a, b and c.

Comparing the σ score of the various outcomes yields:

$$\sigma(a) = n_1 \cdot s_3 + n_2,$$

$$\sigma(b) = n_2 \cdot s_3 + n_2 \Rightarrow \sigma(a) \geq \sigma(b) \geq \sigma(c) > \sigma(x), \quad \text{all other } x,$$

$$\sigma(c) = n_1 + n_2 \cdot s_3.$$

Hence, a belongs to $S_s(u)$. Now consider a profile v such that:

for $1 \leq i \leq n_1$: $\quad u_i(b) > u_i(c) > u_i(a)$,
for $n_1 + 1 \leq i \leq n_1 + n_2$: $u_i(a) > u_i(b) > u_i(c)$,
for $n_1 + n_2 + 1 \leq i \leq n$: $u_i(b) > u_i(a) > u_i(c)$;

all other outcomes being Pareto inferior to a, b and c.

The corresponding scores are:

$$\sigma'(a) = n_1 \cdot s_3 + n_2,$$

$$\sigma'(b) = n_1 + n_2 \quad \Rightarrow \sigma'(b) > \sigma'(a) > \sigma'(c) \geq \sigma(x), \quad \text{all other } x,$$

$$\sigma'(c) = 2n_2 \cdot s_3.$$

Therefore $S_s(u) = \{b\}$. We obtain the desired contradiction by observing that the position of a is preserved from u to v.

Remark. For $p = 3$ and $n = 4$ we check that the plurality correspondence (corresponding to $s_1 = 1$, $s_2 = s_3 = 0$) is strongly monotonic. This justifies the restrictions on the pair (p, n) in the statement of lemma 4.

We prove now that no s.c.c. that generalizes the Condorcet winner(s) is strongly monotonic.

Lemma 5. Let A and N be given such that $p \geqslant 3$ and ($n = 3$ or $n \geqslant 5$). Let S be a Condorcet-type s.c.c.:

$$\forall u \in L(A)^N : [\mathrm{CW}(u) \neq \emptyset] \Rightarrow [S(u) = \mathrm{CW}(u)].$$

Then S is *not* strongly monotonic.

Proof. We assume that S satisfies SPA and derive a contradiction. We pick a triple $\{a, b, c\}$ within A and we consider a profile u as in the proof of lemma 2, Chapter 2: the relevant properties of u are given by $(\cdot)$.

Given u, there is no Condorcet winner so that $S(u)$ is not a priori restricted.

Suppose that $S(u)$ contains a. Then if v is a profile such that

$$\forall i \in N_1 : v_i(a) > v_i(c) > v_i(b) > v_i(d),$$

$$\forall i \in N_2 \cup N_3 : u_i = v_i,$$

outcome c is the unique Condorcet winner of v so that $S(v) = \{c\}$. We note that the position of a is preserved from u to v, therefore SPA would imply $a \in S(v)$. We conclude that $S(u)$ does not contain a. By symmetry it contains neither b nor c. Thus, $S(u)$ contains at least one Pareto-inferior outcome, d.

Let w be a profile where *all* agents are such that

$$w_i(a) > w_i(b) > w_i(c) > w_i(d).$$

Here, a is the Condorcet winner $\mathrm{CW}(w) = \{a\}$ so that $S(w) = \{a\}$. But the position of d is preserved from u to w, so by SPA $S(w)$ contains d – a contradiction.

We give now a less trivial example of a strongly monotonic s.c.c.

Example 2: A family of strongly monotonic s.c.c. Fix two integers k, $1 \leqslant k \leqslant p$, and m, $1 \leqslant m \leqslant n$. We consider the following s.c.c.:

$$S_{m,k}(u) = \{a \in A / a \text{ is ranked at most } k \text{ by at least } m \text{ agents}\}.$$

We can easily check that $S_{m,k}$ is not empty valued (for all profiles) if and only if:

$$m \leqslant [(k/p) \cdot n],$$

where $\lceil z \rceil$ denotes the smallest integer not inferior to z. Moreover, $S_{m,k}$ clearly satisfies SPA. Thus, these s.c.c. all are anonymous, neutral and strongly monotonic (notice that they do not satisfy efficiency when $k \geq 2$).

The next example is an efficient, anonymous and strongly monotonic s.c.c.

Example 3: The imputation s.c.c. We fix a particular outcome a_0 that plays the role of a status quo. Given a profile $u \in L(A)^N$ the socially desirable outcomes are taken to be Pareto optimal and individually rational (every agent gets at least his status quo utility level). Hence, S_{a_0} is given by

$$S_{a_0}(u) = \{a \in A / a \text{ is Pareto optimal and } u_i(a_0) \leq u_i(a), \text{ all } i \in N\}.$$

Clearly S_{a_0} satisfies SPA, and is therefore strongly monotonic. It results from problem 7 below that S_{a_0} is inclusion minimal among the strongly monotonic s.c.c. (a property not shared by any s.c.c. of the form $S_{m,k}$).

Problem 7: Inclusion Minimal Strongly Monotonic s.c.c. We say that a s.c.c. S is *inclusion minimal strongly monotonic* (IMSM) if it satisfies:
(a) S is strongly monotonic; and
(b) no strongly monotonic s.c.c. S' exists such that $S'(u) \subset S(u)$ for all $u \in L(A)^N$, the inclusion being strict for at least one profile u.
We shall use the following notation:

for all $a \in A$ and $u \in L(A) : Z(a, u) = \{b \in A / u(b) \leq u(a)\}$.

Observe that the SPA property can be reformulated as:

$$\forall a \in A, \forall u, v \in L(A)^N : [a \in S(u) \text{ and } Z(a, u_i) \subset Z(a, v_i), \text{ all } i \in N]$$

$$\Rightarrow [a \in S(v)].$$

(1) Let S be a strongly monotonic s.c.c. Prove that S is IMSM if and only if the following property holds true:

$$\forall a \in A, \forall u \in L(A)^N [a \in S(u)]$$

$$\Rightarrow \left[\exists v \in L(A)^N : S(v) = \{a\}, Z(a, v_i) = Z(a, u_i), \text{ all } i \in N \right].$$

(2) Show that an IMSM is efficient.

(3) Show that for all integers k, m such that $m \leq \lceil (k/p) \cdot n \rceil$ the s.c.c. $S_{m,k}$ (see example 2 above) is not IMSM.

(4) Show that for all $a_0 \in A$, the imputation s.c.c. S_{a_0} (see example 3 above) *is* IMSM.

As far as strong monotonicity is concerned, a nice s.c.c. would be an efficient anonymous and neutral IMSM s.c.c. Such s.c.c. do exist for some cardinalities of A and N: see Chapter 6, problem 18.

5. Strongly monotonic s.c.f.: Impossibility result

If A, the set of outcomes, contains at least three elements, then a very mild requirement on an s.c.f. is that every existing outcome could actually be reached for at least one profile:

$$\forall a \in A, \exists u \in L(A)^N, \quad a \in S(u). \tag{8}$$

This condition, called *citizen sovereignty*, is a consequence of the *unanimity* property (if some outcome is the top outcome of every agent, it should belong to the choice set). Citizen sovereignty requires even less than unanimity: no outcome is viewed as bad by the s.c.f. itself and therefore rejected independently of the individual opinions.

Theorem 1 (Muller and Satterthwaite, 1977). Let N be finite and A contains at least three outcomes. Let S be a social choice function satisfying citizen sovereignty. Then S is strongly monotonic if and only if it is dictatorial:

$$\exists i \in N, \forall u \in L(A)^N : S(u) = \{\text{top outcome of } u_i\}.$$

Theorem 1 is a typical "impossibility" result: when at least three outcomes can be elected, only "trivial" social choice functions, i.e. the dictatorial ones, are strongly monotonic. Alternatively we can conclude that the strong monotonicity property *implies* some indeterminacy of collective choice (if S is a strongly monotonic s.c.c. there are some profiles such that the corresponding choice set is not a singleton).

When A, the set of outcomes, is a doubleton, very meaningful strongly monotonic social choice functions (typically majority voting) exist. They will be studied systematically in Chapter 4.

As a final remark we insist that theorem 1 is very powerful: it easily implies the Arrow theorem (theorem 2 below) and (at a low cost) the Gibbard–Satterthwaite theorem (theorem 2, Chapter 4).

Proof of theorem 1. The "if" part of the result is evident. To prove the "only if" statement we fix a strongly monotonic s.c.f. S satisfying citizen sovereignty.

Step 1. S is efficient.

Otherwise we take a profile u and suppose that $S(u)$ is not efficient: $S(u) \notin \text{Par}(u)$. Setting $a = S(u)$ there exists $b \in A$, an outcome Pareto superior to a. Choosing a profile v such that *all* agents in v rank b first and a second, we observe that the position of a is preserved from u to v. Hence, by SPA $a = S(v)$. But citizen sovereignty implies the existence of some profile w such that $S(w) = b$. Since the position of b is preserved from w to v we have, by SPA again, $S(v) = b$ – a contradiction.

Step 2.

We fix a coalition $T \subset N$ and two distinct outcomes, $a, b \in A$. We define a subset $\mathcal{U}(T, a, b)$ of $L(A)^N$ by

$$u \in \mathcal{U}(T, a, b) \Leftrightarrow \begin{array}{l} \forall i \in T: u_i \text{ ranks } a \text{ top, } b \text{ second,} \\ \forall j \in N \setminus T: u_j \text{ ranks } b \text{ top, } a \text{ second.} \end{array}$$

We claim that for all T, a, b the following three statements are equivalent:
(i) $S(\mathcal{U}(T, a, b)) = \{a\}$;
(ii) $\exists u \in L(A)^N S(u) = a$ and $\{i \in N / u_i(a) > u_i(b)\} = T$; and
(iii) $\forall u \in L(A)^N [\{i \in N / u_i(a) > u_i(b)\} = T] \Rightarrow [S(u) \neq b]$.

(i) $\Rightarrow$ (ii) is evident. To prove (ii) $\Rightarrow$ (iii) per absurdum we take two profiles, u and v, such that:

$$S(u) = a \quad \text{and} \quad \{i \in N / u_i(a) > u_i(b)\} = T,$$

$$S(v) = b \quad \text{and} \quad \{i \in N / v_i(a) > v_i(b)\} = T.$$

Choosing any profile $w \in \mathcal{U}(T, a, b)$ we observe that the position of a (and b) is preserved from u to w (and from v to w). Therefore by SPA we must have $S(w) = a$ and $S(w) = b$ – a contradiction.

The implication (iii) ⇒ (i) follows from the efficiency of S (step 1). Namely, if $u \in \mathcal{U}(T, a, b)$ only a and b are Pareto-optimal outcomes so that $S(u) \in \{a, b\}$.

Step 3.

For every pair $\{a, b\}$ of distinct outcomes we define a subset $\mathcal{T}_{a,b}$ of non-empty coalitions of N ($\mathcal{T}_{a,b} \subset 2^N \setminus \{\emptyset\}$). We say that *coalition T blocks b by a* and denote $T \in \mathcal{T}_{a,b}$ if properties (i)–(iii) of step 2 hold. We will derive some set-theoretical properties of $\mathcal{T}_{a,b}$:

(α) $N \in \mathcal{T}_{a,b}$. Namely if u belongs to $\mathcal{U}(N, a, b)$, then Par$(u) = \{a\}$ so that $S(u) = a$ by efficiency of S (step 1). Thus, $N \in \mathcal{T}_{a,b}$ by definition (i).

(β) $T \in \mathcal{T}_{a,b} \Leftrightarrow N \setminus T \notin \mathcal{T}_{b,a}$ (all proper and non-empty subsets of N). The implication $T \in \mathcal{T}_{a,b} \Rightarrow N \setminus T \notin \mathcal{T}_{a,b}$ is obvious from definition (i). To prove the converse implication, we observe that if u and v both belong to $\mathcal{U}(T, a, b)$ then the position of a (and b) is preserved from u to v (and from v to u). Since by efficiency $S(\mathcal{U}(T, a, b)) \subset \{a, b\}$ we conclude by SPA that either $S(\mathcal{U}(T, a, b)) = \{a\}$ or $S(\mathcal{U}(T, a, b)) = \{b\}$. We note $\mathcal{U}(T, a, b) = \mathcal{U}(N \setminus T, b, a)$ so that $S(\mathcal{U}(T, a, b)) = \{b\}$ means $N \setminus T \in \mathcal{T}_{b,a}$.

(γ) For all $a, b, c \in A$ such that $a \ne b$ and $a \ne c$, we have $\mathcal{T}_{b,a} = \mathcal{T}_{c,a}$. Because both b and c play symmetrical roles it suffices to prove $\mathcal{T}_{b,a} \subset \mathcal{T}_{c,a}$. Suppose then that some coalition T is such that $T \in \mathcal{T}_{b,a} T \notin \mathcal{T}_{c,a}$. By property ($\beta$) we obtain $N \setminus T \in \mathcal{T}_{a,c}$. We choose now a profile u such that:

$$\forall i \in T: u_i(c) > u_i(b) > u_i(a) > u_i(x), \quad \text{all other } x,$$
$$\forall i \in N \setminus T: u_i(a) > u_i(c) > u_i(b) > u_i(x), \quad \text{all other } x.$$

The corresponding Pareto set is $\{a, c\}$ so that by efficiency of S: $S(u) \in \{a, c\}$. Next, by definition (iii) of $\mathcal{T}_{a,b}$, we get $S(u) \ne a$ (since $T = \{i / u_i(b) > u_i(a)\}$), and $S(u) \ne c$ (since $N \setminus T = \{i / u_i(a) > u_i(c)\}$). This is the desired contradiction.

Step 4.

We now make use of the assumption that A contains at least three distinct elements. This allows us to prove:

(δ) For all $a, b \in A$ such that $a \ne b$: $\mathcal{T}_{a,b} = \mathcal{T}_{b,a}$.

Per absurdum we choose some coalition T such that

$$T \in \mathcal{T}_{b,a}; \qquad T \notin \mathcal{T}_{a,b}.$$

From property (β) we derive $N \setminus T \in \mathcal{T}_{b,a}$. We introduce now a third outcome, c, distinct from a and b.

Suppose $N \setminus T \in \mathfrak{T}_{a,c}$. Then by ($\beta$) we have $T \notin \mathfrak{T}_{c,a}$ and in view of (γ): $T \notin \mathfrak{T}_{b,a}$ – a contradiction. Hence,

$$N \setminus T \notin \mathfrak{T}_{a,c}. \tag{9}$$

Similarly, suppose $N \setminus T \notin \mathfrak{T}_{b,c}$. Then by ($\beta$) we have $T \in \mathfrak{T}_{c,b}$ and by (γ) we have $\mathfrak{T}_{c,b} = \mathfrak{T}_{a,b}$. Hence, a contradiction again so that

$$N \setminus T \in \mathfrak{T}_{b,c}. \tag{10}$$

Finally, (9) and (10) together contradict (γ). Thus (δ) is proved.

Now properties (γ) and (δ) together imply that $\mathfrak{T}_{a,b}$ does not depend on (a, b):

$$\mathfrak{T}_{a,b} = \mathfrak{T}, \quad \text{all } a, b \in A.$$

Step 5.

We show that $\mathfrak{T}$ is a filter of A, that is to say

$$T, T' \in \mathfrak{T} \Rightarrow T \cap T' \in \mathfrak{T}. \tag{11}$$

Per absurdum we select two elements, T and T', of $\mathfrak{T}$ such that $T \cap T' \notin \mathfrak{T}$. By ($\beta$) this implies $N \setminus (T \cap T') \in \mathfrak{T}$. We choose three distinct outcomes, a, b and c, and a profile u such that:

$$\left. \begin{aligned} \forall i \in T \cap T' &: u_i(a) > u_i(b) > u_i(c) \\ \forall j \in N \setminus T' &: u_j(c) > u_j(a) > u_j(b) \\ \forall k \in T' \setminus T &: u_k(b) > u_k(c) > u_k(a) \end{aligned} \right\},$$

all other outcomes being Pareto inferior to a, b, c.

By definition (iii) of $\mathfrak{T}$ we have successively:

$$\{i \in N / u_i(b) > u_i(c)\} = T' \Rightarrow S(u) \neq c,$$

$$\{i \in N / u_i(c) > u_i(a)\} = N \setminus (T \cap T') \Rightarrow S(u) \neq a,$$

By efficiency of S we have $S(u) \in \{a, b, c\}$, therefore $S(u) = b$. We note now that

$$\{i \in N / u_i(a) > u_i(b)\} \supset T.$$

Then there exists a profile v, obtained from u by an improvement of b, such that $\{i \in N / v_i(a) > v_i(b)\} = T$.

By monotonicity of S we must have $S(v) = b$, which contradicts definition (iii) of $\mathcal{T}$. This proves (1^1). In particular it proves that the intersection of two coalitions in $\mathcal{T}$ is non-empty.

Hence, by the finiteness of N the overall intersection $T_0 = \bigcap_{T \in \mathcal{T}} T$ of the coalitions in $\mathcal{T}$ is non-empty and belongs to $\mathcal{T}$. Suppose that T_0 contains two distinct agents, i and j. Then any partition $T_0 = T_1 \cup T_2$ of T_0 is such that

$$T_1 \notin \mathcal{T}; \quad T_2 \notin \mathcal{T}.$$

By (β) this implies $N \setminus T_1 \in \mathcal{T}$ and $N \setminus T_2 \in \mathcal{T}$; hence, by (11) $(N \setminus T_1) \cap (N \setminus T_2) = N \setminus (T_1 \cup T_2) = N \setminus T_0$ must belong to $\mathcal{T}$. Thus, both T_0 and its complement in N belong to $\mathcal{T}$ – a contradiction of (β).

We have just proved that T_0 is a singleton of N, say $T_0 = \{i\}$. We now prove that i is a dictator for S. Given a profile $\boldsymbol{u}$ we denote by a the top candidate of i. Let $\boldsymbol{v}$ be a profile such that $v_i = u_i$, and for all $j, j \neq i$, a is the bottom outcome of v_j.

Then for all outcomes b, $b \neq a$, we have

$$\{j \in N / v_j(a) > v_j(b)\} = \{i\} \in \mathcal{T}.$$

Hence, by definition (iii) of $\mathcal{T}$ it follows that $S(v) \neq b$. Accordingly, $S(v) = a$. Notice that the position of a is preserved from v to $\boldsymbol{u}$, therefore $S(\boldsymbol{u}) = a$ as well. This proves that for all $\boldsymbol{u}$, $S(\boldsymbol{u})$ is the top outcome of u_i and concludes the proof of theorem 1.

6. Social welfare functions: Arrow's theorem

Technically we will derive Arrow's impossibility theorem as an easy corollary of theorem 1.

A social welfare function is an operator aggregating any set of individual preferences (any profile) into a single preference viewed as the preference of society as a whole.

Definition 5. Given A and N, a *social welfare function* (s.w.f.) is a mapping Σ from $L(A)^N$ into $L(A)$.

Clearly a s.w.f. is a more complex mathematical object than an s.c.c. or an s.c.f. A collectivity capable of designing a social welfare function will be able to derive a "social opinion" over every pair of feasible outcomes: that is to say, an s.w.f. tells us not only which outcome will be looked at as a social optimum, but it tells us also which one is preferred among any two non-socially optimal outcomes. This additional information is of crucial importance if the constitution (the social choice operator) must be agreed upon *before* the set of feasible outcomes is known.

Suppose for instance that N is the (fixed) set of electors and A the set of eligible persons from which the electorate must pick one. Certain well-known criteria (age, status, etc.) define the set of potentially eligible persons. But the set of actual candidates is a strict (in general very small!) subset of A determined by less transparent reasons: indeed, the decision to run or not to run results from mostly tactical considerations which are in essence covert – to say the least. It is an empirical and theoretical fact that, depending on the voting rule to be used, strategic modifications of the final set of candidates can be profitable. In plurality voting when centrist candidates duplicate, an extremist candidate might win, owing to cannibalism of centrist electorate. When outcomes are numerical parameters, the choice of a maximal feasible interval to be voted on can be expected to be bargained upon as harshly as the final vote.

If society is able to set up a social welfare function then it is ready to face any set of "feasible" candidates and still determine one unambiguous winner. Suppose Σ is a s.w.f. and B any (non-empty) subset of A. Given any profile $\mathbf{u} \in L(A)^N$, the social preference $\Sigma(\mathbf{u})$ over A will be simply restricted to B and the election of the top candidate of $\Sigma(\mathbf{u})$ over B recommended. This flexibility is not allowed to s.c.f. nor to s.c.c. since they do not respond to potential variations of the set of actual candidates.

The potential adaptability of social welfare functions to any set of relevant candidates is only a fake if the restriction of the social preference to various subsets of candidates ever depends on the preferences of the individual agents *outside* these subsets – formally if the restriction of $\Sigma(\mathbf{u})$ over B depends on the whole profile $\mathbf{u}$ and not on the restriction of $\mathbf{u}$ over B only. In that case the choice of an initial set A of eligible persons does influence the final decision, even if everybody is aware that most of the members of A are not actual candidates; accordingly, the choice of a particular A is debatable and hence potentially conflictual and we are back to the sensitiveness of s.c.f. with respect to the choice of A.

Notation. For any profile $\mathbf{u} \in L(A)^N$ and any subset B of A we denote by $\mathbf{u}^B$ the restriction of $\mathbf{u}$ to B:

$$\mathbf{u}^B \in L(B)^N, \forall i \in N, \forall b, b' \in B: u_i^B(b) > u_i^B(b') \Leftrightarrow u_i(b) > u_i(b').$$

Definition 6. Given A and N and a social welfare function Σ we say that Σ is *independent of irrelevant alternatives* (IIA) if for all subsets B of A and all profiles $\boldsymbol{u}$ the restriction of $\Sigma(\boldsymbol{u})$ to B depends only on the restriction of $\boldsymbol{u}$ to B:

$$\forall \boldsymbol{u} \in L(A)^N : [\boldsymbol{u}^B = \boldsymbol{v}^B] \Rightarrow \left[\Sigma(\boldsymbol{u})^B = \Sigma(\boldsymbol{v})^B\right]. \tag{12}$$

Clearly, a s.w.f. satisfies IIA iff it satisfies (12) for every pair of outcomes:

$$\forall \boldsymbol{u}, \boldsymbol{v} \in L(A)^N, \forall a, b \in A:$$

$$\left[\forall i \in N\{u_i(a) > u_i(b)\} \Leftrightarrow \{v_i(a) > v_i(b)\}\right]$$
$$\Rightarrow \left[\{\Sigma(\boldsymbol{u})(a) > \Sigma(\boldsymbol{u})(b)\} \Leftrightarrow \{\Sigma(\boldsymbol{v})(a) > \Sigma(\boldsymbol{v})(b)\}\right] \tag{13}$$

Theorem 2 (Arrow, 1963). Let A and N be both finite and A contains at least three outcomes. Let Σ be a Paretian social welfare function:

$$\forall \boldsymbol{u} \in L(A)^N, \forall a, b \in A : \left[\forall i \in N u_i(a) > u_i(b)\right]$$
$$\Rightarrow \left[\Sigma(\boldsymbol{u})(a) > \Sigma(\boldsymbol{u})(b)\right]. \tag{14}$$

Then Σ is independent of irrelevant alternatives if and only if it is dictatorial:

$$\exists i \in N, \forall \boldsymbol{u} \in L(A)^N : \Sigma(\boldsymbol{u}) = u_i.$$

The Paretian character of an s.w.f. (condition (13)) is analogous to the efficiency property of an s.c.f. It implies in particular unanimity of the s.w.f. (if $u_i = u$ for all i, then $\Sigma(\boldsymbol{u}) = u$).

Thus, Arrow's theorem is a negative result that explains why we will not explore further the formalism of s.w.f. It should be interpreted as the strategic statement that in all non-dictatorial voting methods the choice of the set of feasible candidates is potentially conflictual and subject to manipulations: this is so because additional candidates who are irrelevant, since they will not finally be elected, do influence the final result.

Proof of theorem 2. Only the "only if" implication is non-obvious. Let us choose a Paretian s.w.f. Σ satisfying IIA. For all $a, b \in A$ we consider the subset $\mathfrak{T}_{a,b}$ of coalitions "blocking b by a":

$$T \in \mathfrak{T}_{a,b} \Leftrightarrow \forall \boldsymbol{u}\big[\{i \in N / u_i(b) < u_i(a)\} = T\big] \Rightarrow \big[\Sigma(\boldsymbol{u})(a) > \Sigma(\boldsymbol{u})(b)\big].$$

The same argument developed in the proof of theorem 1 could be followed now to obtain a parallel proof of theorem 2: one would show successively that $\mathfrak{T}_{a,b}$ does not depend on (a, b) and that $\mathfrak{T}$ is a filter, and therefore contains a singleton.

Here we simply establish monotonicity of $\mathfrak{T}_{a,b}$ and then derive theorem 2 as a corollary of theorem 1.

Step 1.
For all $a, b \in A$, $\mathfrak{T}_{a,b}$ is *monotonic*:

$$\big[T \in \mathfrak{T}_{a,b} \text{ and } T \subset T'\big] \Rightarrow \big[T' \in \mathfrak{T}_{a,b}\big]. \tag{15}$$

Since Σ is Paretian, $\mathfrak{T}_{a,b}$ contains the grand coalition N.

Let $a, b \in A$ be two given outcomes and T be a coalition in $\mathfrak{T}_{a,b}$. We choose an outcome c different from $\{a, b\}$ and we consider any profile $\boldsymbol{u}$ such that:

$$\begin{cases} \forall i \in T: \quad u_i(a) > u_i(b) > u_i(c), \\ \forall j \in N \setminus T: \ b \text{ is the top outcome of } u_j. \end{cases} \tag{16}$$

Because Σ is Paretian we have:

$$\Sigma(\boldsymbol{u})(b) > \Sigma(\boldsymbol{u})(c).$$

Because T belongs to $\mathfrak{T}_{a,b}$ we have:

$$\Sigma(\boldsymbol{u})(a) > \Sigma(\boldsymbol{u})(b).$$

Because $\Sigma(\boldsymbol{u})$ is transitive this implies:

$$\Sigma(\boldsymbol{u})(a) > \Sigma(\boldsymbol{u})(c).$$

Since $\boldsymbol{u}$ satisfying (16) can be taken arbitrarily we deduce:

$$\forall T' \subset N: T \subset T' \Rightarrow T' \in \mathfrak{T}_{a,c}. \tag{17}$$

In particular, $T \in \mathfrak{T}_{a,c}$ so that $\mathfrak{T}_{a,b} \subset \mathfrak{T}_{a,c}$. Since the roles of c, b can be permuted, this implies $\mathfrak{T}_{a,b} = \mathfrak{T}_{a,c}$. Returning to (17) we deduce the monotonicity of $\mathfrak{T}_{a,b}$ (property (15)).

Step 2.

To the s.w.f. Σ we associate the s.c.f. S:

$S(u) = $ top outcome of $\Sigma(u)$.

The IAA property of Σ implies that S satisfies SPA. That is to say, for any two given profiles u and v and outcome a such that the position of a is preserved from u to v, we have

$$\forall b \in A, b \neq a: \{i \in N / u_i(a) > u_i(b)\} \subset \{i \in N / v_i(a) > v_i(b)\}.$$

In view of IIA, assuming $a = S(u)$ amounts to

$$\forall b \in A, b \neq a: \{i \in N / u_i(a) > u_i(b)\} \in \mathcal{T}_{a,b}$$

This, by monotonicity of $\mathcal{T}_{a,b}$, implies

$$\forall b \in A, b \neq a: \{i \in N / v_i(a) > v_i(b)\} \in \mathcal{T}_{a,b}.$$

Therefore $\Sigma(v)(a) > \Sigma(v)(b)$ for all b and $a = S(v)$ again. We have proved that S satisfies SPA.

Because Σ satisfies unanimity, S satisfies it as well, hence citizen sovereignty holds for S. Thus, by theorem 1 we conclude that S must be dictatorial.

Step 3.

If agent i is a dictator for S, he or she is a dictator for Σ as well.

That is to say, suppose that for some profile u we have

$$\begin{cases} a = S(u) = \text{top outcome of } u_i, \\ b = \text{second outcome of } \Sigma(u) \neq \text{second outcome of } u_i = c. \end{cases} \quad (18)$$

Then consider a profile v such that

$$\begin{cases} c = \text{top outcome of } v_i, \\ v_j = u_j, \quad \text{all } j \neq i. \end{cases}$$

We have $S(v) = c$, therefore $\Sigma(v)(c) > \Sigma(v)(b)$. On the other hand, (18) implies $\Sigma(u)(b) > \Sigma(u)(c)$. The two later inequalities contradict IIA since

$$\{j \in N / u_j(c) > u_j(b)\} = \{j \in N / v_j(c) > v_j(b)\}.$$

We have proved that the second outcome of $\Sigma(u)$ necessarily is the second outcome of u_i. Repeating this argument inductively shows that $\Sigma(u)$ coincides with u_i.

References

Arrow, K., 1963, Social choice and individual values, John Wiley, New York.
Moulin, H., 1980, "Implementing efficient, anonymous and neutral social choice functions", Journal of Mathematical Economics 7, 249–269.
Muller, E. and M. Satterthwaite, 1977, "The equivalence of strong positive association and strategy proofness", Journal of Economic Theory 14, 412–418.
Peleg, B., 1980, Game theoretic analysis of voting in committees, The Institute of Mathematics, The Hebrew University of Jerusalem.
Sraffin, P., 1978, Introduction to the social choice theory for environmental decision making, Department of Mathematics, Beloit College, Beloit, Wisconsin.

CHAPTER 4

STRATEGY-PROOFNESS AND MONOTONICITY

1. Summary of the results

A game form (g.f.) describes any democratic decision rule that can be associated with a fixed society and set of outcomes. It is a more general object than a social choice function.

In section 2 we define a strategy-proof g.f. (resp. s.c.f.) where for each profile each agent is endowed with at least one dominating strategy (resp. where telling the truth always is a dominating strategy).

When there are only two outcomes, strategy-proofness, monotonicity and strong monotonicity are three equivalent properties of a s.c.f. (theorem 1, section 3). We characterize those strategy-proof s.c.f. which are, in addition, neutral and/or anonymous.

When at least three different outcomes exist, the Gibbard–Satterthwaite theorem states that the only strategy-proof g.f. are dictatorial, i.e. endow one particular agent with all decision power (theorem 2, section 4).

To overcome this impossibility result we restrict the domain of feasible preferences profiles (section 5). If a Condorcet winner exists for every feasible profile, it defines a strategy-proof s.c.f (theorem 3, section 5). Therefore we seek restrictions of the domain that systematically avoid the Condorcet paradox. One such restriction is the single peakedness of preferences: the outcomes are linearly ordered and in every agent's preference there is exactly one local maximum (i.e. an outcome that is preferred to its neighbour(s)).

2. Strategy-proof social choice functions and game forms

When society (N) and the outcome space (A) are fixed, we say that a decision process is democratic if it relies only on individual wills. It is formally described by a game form.

A game form distributes exhaustively the decision power among individuals by endowing each agent with a fixed message space and converting any bundle of an agent's messages into a single outcome.

Definition 1. Given A, the set of outcomes, and N, the set of agents, a game form g is an $(N+1)$-tuple $g = (X_i, i \in N; \pi)$, where:
   (a) X_i is the strategy set (or message space) of agent i, and
   (b) π is a (single valued) mapping from $X_N = \prod_{i \in N} X_i$ into A.
The mapping π describes the decision rule: if for all i agent i chooses strategy i, the overall strategy N-tuple is denoted $x = (x_i)_{i \in N}$ and the decision rule π forces the outcome $\pi(x) \in A$.

Any social choice function (definition 2, Chapter 2) can be viewed as a game form where the message space of every agent is $L(A)$, the set of linear orderings of A, and S is the decision rule. Throughout this chapter almost every considered g.f. will be a s.c.f. In fact, lemma 1 below states that the search for strategy proof g.f. is equivalent to that of strategy proof s.c.f. The full generality of the game form concept, which allows in particular the message space to be bigger than $L(A)$, is needed when we explore a more complex strategic behaviour than the dominating strategy equilibrium. This is indeed the case in Chapters 5–7.

Given a game form $g = (X_i, i \in N, \pi)$ we can associate to every preference profile $u = (u_i)_{i \in N}$ the normal form game $g(u) = (X_i, u_i \circ \pi, i \in N)$, where agent i's strategy is x_i and his or her utility level is $u_i(\pi(x))$. This game reflects the interdependence of the individual agents' opinions (utility) and their strategic abilities (agent i is free to send any message within X_i).

In this chapter we focus on those game forms such that for all profiles u every agent has a straightforward non-cooperative strategy whether or not he or she knows of the other agents' preference orderings. This is captured by the notion of dominating strategy.

Notation. We denote

$$X_{\hat{i}} = \prod_{\substack{j \in N \\ j \neq i}} X_j,$$

with current element $x_{\hat{i}}$. Similarly, the current element of $L(A)^{N \setminus (i)}$ is denoted by $u_{\hat{i}}$.

Definition 2. Given A and N and a game form g we say that g is *strategy-proof* if for every agent i there exists a mapping from $L(A)$ into X_i denoted $u_i \to x_i(u_i)$ such that the following hold true:

$$\forall u_i \in L(A), \forall x_{\hat{\imath}} \in X_{\hat{\imath}}, \forall y_i \in X_i: u_i(\pi(y_i, x_{\hat{\imath}})) \leq u_i(\pi(x_i(u_i), u_{\hat{\imath}})). \tag{1}$$

Given a social choice function S, we say that S is *strategy-proof* if for every agent i we have:

$$\forall u_i \in L(A), \forall u_{\hat{\imath}} \in L(A)^{N\setminus\{i\}}, \forall v_i \in L(A): u_i(S(v_i, u_{\hat{\imath}}))$$
$$\leq u_i(S(u_i, u_{\hat{\imath}})). \tag{2}$$

Property (1) says that if agent i's utility is u_i then strategy $x_i(u_i)$ is a best response to every possible strategic behaviour $x_{\hat{\imath}}$ of the other agents, in short x_i is a dominating strategy. Notice that $x_i(u_i)$ is a decentralized behaviour by agent i, who can simply ignore the utility of the other agents.

Similarly, in a strategy-proof s.c.f., "telling the truth" is always a dominating strategy of every agent (property (2)) so that we expect the agents to reveal *sincerely* their utility. Notice that violation of (2) implies that for some agent i, some profile u and some $v_i \in L(A)$:

$$u_i(S(v_i, u_{\hat{\imath}})) > u_i(S(u)).$$

This inequality implies that if the true profile is u, agent i's interest is to manipulate the decision process by pretending that his or her utility actually is v_i. As soon as this possibility arises we are led to the full complexity of the implementation problem, to be explored in the subsequent chapters. So far we merely observe that *among non-cooperative agents* a strategy-proof g.f. or s.c.f. is a dependable decentralization device since the agents' selfish behaviour is unambiguous and therefore predictable.

Remark 1. There are normal form games where cooperative players can do better than using their dominating strategies (if any). This is illustrated by the well-known Prisoner's dilemma or by the game forms proposed in problem 11 (question 2). See, however, remark 3, section 5.

Given a s.c.f. S the property [S is strategy-proof] is more demanding than [S, viewed as a g.f., is strategy-proof] since the later only requires that for all i and all u_i, some utility v_i (that might differ from u_i) is a dominating strategy of i. However, the following result establishes that every strategy-proof g.f. can be equivalently written as a strategy-proof s.c.f. (in the sense of definition 2).

Lemma 1. Let g be a strategy-proof g.f. For all $i \in N$ and all $u_i \in L(A)$, let us denote by $D_i(u_i) \subset X_i$ the set of agent i's dominating strategies:

$$\{x_i \in D_i(u_i)\} \Leftrightarrow \{\forall x_{\hat{\imath}} \in X_{\hat{\imath}} \forall y_i \in X_i u_i(\pi(y_i, x_{\hat{\imath}})) \leq u_i(\pi(x_i, x_{\hat{\imath}}))\}.$$

Then for all profiles $u \in L(A)^N$ the set $\pi(D_i(u_i), i \in N)$ is a singleton and defines a strategy proof s.c.f.

The proof is straightforward and therefore omitted.

3. The case of a binary choice

When the set A of outcomes is a doubleton there are many strategy-proof g.f. and s.c.f. By lemma 1 it suffices to consider s.c.f. Since $L(A)$ contains only two elements we shall use the following notation:

$$A = \{0, 1\} \quad \text{and} \quad L(A) = \{0, 1\},$$

$$\text{where} \begin{cases} u_i = 0 \text{ stands for } u_i(0) > u_i(1), \\ u_i = 1 \text{ stands for } u_i(1) > u_i(0). \end{cases}$$

Thus, a s.c.f. S is written as a mapping from $\{0, 1\}^N$ into $\{0, 1\}$.

The notions of monotonicity (definition 2, Chapter 3) and strong monotonicity (definition 3, Chapter 3) clearly coincide since S is single valued. Thus, S is monotonic iff:

$$\forall x, y \in \{0, 1\}^N : [x_i \leq y_i, \text{ all } i \in N] \Rightarrow [S(x) \leq S(y)],$$

i.e. S is not decreasing with respect to the natural ordering of $\{0, 1\}^N$.

Theorem 1. Let $A = \{0, 1\}$, N and a s.c.f. $S: \{0, 1\}^N \to \{0, 1\}$ be given. Then S is strategy-proof if and only if it is monotonic.

Proof. S is strategy-proof if and only if, for every i:

$$\left. \begin{array}{l} u_i(1) < u_i(0) \Rightarrow u_i(S(1, x_{\hat{\imath}})) \leq u_i(S(0, x_{\hat{\imath}})) \\ u_i(0) < u_i(1) \Rightarrow u_i(S(0, x_{\hat{\imath}})) \leq u_i(S(1, x_{\hat{\imath}})) \end{array} \right\}, \quad \text{all } x_{\hat{\imath}} \in \{0, 1\}^{N \setminus \{i\}}.$$

Thus, S is strategy-proof if and only if it is monotonic with respect to each coordinate. Now monotonicity of S is equivalent to its monotonicity in each coordinate.

The above "theorem", although mathematically trivial, is important in so far as interpretation of the monotonicity properties is concerned.

These properties play a central role until Chapter 7: we provide in the current chapter a direct reformulation of monotonicity in terms of non-manipulability.

To select among strategy-proof s.c.f. we use the criteria of neutrality and anonymity.

In our present context where a s.c.f. is a mapping S from $\{0,1\}^N$ into $\{0,1\}$, definitions 4 and 5 of Chapter 2 are written as:
S is anonymous iff S can be written as

$$S(x) = s\left(\sum_{i \in N} x_i\right), \quad \text{all } x \in \{0,1\}^N;$$

S is neutral iff

$$S(x) = 1 - S(y), \quad \text{where } y_i = 1 - x_i, \quad \text{all } i, \quad \text{for all } x \in \{0,1\}^N.$$

Corollary of theorem 1. Let the society N contain n agents. There are $n+2$ anonymous and strategy-proof s.c.f. given by

$$0 \leqslant q \leqslant n+1 : S_q(x) = \begin{cases} 1, & \text{if } \sum_{i \in N} x_i \geqslant q, \\ 0, & \text{if } \sum_{i \in N} x_i < q. \end{cases}$$

Thus, if n is even, no s.c.f. is simultaneously anonymous, neutral and strategy-proof, whereas if n is odd, exactly one s.c.f., namely $S_{(n+1)/2}$: the binary majority s.c.f., is anonymous, neutral and strategy-proof.

The voting rules S_q are the quota majority methods. For instance, $S_{2n/3}$ says that the status quo (outcome 0) wins unless a two-thirds majority agrees on the proposed revision (outcome 1).

The family of neutral and strategy-proof s.c.f. is much more complex, as illustrated by problem 8 below. Roughly, a neutral monotonic s.c.f. is exhaustively described by a family of "winning" coalitions (a simple game) such that for every partition $N = T_1 \cup T_2$ of N, exactly one among T_1 or T_2 is winning. Then for every profile $x \in \{0, 1\}^N$, the winning coalition of the partition $\{i/x_i = 0\} \cup \{i/x_i = 1\}$ determines the elected outcome.

Problem 8: Neutral and strategy-proof (binary) social choice functions (Fishburn and Gehrlein, 1977). Let $S: \{0, 1\}^N \to \{0, 1\}$ be a fixed s.c.f. We say that a coalition $T(T \subset N)$ is winning (with respect to S) if we have:

$$\left. \begin{array}{l} \forall i \in T, \quad x_i = 1 \\ \forall i \notin T, \quad x_i = 0 \end{array} \right\} \Rightarrow S(x) = 1, \quad \text{for all } x \in \{0, 1\}^N.$$

Let us denote by W the set of winning coalitions.

(1) Show that S is neutral if and only if W satisfies the following property:

$$\forall T \subset N: T \in W \Leftrightarrow T^c \notin W.$$

Show that S is strategy-proof if and only if W is "monotonic" in the following sense:

$$\forall T, T' \subset N: [T \in W, T \subset T'] \Rightarrow [T' \in W].$$

(2) Let W_0 be the subset of W made up of the inclusion minimal elements of W:

$$T_0 \in W_0 \Leftrightarrow [T_0 \in W \text{ and } \{T' \in W, T \subset T_0\} \Rightarrow \{T = T_0\}].$$

Show that if S is neutral and strategy-proof, its associated set W_0 satisfies

$$\forall T \subset N: [\exists T_0 \in W_0, T_0 \subset T] \Leftrightarrow [\forall T_0' \in W_0: T_0' \cap T \neq \emptyset].$$

(3) Conversely, let W_1 be a subset of 2^N such that

$$\forall T, T' \in W_1: (T \subset T') \Rightarrow (T = T') \tag{3}$$

and

$$\forall T \subset N: [\exists T_1 \in W_1, T_1 \subset T] \Leftrightarrow [\forall T_1' \in W_1: T_1' \cap T \neq \emptyset]. \tag{4}$$

Then prove that the following s.c.f. S_1 is neutral and strategy-proof:

$$\forall x \in \{0, 1\}^N: \pi(x) = 1, \quad \text{iff } \exists T_1 \in W_1: \forall i \in T_1, x_i = 1.$$

(4) Describe all subsets W_1 sharing (3) and (4) for $n \leq 5$ (n is the cardinality of N).

For a given cardinality of N, the neutral and strategy-proof s.c.f. can be distinguished by the amount of discrimination that they introduce among agents. At one extreme are the dictatorial s.c.f. and at the other extreme the majority binary vote which is uniquely anonymous (for odd n). One way to generate a family of neutral and strategy-proof s.c.f. is to allocate a (non-negative) weight α_i to agent i and declare that a winning coalition is one of which the total weight does not exceed $\frac{1}{2}[\sum_{i \in N} \alpha_i]$ (to avoid "ties" one requires that the total weight $\sum_{i \in T} \alpha_i$ of a coalition T never equals $\frac{1}{2}[\sum_{i \in N} \alpha_i]$). However, not all neutral and strategy-proof s.c.f. can be obtained in such a way.

4. The Gibbard–Satterthwaite theorem

We say that the game form $g = (X_i, i \in N; \pi)$ satisfies citizen sovereignty if

$$\pi\left(\prod_{i \in N} X_i\right) = A.$$

This generalizes straightforwardly the notion of citizen sovereignty for s.c.f. (Chapter 3, section 5).

Theorem 2 (Gibbard, 1973, and Satterthwaite, 1973). Let N be finite and A contain at least three outcomes. Let $g = (X_i, i \in N, \pi)$ be a game form satisfying citizen sovereignty. Then g is strategy-proof if and only if it is dictatorial:

$$\exists i \in N, \forall a \in A; \exists x_i \in X_i, \forall x_{\hat{i}} \in X_{\hat{i}}: \pi(x_i, x_{\hat{i}}) = a.$$

In view of lemma 1 an equivalent formulation of this result is as follows:

> if A and N are finite and A contains at least three distinct elements and if S is a s.c.f. satisfying citizen sovereignty, then S (5) is strategy-proof if and only if it is dictatorial.

Theorem 2 shows that only binary choices can actually be made via a strategy-proof voting method (unless we allow one dictator to decide in the name of the whole society). Its proof is easily derived from the Muller–Satterthwaite theorem (theorem 1, Chapter 3).

Proof of theorem 2. By lemma 1 it suffices to prove (5). The "if" statement is clear. Conversely, we will prove: a strategy-proof s.c.f. S is strongly monotonic (definition 3, Chapter 3).

By theorem 1 of Chapter 3 this is enough to complete the proof of theorem 2.

Let S be a s.c.f. which is not strongly monotonic. Then there exist $a \in A$ and $u, v \in L(A)^N$ such that v is obtained from u by an *elementary* improvement of a, whereas $S(v)$ differs from a and $S(u)$. Say that from u to v, outcome a jumps above outcome b in the ordering of agent i. We denote $S(u) = c$, $S(v) = d$ ($c \neq d$) and we distinguish two cases:

(α) if $\{c, d\} \neq \{a, b\}$ then the relative ordering of c and d is the same in u_i and v_i, so that one among the two following inequalities holds:

$$u_i(c) < u_i(d), \quad \text{i.e. } u_i(S(u)) < u_i(S(v_i, u_{\hat{i}})),$$

or

$$v_i(d) < v_i(c), \quad \text{i.e. } v_i(S(v_i, u_{\hat{i}})) < v_i(S(u)).$$

In each case we deduce that S violates strategy-proofness.

(β) if $\{c, d\} = \{a, b\}$ since $d \neq a$ we get $a = c$ and $b = d$; hence:

$$u_i(S(u)) = u_i(a) < u_i(b) = u_i(S(v_i, u_{\hat{i}})),$$

and strategy-proofness of S is again impossible. ∎

The Gibbard–Satterthwaite theorem shows that voting rules (as formalized by game forms) cannot achieve informationally decentralized aggregation of profiles unless they are dictatorial and/or binary. This negative result suggests two lines of investigation.

Suppose first we insist on the strategy-proofness requirement, that is we want our mechanisms to allow "pure" decentralization of the decision process, therefore requiring that an agent's optimal strategy is unambiguous even if he or she ignores the other preferences, and is still unaffected if this agent happens to know the preferences of some among his or her fellow agents. Then, by the Gibbard–Satterthwaite theorem we must *restrict the domain* of feasible profiles, just as standard assumptions of microeconomics severely restrict the possible configuration of the utility profile. This line will be explored in section 5 below.

Another way of escaping the Gibbard–Satterthwaite result is to weaken the equilibrium concept: not demanding that a dominating strategy equilibrium exists for all profiles still leaves room for patterns of behaviour that are, to a large extent, non-cooperatively decentralized (see Chapters 5 and 6). Next we take a cooperative view of the decision-making mechanism so that specific equilibrium concepts will be in order (see Chapters 6 and 7).

Problem 9: Strategy-proof social choice correspondences. We extend definition 2 to s.c.c. in two ways. Given A and N and a s.c.c. S, we say that S is *strategy-proof* (SP) if:

$$\forall i \in N, \forall u \in L(A)^N, \forall v_i \in L(A): \inf\{u_i(a)/a \in S(v_i, u_{\hat{i}})\}$$

$$\leqslant \inf\{u_i(b)/b \in S(u)\}.$$

We say that S is *weakly strategy-proof* (WSP) if:

$$\forall i \in N, \forall u \in L(A)^N, \forall v_i \in L(A): \exists a \in S(v_i, u_{\hat{i}}),$$

$$\exists b \in S(u), u_i(a) \leqslant u_i(b).$$

(1) Interpret properties SP and WSP, check that they both generalize definition 2 and that SP implies WSP.

(2) Show that for $p \geqslant 3$ and ($n = 3$ or $n \geqslant 5$) a scoring correspondence S_s such that $s_1 > s_2$ does not satisfy WSP (see lemma 4, Chapter 3).

Show that for $p \geqslant 3$ and ($n = 3$ or $n \geqslant 5$) a Condorcet-type s.c.c. cannot satisfy SP.

Show next that for $p \geqslant 4$ and ($n = 3$ or $n \geqslant 5$) the Condorcet cycle s.c.c. (problem 3, Chapter 2) is weakly strategy-proof, whereas the Copeland s.c.c. and the Kramer s.c.c. (definition 7, Chapter 2) both violate WSP.

(3) If a s.c.c. S is strongly monotonic, prove that it is weakly strategy-proof.

Using example 2, Chapter 3, give an example of a strongly monotonic s.c.c. that is not strategy-proof.

(4) Show that the Pareto s.c.c. and the s.c.c. $S_{1,1}$ of example 2, Chapter 3, are both anonymous, neutral and strategy-proof.

5. Restricted domains

Let us denote by S_2 a neutral and strategy-proof binary social choice function (see section 3). Suppose now the set A containing at least three elements, the society N and a profile $\boldsymbol{u} \in L(A)^N$ are given. Then for every pair of outcomes, a and b, the binary s.c.f. S_2 can be applied to the restriction of profile $\boldsymbol{u}$ to $\{a, b\}$ so as to determine a binary relation:

$$aB_{S_2}b\,(a \text{ beats } b \text{ w.r.t. } S_2) \Leftrightarrow S_2(\boldsymbol{u}/_{\langle a,b \rangle}) = a.$$

This binary relation has not necessarily a maximal element: if, for instance, S_2 is the majority binary s.c.f. (for odd n) then a maximal element is a Condorcet winner of profile $\boldsymbol{u}$, which, as we have seen (lemma 2, Chapter 2), may fail to exist.

Definition 3. Given A and N, a neutral strategy-proof binary s.c.f. S_2 and for every agent i a subset U_i of $L(A)$, we say that $\mathcal{D} = (U_i, i \in N)$ is a *domain consistent with* S_2 if for every profile in $\prod_{i \in N} U_i$ the associated binary relation B_{S_2} has a (necessarily unique) maximal element:

$$\forall \boldsymbol{u} \in \prod_{i \in N} U_i, \exists a \in A; \forall b \in A, b \neq a: S_2(\boldsymbol{u}/_{\langle a,b \rangle}) = a.$$

In this case we denote this maximal element by $m(S_2, \boldsymbol{u})$.

Theorem 3. Let $\mathcal{D} = (U_i, i \in N)$ be a domain consistent with S_2. Then the maximal element $m(S_2, \boldsymbol{u})$ is a strategy-proof s.c.f. on $\prod_{i \in N} U_i$:

$$\forall \boldsymbol{u} \in \prod_{i \in N} U_i, \forall j \in N, \forall v_j \in U_j: u_j\big(m(S_2, (v_j, u_{\hat{\jmath}}))\big) \leq u_j\big(m(S_2, \boldsymbol{u})\big). \tag{6}$$

Proof. Suppose that (6) is violated for some profile $\boldsymbol{u}$, some agent j and some v_j within U_j:

$$\left.\begin{array}{l} m(S_2, \boldsymbol{u}) = a \\ m(S_2, (v_j, u_{\hat{\jmath}})) = b \end{array}\right\} \text{ and } u_j(b) > u_j(a). \tag{7}$$

By definition of $m(S_2, \boldsymbol{u})$ we have $S_2(\boldsymbol{u}/_{\langle a,b \rangle}) = a$; hence, $T = \{i \in N / u_i(a) > u_i(b)\}$ is a winning coalition for S_2 (see problem 8, section 3). From

(7), j does not belong to T, hence $T = \{i \in N \setminus \{j\} / u_i(a) > u_i(b)\}$ so that $S_2((v_j, u_j)/_{\langle a, b \rangle}) = a$ since the set of agents preferring a to b, if the profile is (v_j, u_j), contains T. Thus, we derive a contradiction with $m(S_2(v_j, u_j)) = b$. ∎

Theorem 3 yields the most profound justification of the "majority principle": the society should select a Condorcet winner if one exists. To make this point clear, suppose first n the number of agents is odd. Then the majority binary s.c.f. $\tilde{S}_2$ is the unique anonymous and neutral strategy-proof s.c.f. Moreover, a domain $\mathcal{D}$ is consistent with $\tilde{S}_2$ if and only if a (necessarily unique) Condorcet winner exists for all profiles contained in $\mathcal{D}$, and the maximal element $m(\tilde{S}_2, \boldsymbol{u})$ is this Condorcet winner. If now n is even there is no anonymous and neutral strategy-proof s.c.f. but a "nearly anonymous", neutral and strategy-proof s.c.f. is obtained by letting a particular agent, say 1, break ties in his or her favour:

$$S_2(\boldsymbol{u}/_{\langle a, b \rangle}) = a, \quad \text{iff} \quad \begin{cases} |\{i \in N / u_i(a) > u_i(b)\}| \geq \dfrac{n}{2} + 1 \\ \text{or} \\ |\{i \in N / u_i(a) > u_i(b)\}| = \dfrac{n}{2} \text{ and } u_1(a) > u_1(b). \end{cases}$$

(8)

Clearly, for every domain $\mathcal{D}$ consistent with S_2 the maximal element $m(S_2, \boldsymbol{u})$, $\boldsymbol{u} \in \mathcal{D}$ is a (possibly non-unique) Condorcet winner. Conversely, if $\mathcal{D}$ is a domain such that at least one Condorcet winner exists for all profiles in $\mathcal{D}$ then $\mathcal{D}$ is consistent with S_2 and $m(S_2, \boldsymbol{u})$, $\boldsymbol{u} \in \mathcal{D}$, is agent 1's most preferred Condorcet winner.

The above remarks emphasize the role of the Condorcet-type s.c.f. when strategy-proofness is combined with the requirements of neutrality and anonymity. However, if anonymity is no longer in order, then other neutral monotonic binary s.c.f. can be aggregated (see problem 8, section 3). By theorem 3, as long as this aggregation is consistent (i.e. there exists a maximal element for all $\boldsymbol{u}$ in the considered domain), then the resulting s.c.f. will be strategy-proof as well.

Remark 2. Theorem 3 can be extended straightforwardly to the aggregation of monotonic (non-necessarily neutral) binary s.c.f. In that case a different binary s.c.f. is in order for each pair of alternatives.

Remark 3. When cooperation of the agents allows them to form coalitions (a possibility that will be systematically explored in Chapters 6 and 7) then in order to assert that sincere behaviour is optimal, a more demanding equilibrium concept is needed (namely telling the truth must be a strong equilibrium). However, under the assumption of theorem 3 we leave as an exercise for the reader to check the following property:

$$\forall u \in \prod_{i \in N} U_i, \forall T \subset N, \forall v_T \in \prod_{i \in T} U_i:$$

$$\text{No}\left[u_i(m(S_2, u)) < u_i(m(S_2, v_T, u_{T^c})), \text{ all } i \in T \right].$$

In other words, a Condorcet winner telling the truth is immune against manipulations by individuals and/or coalitions whenever a Condorcet winner exists for every admissible set of messages.

We give now a fundamental example of restricted domains illustrating theorem 3.

Definition 4. Let A be finite with cardinality p and let $\sigma = \{a_1, \ldots, a_p\}$ be an ordering of the elements in A. We say that a preference ordering $u \in L(A)$ is *single-peaked* with respect to σ if there exists an outcome a, the *peak* of u, such that:

$$a = a_{j_0} \text{ and } \begin{cases} k < j \leq j_0 \Rightarrow u(a_k) < u(a_j) \leq u(a_{j_0}), \\ j_0 \leq j < k \Rightarrow u(a_{j_0}) \geq u(a_j) > u(a_k). \end{cases}$$

Equivalently, u is single-peaked if it has a unique local maximum (an outcome that is preferred to its neighbour(s)).

We denote by $U_\sigma \subset L(A)$ the set of single-peaked profiles w.r.t. σ.

Given a society N and a profile $u \in U_\sigma^N$, where each preference is single-peaked w.r.t. σ, let us denote by a_{k_i} the peak of ordering u_i. Assuming first that $n = 2m + 1$ is odd, then profile u has a unique Condorcet winner. It is the agent i whose peak a_{k_i} is the median of $\{a_{k_j}, j \in N\}$ w.r.t. σ. Thus, a_{k_i} is defined by

$$|\{j \in N / k_j \leq k_i\}| \geq m + 1,$$

$$|\{j \in N / k_j \geq k_i\}| \geq m + 1.$$

The Condorcet winner is where the middle-man agent's dreams are fulfilled.

In case $n = 2m$ is even then one or two Condorcet winner(s) do exist, and are characterized again by:

$$\begin{cases} |\{j \in N/k_j \leq k_i\}| \geq m, \\ |\{j \in N/k_j \geq k_i\}| \geq m. \end{cases}$$

By theorem 3 the s.c.f. with restricted domain U_σ^N associating to every profile its highest ranked (resp. its lowest ranked) Condorcet winner is strategy-proof. In problem 11 below we explore in more detail the strategy-proof s.c.f. with restricted domain U_σ^N. Now we provide a general result which throws more light on the single peakedness property.

Definition 5. Let A be the finite set of outcomes. We shall say that a subset U of $L(A)$ is a *transitive majority* domain if for every finite society N and every profile the associated binary majority relation R is transitive over A:

$$\forall u \in U^N : aRb, \quad \text{iff } |\{i \in N/u_i(a) > u_i(b)\}| \geq n/2.$$

A transitive majority domain U is in particular consistent with the binary majority s.c.f. S_2 given by (8). That is to say, for a given profile u in U^N, agent 1's most preferred outcome among the maximal elements of the binary majority relation clearly is a maximal element of B_{S_2}.

Theorem 4 (Inada, 1969; Sen and Pattanaik, 1969). The subset U of $L(A)$ is a transitive majority domain if and only if for every triple a, b, c in A, there exists an outcome $x \in \{a, b, c\}$ and a rank $i \in \{1, 2, 3\}$ such that

$$\forall u \in U \text{ the rank of } x \text{ among } \{a, b, c\} \text{ is not } i.$$

Proof. Since transitivity of a relation is a condition on triples of outcomes it is enough to prove the theorem when $A = \{a, b, c\}$ has cardinality 3. For every N and every profile $u \in L(A)^N$, the set N is partioned into six subsets corresponding to the six elements of $L(A)$ with respective cardinalities

$n_1, \ldots, n_6$:

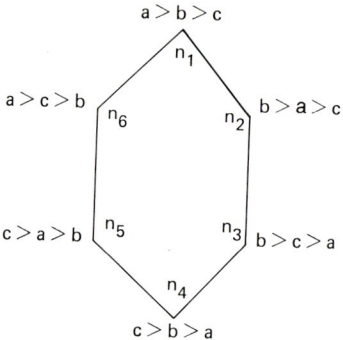

The binary majority relation is *not* transitive if and only if system (9) or system (10) holds true:

$$\begin{cases} n_2 + n_3 + n_4 < n_1 + n_5 + n_6 : aRb, \\ n_4 + n_5 + n_6 < n_1 + n_2 + n_3 : bRc, \\ n_1 + n_2 + n_6 < n_3 + n_4 + n_5 : cRa. \end{cases} \qquad (9)$$

$$\begin{cases} n_2 + n_3 + n_4 > n_1 + n_5 + n_6 : bRa, \\ n_4 + n_5 + n_6 > n_1 + n_2 + n_3 : cRb, \\ n_1 + n_2 + n_6 > n_3 + n_4 + n_5 : aRc. \end{cases} \qquad (10)$$

Now if U is a subset of $L(A)$ and $\boldsymbol{u}$ belongs to U^N, some of the integers $n_1, \ldots, n_6$ must be zero. If only one such n_α is zero, then one of the above two systems is impossible, but not both. For instance, $n_1 = 0$ implies that (9) is absurd (add up the first two inequalities) but (10) is still possible (for N large enough). Therefore no subset of $L(A)$ with cardinality 5 is a transitive majority domain. Suppose next that two among $n_1, \ldots, n_6$ are zero, then it is possible that both above systems are impossible.

We fix $n_1 = 0$ and $n_i = 0$ with i varying from 2 to 6.

Observe that $n_1 = n_3 = n_5 = 0$ does not contradict system (10) (choose, for instance, $n_2 = 2$, $n_4 = 2$, $n_6 = 1$). On the other hand, $(n_1 = n_2 = 0)$, $(n_1 = n_4 = 0)$ and $(n_1 = n_6 = 0)$ all contradict (9) and (10). For instance, $n_1 = n_6 = 0$ together with (10) imply $n_2 > n_3 + n_4 + n_5$ and $n_2 + n_3 < n_4 + n_5$.

This yields the three following transitive majority domains:

$n_1 = n_2 = 0$: $U = \{u \in L(A)/c \text{ is not ranked last}\}$,
$n_1 = n_4 = 0$: $U = \{u \in L(A)/b \text{ is not ranked second}\}$,
$n_1 = n_6 = 0$: $U = \{u \in L(A)/a \text{ is not ranked first}\}$.

Fixing next $n_3 = 0$, $n_i = 0$, $i = 2, \ldots, 6$, and finally $n_5 = 0$, $n_i = 0$, $i = 2, 4, 6$, we obtain all subsets of the form $U = \{u \in L(A)/x \text{ is not ranked } i\}$ for some $x \in A$ and some $i = 1, 2, 3$. ■

As an immediate application of theorem 4 the reader can check that the subset $U_\sigma \subset L(A)$ of single-peaked preferences w.r.t. an arbitrary ordering σ of A is a transitive majority domain. The next problem provides an example of a subset U of $L(A)$ such that for all N, U^N is a domain consistent with a majority s.c.f. S_2, whereas U is not a transitive majority domain.

Problem 10: Single-peaked preferences on a tree (Demange, 1980a, 1980b). Given A, the finite set of outcomes, an *undirected graph* on A is a subset G of

$$A \times A - \{(a, a), a \in A\}$$

such that $(a, b) \in G$ iff $(b, a) \in G$. A *path* between two distinct outcomes, a and b, is a sequence $\{a_0 = a, a_1, \ldots, a_k, a_{k+1} = b\}$ such that $(a_i, a_{i+1}) \in G$ for $i = 0, 1, \ldots, k$.

An undirected graph G is a *tree* if there is a unique path between any two distinct outcomes. This implies that all a_i in any path $\{a_0, \ldots, a_{k+1}\}$ are distinct.

Notation. For a given tree G on A, and any two outcomes a or b in A, we denote by $P(a, b)$ the path between a and b. We say that outcome c belongs to $P(a, b)$ if it belongs to the range of sequence $P(a, b)$.

Now we say that an ordering $u \in L(A)$ with top outcome a is *single-peaked* with respect to G if the following property holds:

$$\forall b, c \in A, b \neq c : b \in P(a, c) \Rightarrow u(c) < u(b).$$

We denote by $U_G \subset L(A)$ the subset of single-peaked orderings, with respect to G.

(1) Given an ordering σ of A prove that the subset U_σ of single-peaked orderings w.r.t. σ (definition 4) takes the form U_G for some tree G.

(2) For any tree G and any outcome a, prove that U_G contains at least one ordering with top outcome a.

(3) For any tree G any society N and any profile $\boldsymbol{u} \in U_G^N$, prove the existence of at least one Condorcet winner a:

$$\forall b \in A, b \neq a : |\{i \in N / u_i(a) > u_i(b)\}| \geq n/2.$$

(4) Prove that U_G is a transitive majority domain only if G is as in question 1.

Hint for question 3. Say that a subset B of A is connected if for all b, $b' \in B$, we have $P(b, b') \subset B$. If B is a connected subset of A and a any outcome, prove the existence of a unique outcome a' in B such that for every b in B, a' belongs to $P(a, b)$. Next prove by induction on the cardinality of B that the restriction of $\boldsymbol{u}$ to the connected hull $\mathcal{B}$ of B has at least one Condorcet winner.

In the next problem we explore the family of strategy-proof game forms when agents' preferences are single-peaked with respect to a fixed ordering.

Problem 11: Strategy-proof game forms on U_σ (Moulin, 1980). We fix A, the finite set of outcomes, an ordering $\sigma = \{b_1, \ldots, b_p\}$ of A, and a finite society N with cardinality n.

We restrict ourselves to those game forms $g = (A, i \in N; \pi)$ where each agent's message is made up of a single outcome – presumably his or her peak.

We say that g is strategy-proof on U_σ if we have:

$$\forall i \in N, \forall u_i \in U_\sigma, \forall a_{\hat{\imath}} \in A^{N \setminus \{i\}} : [a_i \text{ is the peak of } u_i] \Rightarrow$$

$$[u_i(\pi(a_i, a_{\hat{\imath}})) \geq u_i(\pi(a, a_{\hat{\imath}})), \text{ all } a \in A].$$

For any sequence $\{a_1, \ldots, a_{2k+1}\}$ of A with an odd number of terms we denote by $m(a_1, \ldots, a_{2k+1})$ the median of $a_1, \ldots, a_{2k+1}$ with respect to σ (see the discussion following definition 4).

(1) Given $\alpha_1, \ldots, \alpha_{n-1}$ some fixed (and non-necessarily distinct) elements of A prove that the following game form:

$$\forall (a_1, \ldots, a_n) \in A^N : \pi(a_1, \ldots, a_n) = m(a_1, \ldots, a_n, \alpha_1, \ldots, \alpha_{n-1}) \qquad (11)$$

is strategy-proof on U_σ, anonymous and efficient (when everyone tells the truth, the selected outcome is Pareto optimal).

Compute π when $\alpha_1, \ldots, \alpha_{n-1}$ all are b_1 or b_p.

(2) Let us denote by S_n the set of those game forms $(A, i \in N, \pi)$ that can be written as:

$$\forall (a_1, \ldots, a_n) \in A^N: \pi(a_1, \ldots, a_n) = m(a_1, \ldots, a_n; \alpha_1, \ldots, \alpha_{n+1})$$

for some fixed (and non-necessarily distinct) elements $\alpha_1, \ldots, \alpha_{n+1}$ of A. Prove that every game form in S_n is anonymous and strategy-proof on U_σ, but not necessarily efficient.

(3) Prove, conversely, that every game form that is strategy-proof on U_σ and anonymous must belong to S_n. (*Hint*: induction on n.)

(4) Prove that every game form that is simultaneously

- strategy-proof on U_σ,
- anonymous, and
- efficient,

can be written as (11) for some $\alpha_1, \ldots, \alpha_{n-1}$.

References

Demange, G., 1980a, "Single peaked orders on a tree", forthcoming in Mathematical Social Sciences.
Demange, G., 1980b, Gagnant à la majorité et généralisation dans les modèles spatiaux, Thèse, CEREMADE, Université Paris IX.
Fishburn, P.C. and W. Gehrlein, 1977, "Collective rationality versus distribution of power for binary social choice functions", Journal of Economic Theory 15, 72–91.
Gibbard, A., 1973, "Manipulation of voting schemes: A general result", Econometrica 41, 587–601.
Inada, K.I., 1969, "A note on the simple majority rule", Econometrica 37, 490–506.
Moulin, H., 1980, "On strategy-proofness and single peakedness", Public Choice 35, 437–455.
Satterthwaite, M.A., 1973, The existence of strategy-proof voting procedures, a topic in social choice theory, Ph.D. Dissertation, University of Wisconsin, Madison.
Sen, A. and P.K. Pattanaik, 1969, "Necessary and sufficient conditions for rational choice under majority decision", Journal of Economic Theory 1, 178–202.

CHAPTER 5

SOPHISTICATED VOTING

1. Summary of the results

Given a game form and a fixed profile, a dominating strategy of a particular agent i is an optimal decentralized behaviour for this agent whatever the information he or she possesses on the other agents' preferences. If i is completely informed of the whole profile or if he is only aware of his own preference ordering, he will still use his dominating strategy as long as cooperation with the rest of the society is not possible. This is how strategy-proof game forms achieve full decentralization of collective decisions: not creating any incentive for individual agents to acquire information about their respective opinions.

Thus, the Gibbard–Satterthwaite impossibility result can be interpreted as: if we want our decentralizing procedure to work irrespective of the informational context (with the only restriction that an agent knows is his or her own utility) then only dictatorial or binary s.c.f. can be implemented.

Here we make the (somehow extreme) assumption that *every agent is completely informed of the whole preference profile* and explore the strategic implications of it in a *non-cooperative* society. The main consequence is that every agent is now able to anticipate the behaviour of the others and the process of mutual anticipation might converge to the selection of a unique outcome for every profile. When this property holds we say that the considered game form is dominance solvable and the corresponding unambiguous choice of an outcome for every profile is called a sophisticated social choice function (section 2).

In section 3 a rich class of dominance solvable game forms, namely voting by binary choices, is proposed. It is shown that the corresponding sophisticated s.c.f. all generalize the Condorcet winner.

In section 4 we make a few steps toward the–wide open–problem of characterizing all sophisticated s.c.f. The main result is that a sophisticated s.c.f. arbitrates optimally when society splits into two antagonistic coalitions. This in turn implies that several familiar s.c.f. (like the Borda-type s.c.f.) are *not* sophisticated.

2. Sophisticated implementation

In most familiar voting methods an agent can profitably use information about other agents' opinions. A simple example makes this intuition precise.

Example 1: Voting by successive veto. Let the set $A = \{a, b, c, d\}$ of candidates contain four outcomes and society $N = \{1, 2, 3\}$ is made up of three agents. The following game form is in order: each agent successively vetoes one among the non-vetoed candidates. The (necessarily unique) remaining candidate is elected. Suppose next that the following profile holds:

u_1	u_2	u_3
a	b	d
b	a	b
c	d	a
d	c	c

Agent 3 clearly has a dominating strategy. When facing a pair $\{\alpha, \beta\}$ of candidates he vetoes the one he prefers less. This "sincere" strategy is (non-cooperatively) optimal whatever the utility, and therefore the strategy, of the other two agents. On the other hand, agents 1 and 2 have no dominating strategy. Actually, every strategy of agent 2, where he never vetoes his best preferred candidate among the three left by agent 1, is undominated. Hence, he has 2^4 undominated strategies among 3^4 possible strategies. Finally, among the 4 possible strategies of agent 1 not one is dominated (exercise: check that "veto a" is not a dominated strategy). Thus, if he ignores the others' utilities, no good choice emerges and he will presumably use the secure strategy: veto d, the unique best choice of a risk-averse agent. After d is vetoed, the preferences of agents 2 and 3, restricted to a, b, c, do coincide and b will be elected by *any* pair of undominated strategies.

Let us assume now that agent 1 is aware of the whole profile: in particular he knows that by vetoing d he guarantees the election of b. Vetoing b might be a better strategy for agent 1. The restrictions of u_2 and

u_3 to a, c, d are:

u_2	u_3
a	d
d	a
c	c

The two undominated strategies of agent 2, namely to veto c or d, yield the election of d and a, respectively. If agent 2 ignores agent 3's preferences, he will risk-avertedly veto c, and d will be the final outcome – a complete failure for agent 1's ruse! If, on the contrary, agent 2 is completely informed, he can anticipate the output of his own veto, therefore optimally vetoing d to enforce the election of a. This ultimately justifies that agent 1's best strategy is to veto b.

Notice that no explicit communication between agents is needed during this play. The crucial assumption is completeness of the information (I know your preferences, you know that I know your preferences, I know that you know...).

We formalize as follows the strategic mutual anticipation exemplified above.

Notation: Undominated strategies. Given A and N, both finite, let $g = (X_i, i \in N; \pi)$ be a game form and $\boldsymbol{u} \in L(A)^N$ be a fixed profile. For any subsets $Y_i \subset X_i$, $i \in N$, and any agent $j \in N$, we denote by $\mathcal{D}_j(u_j; Y_i, i \in N)$ the set of agent j's undominated strategies when the strategy spaces are restricted to Y_i, $i \in N$. Thus, x_j belongs to $\mathcal{D}_j(u_j; Y_i, i \in N)$ if and only if

$$x_j \in Y_j \text{ and for no } y_j \in Y_j \begin{cases} \forall x_{\hat{j}} \in Y_{\hat{j}}: u_j(\pi(x_j, x_{\hat{j}})) \leq u_j(\pi(y_j, x_{\hat{j}})), \\ \exists x_{\hat{j}} \in Y_{\hat{j}}: u_j(\pi(x_j, x_{\hat{j}})) < u_j(\pi(y_j, x_{\hat{j}})) \end{cases}$$

Definition 1. Given a game form g and a profile $\boldsymbol{u} \in L(A)^N$ the *successive elimination of dominated strategies* is the following N-tuple of decreasing sequences: X_j^t, $j \in N$, $t \in \mathbf{N}$:

$$X_j^0 = X_j; \qquad X_j^{t+1} = \mathcal{D}_j(u_j; X_i^t, i \in N) \subset X_j^t.$$

We say that g is *dominance-solvable* at $\boldsymbol{u}$ if there is an integer t such that $\pi(\mathsf{X}_{i \in N} X_i^t)$ is a singleton, denoted $S(\boldsymbol{u})$. We say that g is dominance solvable if it is so at every profile. In that case we say that *g sophisticatedly implements* the social choice function *S*.

The crucial behavioural assumptions underlying the concept of sophisticated voting are complete information (every agent is aware of the whole profile) and non-cooperation (agent i's strategic choice is made independently of the other agents' choices). Hence, a dominance-solvable game form is a decentralization device to the extent that it gives an incentive to the agents to acquire information on their mutual preferences, which in turn yields the selection of an unambiguous outcome. Thus, it is a realistic equilibrium concept only when the relevant information can be obtained at a relatively low cost (by polls). This restriction did not apply to strategy-proof game forms.

Actually, at any fixed profile, dominance-solvability is a generalization of strategy-proofness: if every agent has a dominating strategy in the normal form game ($X_i, u_i \circ \pi, i \in N$), then X_i^1 is made up of agent i's dominating strategies and $\pi(\mathbf{X}_{i \in N} X_i^1)$ is a singleton. The key observation is that dominance-solvable game forms are a rich class of decision-making procedures (allowing great flexibility in the distribution of power) and therefore implement a great variety of social choice functions. By weakening strategy-proofness into dominance-solvability we convert the Gibbard–Satterthwaite impossibility theorem into a wide possibility result. We shall make this point clear in sections 3 and 4 below.

Remark. The above terminology and definitions were first formally defined in Moulin (1979), whereas the idea of sophisticated voting is due to Farquharson (1969). In Rochet (1980) the connection between successive elimination of dominated strategies and the perfect equilibrium of games in extensive form was drawn precisely.

In the next example we illustrate the non-cooperative character of sophisticated voting.

Example 2: A disadvantageous privilege. Assume $A = \{a, b, c\}$ and $N = \{1, 2, 3\}$ both have cardinality 3. The voting rule is plurality voting where one "privileged" agent – say agent 1 – breaks ties:

$$X_1 = X_2 = X_3 = A: \pi(x_1, x_2, x_3) = x_2, \quad \text{if } x_2 = x_3,$$

$$= x_1, \quad \text{otherwise.}$$

Given the following profile (where the Condorcet paradox arises):

u_1	u_2	u_3
a	c	b
b	a	c
c	b	a

we explore the corresponding successive elimination of dominated strategies. Agent 1 has a unique dominating strategy: vote for a. That is to say:

$$\pi(a, x_2, x_3) = \pi(b, x_2, x_3), \qquad \text{if } x_2 = x_3,$$

$$u_1(\pi(a, x_2, x_3)) = u_1(a) > u_1(b) = u_1(\pi(b, x_2, x_3)), \quad \text{otherwise.}$$

Thus, $X_1^1 = \{a\}$.

However, agents 2 and 3 can only eliminate one dominated strategy, not both. For instance:

$$\left. \begin{array}{l} u_2(\pi(a,a,c)) < u_2(\pi(a,c,c)) \\ u_2(\pi(b,a,a)) > u_2(\pi(b,c,a)) \end{array} \right\} \Rightarrow X_2^1 = \{a, c\},$$

and similarly $X_3^1 = \{b, c\}$.

The next elimination of dominated strategies requires complete information of agents 2 and 3. Indeed, given that 1's vote is a, agent 2's strategy a is now dominated by c:

$$u_2(\pi(a,a,x)) \leq u_2(\pi(a,c,x)), \quad \text{all } x \in X_3^1;$$

this inequality being strict for $x = c$.

Similarly, given that b can no longer be elected (which results from $(x_1, x_2) \in X_1^1 \times X_2^1$) the strategy b of agent 3 is dominated by c.

Thus, we have:

$$X_1^2 \times X_2^2 \times X_3^2 = \{(a,c,c)\} \Rightarrow \pi(X_1^2 \times X_2^2 \times X_3^2) = \{c\}.$$

Hence, g is dominance-solvable at $\boldsymbol{u}$ and the corresponding equilibrium outcome is the worst outcome for the privileged agent! (Since the situation is symmetrical, a similar argument applies if agent 2 or 3 has the privilege to break ties.) During the successive elimination of dominated strategies, agents 2 and 3 implicitly cooperate (although they do not communicate) since agent i's behaviour is at once predictable. We note, moreover, that explicit cooperation within this voting method is unlikely as long as the ballot is secret. For instance, if agent 1 proposes to join agent 3 and force the election of b, then this promise by 1 is hardly believable since, given that 3's vote is b and 2's vote is c, agent 1 has a strong incentive to vote for a! If the ballot is secret, the possibility of double-crossing cannot be avoided and in turn weakens the incentives for cooperation.

Notice that the above game form is *not* dominance-solvable at every profile, as the following situation shows:

v_1	v_2	v_3
a	b	c
b	c	b
c	a	a

Here $X_1^1 = \{a\}$ and $X_2^1 = X_3^1 = \{b, c\}$ so that the remaining game among agents 2 and 3 is a typical "battle of the sexes" situation, where no strategy of any agent is ever dominated:

agent 2's vote

	b	a
b	b	a
c	a	c
	b	c

agent 3's vote

In the next example we analyse a dominance-solvable game form that sophisticatedly implements a well-known social choice function. This illustrates how a game form can sharply differ from its implemented s.c.f.

Example 3: Implementing a two-person Rawlsian rule. Given A and $N = \{1, 2\}$ we assume that a linear ordering u is written as a fixed scale utility, namely a one-to-one mapping from A into $\{0, \ldots, p-1\}$. For a given profile (u_1, u_2) we denote $R(u_1, u_2)$ the set of *Rawlsian maximal candidates*:

$$a \in R(u_1, u_2) \Leftrightarrow \min\{u_1(a), u_2(a)\} = \max_{b \in A} \min\{u_1(b), u_2(b)\}.$$

We say that a s.c.f. S is Rawlsian if $S(u_1, u_2) \in R(u_1, u_2)$ for all profiles. The underlying ethics is maximally risk-averse: the utility level of the worse-off agent should be as high as possible (given full intercomparability of the utility levels).

In order to sophisticatedly implement a Rawlsian s.c.f. we define a suitable game form. This definition is given in *extensive* form but can easily be translated as a pair of strategy sets and a decision operator.[1]

Step 1
Agent 1 selects an integer k, $0 \leq k \leq p-1$.

Step 2
Agent 2 selects one from two possible g.f. $G_1(k)$ or $G_2(k)$:
$G_1(k)$: first agent 1 vetoes k candidates and then agent 2 vetoes $p-1-k$ of the remaining candidates.
$G_2(k)$: first agent 2 vetoes k candidates and then agent 1 vetoes $p-1-k$ of the remaining candidates.

Intuitively, agent 1 cannot select too high a value for the integer k (for $k = p-1$, agent 2 is a dictator when choosing $G_2(p-1)$) nor can he or she select too low a value (for $k = 0$, agent 2 is again a dictator when choosing $G_1(0)$).

To check that this neutral g.f. implements a two-person Rawlsian rule we fix a profile $(u_1, u_2) \in L(A)^2$ and compute the successive elimination of dominated strategies that can be obtained by going backwards along the decision tree of the game (for more details on this equivalence see section 3).

For instance, suppose that $G_1(k)$ is to be played. Anticipating that agent 2 always vetoes his or her least preferred candidates among the $(p-k)$ remaining ones, then agent 1's optimal strategy in $G_1(k)$ is to veto the subset A_1 of A and let agent 2 veto the subset A_2 of A, where A_1 and A_2 are defined by

$$A_2 = u_2^{-1}(\{0, \ldots, (p-k-2)\}).$$

If a_1^k is a solution of $\max_{a \in A \setminus A_2} u_1(a)$, then $A_1 = A \setminus (A_2 \cup \{a_1^k\})$.

Therefore if $G_1(k)$ is played the expected candidate is the solution a_1^k of the following problem:

$$\sup u_1(a),$$

$$u_2(a) \geq p-1-k.$$

---

[1] A game in extensive form (with perfect information) is described by a decision tree and a partition of the nodes of the tree specifying who has the move. These games can be converted into normal (strategic) form games in several ways. For more details see Owen (1971).

Similarly, the expected outcome of $G_2(k)$ is the election of this candidate's a_2^k solution of the maximization problem:

$$\sup u_2(a),$$

$$\{u_1(a) \geq p - 1 - k\}.$$

Agent 2 at step 2 will select $G_i(k)$ rather than $G_j(k)$ if he or she prefers a_i^k to a_j^k. Since a_1^k and a_2^k are both Pareto optimal candidates, the best preferred for agent 2 among $\{a_1^k, a_2^k\}$ is the least preferred for agent 1 among $\{a_1^k, a_2^k\}$.

The problem of agent 1 at step 1 is now to select k so as to maximize the function

$$\varphi(k) = \inf\{u_1(a_1^k), u_1(a_2^k)\}.$$

Lemma 1. If k maximizes φ on $\{0, \ldots, (p-1)\}$, then every a_i^k such that $\varphi(k) = u_1(a_i^k)$ belongs to the set $R(u_1, u_2)$ of Rawlsian maximal candidates. Conversely, if a belongs to $R(u_1, u_2)$, then there exists k maximizing φ such that $a = a_1^k$ and/or $a = a_2^k$.

Proof. We distinguish two cases.

Case 1

There exists an element a^* of $R(u_1, u_2)$ (i.e. a^* maximizes over A the function $\min\{u_1(a), u_2(a)\}$) such that

$$u_1(a^*) = u_2(a^*).$$

We set $u_i(a^*) = p - 1 - k^*$ and observe that

$$a^* = a_1^{k^*} = a_2^{k^*}.$$

That is, $a^* \neq a_1^{k^*}$ would imply $u_1(a^*) < u_1(a_1^{k^*})$ since $u_2(a^*) \geq p - 1 - k$. Moreover, $u_2(a^*) = p - 1 - k^* \leq u_2(a_1^{k^*})$, therefore $u_i(a^*) < u_i(a_1^{k^*})$ for $i = 1, 2$ (since $a \neq a_1^{k^*}$). This contradicts the definition of a^*. By the definition of a_i^k, we note that $u_1(a_1^k)$ is non-decreasing with respect to k, whereas $u_1(a_2^k)$ is non-increasing (since $u_2(a_2^k)$ is non-decreasing). Since $u_1(a_1^{k^*}) = u_1(a_2^{k^*})$ we deduce that k^* maximizes $\varphi(k)$ on $\{0, \ldots, (p-1)\}$. Conversely, let k maximize φ on $\{0,\ldots,(p-1)\}$. Then $\varphi(k)=\varphi(k^*)$. We have:

$$u_1(a^*)=\varphi(k^*)=\inf\{u_1(a_1^{k^*}),u_1(a_2^{k^*})\}.$$

Hence, any $a_i^k(i=1,2)$ such that $u_1(a_i^k)=\varphi(k)$ equals a^* and therefore belongs to $R(u_1,u_2)$. Moreover $R(u_1,u_2)=\{a^*\}$.

Case 2

There exists an element a^* of $R(u_1,u_2)$ such that $u_1(a^*)\neq u_2(a^*)$, for instance $u_1(a^*)<u_2(a^*)$.

We set $u_1(a^*)=p-1-k^*$ and observe by the same argument as in case 1 (where the roles of 1 and 2 are exchanged) that $a^*=a_2^{k^*}$.

Suppose $a^*=a_1^{k^*}$ as well. Then the same argument as in case 1 applies (starting from "By the definition of a_i^k, we note that...") and the lemma is proved.

Thus, we assume $a^*\neq a_1^{k^*}$. Since $p-1-k^*=u_1(a^*)\leq u_2(a^*)$ the definition of $a_1^{k^*}$ implies $u_1(a^*)<u_1(a_1^{k^*})$.

Therefore we have

$$\varphi(k^*)=\inf\{u_1(a_1^{k^*}),u_1(a_2^{k^*})\}=u_1(a^*)=p-1-k^*.$$

We prove now that k^* maximizes φ on $\{0,\ldots,(p-1)\}$. Suppose, on the contrary, that for some k we have

$$u_1(a^*)=\varphi(k^*)<\inf\{u_1(a_1^k),u_1(a_2^k)\}. \tag{1}$$

From this we deduce

$$u_1(a_2^{k^*})=u_1(a^*)<u_1(a_2^k).$$

Since $u_1(a_2^k)$ is non-increasing in k, this implies $k<k^*$.

From (1) we again deduce $u_1(a^*)<u_1(a_1^k)$. Since a^* is a Rawlsian maximum, $u_2(a^*)<u_2(a_1^k)$ would be a contradiction. Hence

$$u_2(a_1^k)\leq u_1(a^*)=p-1-k^*<p-1-k.$$

The above inequality contradicts the definition of a_1^k. We have proved that k^* maximizes φ on $\{0,\ldots,(p-1)\}$. Conversely, if k maximizes φ and i ($i=1,2$) is such that $u_1(a_i^k)=\varphi(k)$, then $u_1(a_i^k)=u_1(a^*)$ so that $a_i^k=a^*$ is a Rawlsian maximum of profile (u_1,u_2). ∎

Problem 12: Implementation by risk-averse agents. Given A and N, both finite, we consider a game form $(X_i, i \in N; \pi)$ where agent i's strategy space X_i is finite (all i).

Given an ordering $u \in L(A)$, an agent i, and a strategy x_i of agent i, we denote

$$\varphi_k(u, x_i) = |\{x_{\hat{i}} \in X_{\hat{i}}/\pi(x_i, x_{\hat{i}}) \text{ is ranked } k \text{ by } u\}|,$$

where $k = 1, \ldots, p$ and $p = |A|$.

Next we set $\varphi(u, x_i) = (\varphi_p(u, x_i), \varphi_{p-1}(u, x_i), \ldots, \varphi_1(u, x_i))$ and we denote by $P_i(u)$ the set of agent i's strategies x_i that lexicographically minimize the vector $\varphi(u, x_i)$. We say that the game form g risk-aversedly implements the social choice correspondence (or function) S if we have:

$$\forall u \in L(A)^N : \pi(P_1(u_1) \times \cdots \times P_n(u_n)) = S(u).$$

(1) Interpret the strategies in $P_i(u_i)$ as optimal for agent i if no information is available to him about the preferences of other agents, whereas he is totally risk-averse.

(2) Prove that if a neutral social choice *function* S is risk-aversedly implemented by itself, then S satisfies the following property of *average-monotonicity*:

$$\left.\begin{array}{l} \forall i \in N \\ \forall u_i \in L(A) \\ \forall a, b \in A \end{array}\right\} \{u_i(a) < u_i(b)\} \Rightarrow \left|\{u_{\hat{i}} \in L(A)^{N_{\hat{i}}}/S(u_i, u_{\hat{i}}) = a\}\right|$$

$$\leq \left|\{u_{\hat{i}} \in L(A)^{N_{\hat{i}}}/S(u_i, u_{\hat{i}}) = b\}\right|.$$

(3) Conversely, prove that every neutral and strictly average-monotonic s.c.f. is risk-aversedly implementable.

(4) Give an example of a dominance-solvable game form that does not risk-aversedly implement a social choice function.

(5) To every social choice function S we associate the following vectors in $\mathbf{R}^p$:

$$\alpha_s = (\alpha_s(p), \ldots, \alpha_s(1)); \quad \beta_s = (\alpha_s(1), \ldots, \alpha_s(p)),$$

where

$$\alpha_s(k) = \left|\{(i, u) \in N \times L(A)^N / S(u) \text{ is ranked } k \text{ by } u_i\}\right|.$$

Show that the three following statements are equivalent:
(i) S lexicographically minimizes α_s.
(ii) S lexicographically maximizes β_s.
(iii) For all $\boldsymbol{u} \in L(A)^N$, $a = S(\boldsymbol{u})$ lexicographically minimizes the vector $r(a)$ over A, where

$$r(a) = \big(r_p(a), \ldots, r_1(a)\big),$$

$r_k(a) = |\{i \in N / a \text{ is ranked } k \text{ by } u_i\}|.$

Interpretation?

3. Voting by binary choices

We explore a family of dominance-solvable game forms that sophisticatedly implement several Condorcet-type social choice functions. We start with an example.

Example 4: Sequential elimination among outcomes. Three outcomes $\{a, b, c\}$ are on the floor and the number of voters is odd. The procedure goes in two steps. The first step is the majority voting to decide whether b or c should be eliminated. The second step is the majority voting to elect a or the outcome that survived the first step. Fig. 5.1 visualizes this procedure.

By the Gibbard–Satterthwaite theorem not every agent at every profile has a dominating strategy. In particular, the sincere strategy of an agent (eliminate first the least preferred among b and c, next eliminate the least preferred among the last two outcomes) can be profitably manipulated for some preference ordering. Clearly, this manipulation occurs only in the first

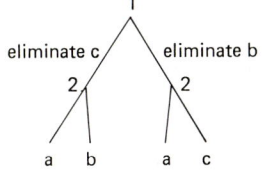

Fig. 5.1.

step. More precisely, if agent i's preferences are

$$u_i(b) > u_i(a) > u_i(c) \quad \text{or} \quad u_i(c) > u_i(a) > u_i(b),$$

then the sincere strategy *is* dominating (if $u_i(b) > u_i(a) > u_i(c)$, elimination of b allows at most the election of a, whereas elimination of c forces at least the election of a).

Suppose now that agent i has preferences

$$u_i(b) > u_i(c) > u_i(a). \tag{2}$$

The crucial piece of information is the expected result of the second round of voting: since this second vote is a strategy-proof binary voting, complete knowledge of the profile allows a straightforward prediction of the result of this vote. If, for instance, a majority of agents prefer b to a, then b would be elected for sure if c is eliminated in the first round. Thus, a vote against c in the first round is a dominating strategy of any agent with preference (2) given that only non-dominated strategies will be used by the others.

Suppose, on the contrary, that a majority of agents prefers a to b. Then an agent of type (2) no longer has any incentive to vote against c in the first round. If, moreover, a majority of agents prefers c to a, then he has a strict incentive to vote against b in the first round: after one round of elimination of dominated strategies, his vote against c becomes a dominated strategy.

The above discussion is precisely formulated as: our procedure is dominance-solvable and its sophisticated outcome is computed as follows. Given a profile u, denote by m_u the binary operation

$$m_u(\alpha, \beta) = \begin{cases} \alpha, & \text{if } |\{i \in N / u_i(\alpha) > u_i(\beta)\}| > n/2, \\ \beta, & \text{if } |\{i \in N / u_i(\beta) > u_i(\alpha)\}| > n/2 \end{cases} \tag{3}$$

(remember that the cardinality of N is odd).

Then voting by sequential elimination sophisticatedly implements the s.c.f. S:

$$S(u) = m_u[m_u\{a, b\}, m_u\{a, c\}].$$

Let us define voting by binary choice mechanisms. We consider a finite binary tree Γ, that is to say a connected graph with no cycles where a particular node m_0 is taken to be the origin of Γ (fig. 5.2). Then we say that node m follows node m' if the (unique) path from m_0 to m ends at m'. To say that Γ is binary amounts to saying that every node either is a terminal node (removing this node still leaves a tree) or has exactly two followers. Thus, Γ is entirely described by a finite set M of nodes and a mapping σ from M into M that associates to every node its immediate predecessor. We assume that σ satisfies:

(α) $\left.\begin{array}{l}\sigma(m) \neq m, \text{ for all } m \neq m_0 \\ \sigma(m_0) = m_0\end{array}\right\}$ m_0 is the origin of Γ.

(β) $\sigma^{-1}(m)$ is a doubleton or is empty: a node m such that $\sigma^{-1}(m) = \varnothing$ is called a terminal node, their set is denoted Z.

Given a binary tree $\Gamma = (M, \sigma)$ we consider a mapping θ from Z, the set of terminal nodes *onto* A being a fixed set of outcomes. Then to every fixed society with an *odd* number of agents we associate the following mechanisms.

(a) First a majority vote is taken to pick one among the two successors of m_0. Let $m \in \sigma^{-1}(m_0)$ be the chosen node.

(b) If m is a terminal node, outcome $\theta(m)$ is elected. Otherwise a majority vote is taken to pick one among the two successors of m.

This process goes on until a terminal node is reached, say m, in which case $a = \theta(m)$ is the finally elected outcome.

It is easy to extend this definition to the case of an *even* number of agents and still preserve anonymity of the procedure (all agents have equal influence on the collective decision). It suffices to incorporate a tie-breaking rule, i.e. a selection of σ^{-1}.

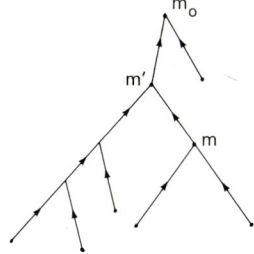

Fig. 5.2. A typical binary tree. (An arrow between m and m' means $m' = \sigma(m)$. Terminal nodes receive no arrow.)

3.1. Voting by successive amendments

Outcomes in A are ranked $(a_1,\ldots,a_p)$. A vote is taken first to adopt a_1 or reject it. If a_1 has been rejected, the next vote is to adopt a_2 or reject it, and so on.

We suppose that ties are broken by rejecting the currently proposed outcome (ties between a_p and a_{p-1} are broken in favour of a_p). The tree shown in fig. 5.3 visualizes this procedure.

3.2. Voting by sequential elimination

Outcomes in A are ranked $(a_1,\ldots,a_p)$. The first vote is to eliminate a_1 or a_2. If α_2 denotes the surviving outcome, the second vote is to eliminate α_2 or a_3. The kth vote is to eliminate α_k or a_{k+1}. After $(p-1)$ rounds of voting, the overall surviving outcome is elected. Assume, finally, that ties are broken in favour of the more ancient (i.e. with smallest index) candidate. The tree describing this procedure clearly has $2^p - 1$ nodes (since $(p-1)$ rounds of voting always occur) and is therefore hardly visualizable. See fig. 5.1 for the case $p = 3$.

To a particular voting by binary choice mechanism (M, σ, θ) and a fixed society N, we associate an anonymous game form $(X_i, i \in N; \pi)$ in the obvious way.

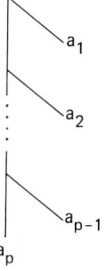

Fig. 5.3.

The strategy set X_i of any agent is the set of single-valued selections of the correspondence σ^{-1}: $X_i \subset M^{M \setminus Z}$, where $x_i \in X_i$ iff $x_i(m) \in \sigma^{-1}(m)$ for all non-terminal nodes m. Given a strategy N-tuple $(x_i, i \in N)$, the elected outcome $a = \pi(x_i, i \in N)$ is computed as follows.

For every non-terminal node m we denote by $y(m)$ the majority successor of m according to $(x_i, i \in N)$:

$$y(m) = m', \quad \text{iff} \begin{cases} |\{i \in N/x_i(m) = m'\}| > |N|/2, \\ \text{or} \\ |\{i \in N/x_i(m) = m'\}| = |N|/2 \text{ and } t(m) = m', \end{cases}$$

where t is the tie-breaking rule.

Then $a = \theta(m_T)$, where m_T is the first terminal node of the sequence

$$m_1 = y(m_0); \quad m_2 = y(m_1), \ldots, m_{t+1} = y(m_t), \text{ etc.}$$

Theorem 1 (McKelvey and Niemi, 1978; Moulin, 1979; and Gretlein, 1980a). Given the finite set A of outcomes, every voting by binary choice mechanism (M, σ, θ) defines for every society N a dominance-solvable game form.

The sophisticatedly implemented s.c.f. S is a Condorcet-type s.c.c. for $|N|$ odd:

$$\forall u \in L(A)^N, S(u) \in \mathrm{CW}(u), \quad \text{if } \mathrm{CW}(u) \neq \emptyset.$$

For $|N|$ even, S selects the *strict* Condorcet winner if there is one:

$$\exists a \in A \forall b \neq a |\{i \in N/u_i(a) > u_i(b)\}| > |N|/2 \Rightarrow S(u) = a.$$

Proof. The proof consists of exhibiting an algorithm to compute the sophisticated outcome at any fixed profile u. Intuition of this algorithm can be taken from the proofs of lemma 3 and theorem 2 below.

We remark first that some non-terminal nodes m, $m \in M \setminus Z$, are followed by two terminal nodes: $\sigma^{-1}(m) \subset Z$ (exercise: prove this claim). Let Z^1 be the set of such nodes. To each node $m \in Z^1$ we associate the binary choice between the pair $\sigma^{-1}(m) = \{m_1, m_2\}$, i.e. between $\theta(m_1)$ and $\theta(m_2)$. This choice is a strategy-proof (partial) game form so that the use by any agent of an insincere strategy if the decision process ever goes through m is a dominated strategy – actually in the global game form itself. Therefore given u we can predict the node that will be reached after m as:

$$\eta_u(m) = m_k,$$

$$\text{if} \begin{cases} |\{i \in N / u_i(\theta(m_k)) > u_i(\theta(m_{k'}))\}| > |N|/2, \\ |\{i \in N / u_i(\theta(m_k)) > u_i(\theta(m_{k'}))\}| = |N|/2 \text{ and } t(m) = m_k, \end{cases}$$

where $\{k, k'\} = \{1, 2\}$.

This in turn allows us to drop the nodes m_1 and m_2 and make m a terminal node to which outcome $\theta(\eta_u(m))$ is associated. Doing so for every element of Z^1 we get the following reduced voting by binary choice:

set of nodes: $M \setminus Z^0$, where $Z^0 = \{m \in Z/\sigma(m) \in Z^1\}$;
terminal nodes: $Z^1 \cup (Z \setminus Z^0)$;
the mapping σ is simply restricted to $M \setminus Z^0$;
the mapping θ^1 is given by $\theta^1(m) = \theta(m)$ if $m \in Z \setminus Z_0$, and by $\theta^1(m) = \theta(\eta_u(m))$ if $m \in Z^1$.

Notice that in the mechanism $(M \setminus Z^0, \sigma, \rho, \theta^1)$ not all outcomes are necessarily feasible: θ^1 is not necessarily *onto* A, some outcomes possibly being eliminated at once. In that case we understand that the reduced set of outcomes is $A^1 = \theta^1(Z^1 \cup (Z \setminus Z^0))$.

The key argument is that our original voting by binary choice mechanism is dominance-solvable if the reduced mechanism is; in order to prove this (seemingly innocuous) claim we need a robustness result on the successive elimination of dominated strategies; this is lemma 2 below. For the time being we assume that the above claim is true, and observe that the length of the reduced tree $(M \setminus Z^0, \sigma)$ equals the length of (M, σ) minus one (where the *length* of a tree (M, σ) is the greatest integer k such that $\sigma^k(m) \neq \sigma^{k-1}(m)$ for some m). Therefore after finitely many – say t – repetitions of the reduction operation, we get a 0-length tree $\{m_0\}$ and $\theta^t(m_0)$ is the sophisticated outcome of our mechanism at u.

If a is a strict Condorcet winner of profile u, then a is the sophisticated outcome of voting by binary choices. That is, consider any terminal node m such that $\theta(m) = a$ (such a node exists since θ is onto). Then if $\sigma(m) = m'$ belongs to $Z^1 (m \in Z^0)$ we have $\eta_u(m') = m$ and therefore $a \in \theta^1(Z^1 \cup (Z \setminus Z^0))$. If m does not belong to $Z^0 (m \in Z \setminus Z^0)$ then $a \in \theta^1(Z^1 \cup (Z \setminus Z^0))$ still holds. Hence, a is still a feasible outcome in the reduced voting by binary choice mechanism. By an induction argument we conclude that $\theta^t(m_0) = a$.

It remains to prove that the game form $(X_i, i \in N; \pi)$ is dominance-solvable and actually selects that outcome defined by the above algorithm. As already pointed out, given a profile u, any strategy x_i of agent i such that for some node m in Z^1, $x_i(m)$ is not agent i's best preferred successor of m, is a dominated strategy. Denoting $\mathcal{D}_i(u_i)$ the set of agent i's undominated strategies in game $(X_j, u_j \circ \pi, j \in N)$, we have:

$$\left. \begin{array}{l} \forall u_i \in L(A) \\ \forall m \in Z^1 \end{array} \right\} \forall x_i \in X_i [x_i \in \mathcal{D}_i(u_i)]$$

$$\Rightarrow [u_i(\theta(x_i(m))) = \sup_{m' \in \sigma^{-1}(m)} u_i(\theta(m'))].$$

Let us denote by $A_i(u_i)$ the set of agent i's strategies where he votes sincerely at every node of Z^1:

$$A_i(u_i) = \left\{ x_i \in X_i / \forall m \in Z^1 : u_i(\theta(x_i(m))) = \sup_{m' \in \sigma^{-1}(m)} u_i(\theta(m')) \right\}.$$

We have $\mathcal{D}_i(u_i) \subset A_i(u_i) \subset X_i$, where the right-hand inequality is strict whereas the left-hand inequality *can* be strict (exercise: prove this claim).

Moreover, the game form $(Y_i, i \in N, \bar{\pi})$ associated with the reduced mechanism $(M \setminus Z^0, \sigma, \rho, \theta^1)$ is clearly isomorphic to the game form $(A_i(u_i), i \in N, \pi)$.

In order to use the induction argument $((M \setminus Z^0, \sigma, \rho, \theta^1)$ dominance-solvable $\Rightarrow (M, \sigma, \rho, \theta)$ dominance-solvable) it suffices then to prove the following result.

Lemma 2 (Gretlein 1980a and b; Rochet, 1980).   Let $g = (X_i, i \in N; \pi)$ be any finite game form and $u \in L(A)^N$ be any fixed profile. For every i, let A_i be such that

$$\mathcal{D}_i(u_i) \subset A_i \subset X_i, \quad \text{all } i \in N.$$

Then g is dominance-solvable at u if and only if $(A_i, i \in N; \pi)$ is dominance-solvable at u. In that case their sophisticated outcomes coincide.

Proof.   Throughout the proof we fix the game form g and a profile u. We denote by $B = \prod_{i \in N} B_i$, $C = \prod_{i \in N} C_i$, etc. some rectangular subsets of

$X = \prod_{i \in N} X_i$. We denote by $G(B)$ the normal form game $(B_i, u_i \circ \pi, i \in N)$ and by $G(B^t) = (B_i^t; u_i \circ \pi, i \in N)$ the game obtained from $G(B)$ after t successive eliminations of dominated strategies (see definition 1). Thus, $G(B)$ is dominance solvable if $\pi(B^t)$ is a singleton for some t.

For any two B, C we denote $C \to B$ if the following property holds:

$$\left. \begin{array}{l} C_i \subset B_i \\ \forall x_i \in B_i, \exists y_i \in C_i : \forall x_{\hat{i}} \in B_{\hat{i}} \pi(x_i, x_{\hat{i}}) = \pi(y_i, x_{\hat{i}}) \end{array} \right\}, \quad \text{all } i \in N.$$

Step 1

Suppose $C \to B$. Then $G(B)$ is dominance-solvable iff $G(C)$ is. In that case their sophisticated outcomes coincide.

First $C \to B$ implies $C^1 \to B^1$. Namely, if $x_i \in C_i^1$ and $x_i \notin B_i^1$, then for some $y_i \in B_i$ we have

$$\forall x_{\hat{i}} \in B_{\hat{i}} : u_i(\pi(x_i, x_{\hat{i}})) \leq u_i(\pi(y_i, x_{\hat{i}})),$$

$$\exists x_{\hat{i}} \in B_{\hat{i}} : u_i(\pi(x_i, x_{\hat{i}})) < u_i(\pi(y_i, x_{\hat{i}})).$$

From $C \to B$ there exists $z_i \in C_i$ such that $\pi(y_i, x_{\hat{i}}) = \pi(z_i, x_{\hat{i}})$, all $x_{\hat{i}} \in B_{\hat{i}}$. Choose $x_{\hat{i}} \in B_{\hat{i}}$ such that $u_i(\pi(x_i, x_{\hat{i}})) < u_i(\pi(z_i, x_{\hat{i}}))$. From $C \to B$ we can associate to each $x_j \in B_j$ a $z_j \in C_j$ in such a way that

$$u_i(\pi(x_i, z_{\hat{i}})) = u_i(\pi(x_i, x_{\hat{i}})) < u_i(\pi(z_i, x_{\hat{i}})) = u_i(\pi(z_i, z_{\hat{i}})).$$

We conclude that z_i dominates x_i in $G(C)$, a contradiction. We have proved $C_i^1 \subset B_i^1$ all i. We pick now $x_i \in B_i^1 \subset B_i$. There exists $y_i \in C_i$ such that $\pi(x_i, x_{\hat{i}}) = \pi(y_i, x_{\hat{i}})$, all $x_{\hat{i}} \in B_{\hat{i}}$. It remains to prove that $y_i \in C_i^1$. Suppose the contrary: there exists $z_i \in C_i$ such that $u_i(\pi(y_i, x_{\hat{i}})) \leq u_i(\pi(z_i, x_{\hat{i}}))$, all $x_{\hat{i}} \in C_{\hat{i}}$ the inequality being strict for at least one $x_{\hat{i}} \in C_{\hat{i}}$. We remark again that for all $y_{\hat{i}} \in B_{\hat{i}}$ we can find (by $C \to B$) an $x_{\hat{i}} \in C_{\hat{i}}$ such that $\pi(\alpha_i, y_{\hat{i}}) = \pi(\alpha_i, x_{\hat{i}})$, all $\alpha_i \in B_i$. In particular, $u_i(\pi(x_i, y_{\hat{i}})) = u_i(\pi(y_i, y_{\hat{i}})) \leq u_i(\pi(z_i, y_{\hat{i}}))$. This being true for all $y_{\hat{i}} \in B_{\hat{i}}$ and the inequality being strict at least once, we conclude that x_i does not belong to B_i^1, a contradiction. We have thus proved that $C \to B$ implies $C^t \to B^t$, all $t \in \mathbf{N}$.

If $G(B)$ is d-solvable, $\pi(B^t)$ is a singleton for some t, hence the inclusion $\pi(C^t) \subset \pi(B^t)$ actually is an equality (remember that C^t is never empty by the finiteness of X). Thus, $G(C)$ is d-solvable as well, with the same sophisticated outcome.

If now $G(C)$ is d-solvable, then $\pi(C^t)$ is a singleton for some t. We remark again, by $C^t \to B^t$, that to every $x \in B^t$ we can associate $y \in C^t$ such that $\pi(y) = \pi(x)$. This implies $\pi(B^t) = \pi(C^t)$ and step 1 is proved.

Step 2

We fix an integer r and we assume the theorem to be true when the cardinality of X does not exceed $r - 1$. Now, let x with cardinality r and $A = \prod_{i \in N} A_i$ be such that

$$\mathcal{D}_i(u_i) = X_i^1 \subset A_i \subset X_i.$$

If $|A| = |X|$ there is nothing to prove, therefore we assume $|A| \leq r - 1$. We set $B = A^1 \cup X^2$ and observe that

$$A^1 \subset B \subset A.$$

Thus by the induction assumption, we have

$G(B)$ is d-solvable iff $G(A)$ is, and their sophisticated outcomes coincide. (4)

Next we set $C = (A^1 \cap X^1) \cup X^2$ and we prove $C \to B$. Inclusion $C \subset B$ is clear. Now, fix $i \in N$ and some $x_i \in B_i \setminus C_i = (A_i^1 \cup X_i^2) \setminus ([A_i^1 \cap X_i^1] \cup X_i^2)$. We have $x_i \in A_i^1$ and $x_i \notin X_i^1$. By the finiteness of X this implies the existence of some $y_i \in X_i^1$ such that

$$u_i(\pi(x_i, x_{\hat{\imath}})) \leq u_i(\pi(y_i, x_{\hat{\imath}})), \quad \text{all } x_{\hat{\imath}} \in X_{\hat{\imath}}$$

(the inequality being strict at least once).

Since $y_i \in A_i$ and $x_i \in A_i^1$ the above inequality must be an equality for all $x_{\hat{\imath}} \in A_{\hat{\imath}}$. Hence,

$$u_i(\pi(x_i, x_{\hat{\imath}})) = u_i(\pi(y_i, x_{\hat{\imath}})), \quad \text{all } x_{\hat{\imath}} \in A_{\hat{\imath}}.$$

This implies $y_i \in A_i^1$, so that finally $y_i \in C_i$.

We have proved the existence of $y_i \in C_i$ such that $\pi(x_i, x_{\hat{\imath}}) = \pi(y_i, x_{\hat{\imath}})$, all $x_{\hat{\imath}} \in B_{\hat{\imath}}$. Thus, $C \to B$ is true.

By step 1 and property (4) we get now that $G(A)$ is d-solvable iff $G(C)$ is, with the same sophisticated outcomes.

We remark finally that

$$X^2 \subset C \subset x^1.$$

Thus, by the induction assumption, $G(C)$ is d-solvable iff $G(X^1)$ is, with the same sophisticated outcomes. By definition of d-solvability, $G(X^1)$ is d-solvable iff $G(X)$ is, which concludes the proof of lemma 2. ∎

Theorem 1 yields the most important strategic feature of the widely used voting by binary choices method. Their underlying power structure relies on the majority principle: any strict majority of agents has a dictatorial control over the outcome of the decision-making mechanism. If, indeed, all agents of a strict majority agree on their top outcome a, then a is the (unique) Condorcet winner; using the terminology to be introduced in Chapter 7, we could say that the effectivity function of any voting by binary choices mechanism is the simple majority game.

Although all s.c.f.s sophisticatedly implemented by voting by binary choices are of the Condorcet type, not all of them satisfy more elementary ethical criteria like efficiency and monotonicity (definition 1, Chapter 2).

Lemma 3. Not every s.c.f. sophisticatedly implemented by a voting by binary choices method is efficient. For instance, if $|A| = p \geqslant 4$ and $|N| = n \geqslant 3$, the s.c.f. sophisticatedly implemented by voting by successive amendments is not efficient.

Not every s.c.f. sophisticatedly implemented by a voting by binary choice method is monotonic. Counter-examples can be found if $|A| = p \geqslant 4$ and $|N| = n \geqslant 3$.

Proof. For $|A| = 4$ and $|N| = 3$ we consider voting by successive amendments associated with the ranking $\{a, b, c, d\}$ and the following profile:

u_1	u_2	u_3
c	d	b
d	a	c
a	b	d
b	c	a

To compute the sophisticated outcome we use the algorithm developed in the proof of theorem 1: the only two terminal nodes correspond to $\{c, d\}$. Anticipating the (strategy-proof) majority duel between c and d yields c since $\{1, 3\}$ is a majority. Next, the majority $\{2, 3\}$ enforces b against c (since rejecting b amounts to enforcing c, the informed agents really are voting c against b). Finally, $\{1, 2\}$ enforces a against b (fig. 5.4).

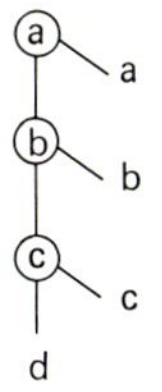

```
        ⓐ
         ╲ a
        ⓑ
         ╲ b
        ⓒ
        │ ╲ c
        d
```

Fig. 5.4.

Observe now that d Pareto dominates a. We let the reader check that for $|A| \geq 4$ and $|N| \geq 3$ a similar counter-example can always be found (for $|A| = |N| = 4$ remember that ties are broken to the detriment of the currently proposed outcome).

Choosing, again, without loss of generality, $|A| = 4$ and $|N| = 3$, we claim that the voting by binary choices method proposed in fig. 5.5 sophisticatedly implements a non-monotonic s.c.f.

That is, consider the switch from profile (u_1, u_2, u_3) to (v_1, u_2, u_3) obtained by an improvement of the position of a:

u_1	u_2	u_3	v_1
c	a	d	c
d	c	b	d
b	d	a	a
a	b	c	b

Twice applying the above algorithm to compute the sophisticated outcomes gives the results shown in fig. 5.6.

This concludes the proof of lemma 3. ∎

Fortunately, some voting by binary choices methods do implement efficient and monotonic s.c.f.

Theorem 2 (Miller, 1977; Moulin, 1979). For every cardinality of A and N (both finite) the voting by sequential elimination method does implement an efficient and monotonic s.c.f.

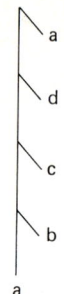

Fig. 5.5. $A = \{a, b, c, d\}$.

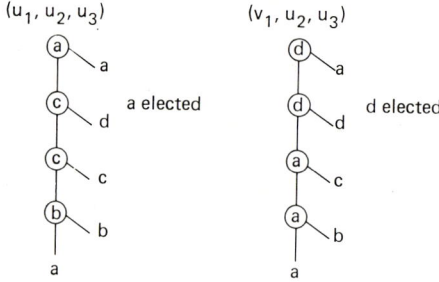

Fig. 5.6.

Proof. The proof goes by making explicit the general inductive algorithm introduced in the proof of theorem 1.

To a fixed profile **u** we associate the binary majority relation $ma(\cdot,\cdot)$, where ties are broken in favour of the left-hand outcome:

$$ma(a,b) = \begin{cases} a, & \text{if } |\{i \in N / u_i(a) \geq u_i(b)\}| \geq n/2, \\ b, & \text{if } |\{i \in \dot{N} / u_i(b) \geq u_i(a)\}| > n/2. \end{cases}$$

The sequential elimination occurs with the following ordering of the outcomes:

$$A = \{a_1, \ldots, a_p\}.$$

There are $(p-1)$ rounds of voting. In the kth round, candidate α_k, that is one among $\{a_1,\ldots,a_k\}$, is opposed to a_{k+1}. Let us denote by $\varphi^k(\alpha_k)$ the sophisticated outcome of voting by sequential elimination among $\{\alpha_k, a_{k+1},\ldots,a_p\}$. Thus, φ^k is a mapping from $\{a_1,\ldots,a_k\}$ into A. Sophisticated players in round k do not vote against α_k or against a_{k+1}: they anticipate that eliminating α_k raises the election of $\varphi^{k+1}(a_{k+1})$, whereas eliminating a_{k+1} raises the election of $\varphi^{k+1}(\alpha_k)$. Hence, strategy-proof binary majority voting between these last two outcomes leads to the induction formula:

$$\begin{cases} \varphi^k(\alpha_k) = ma\big(\varphi^{k+1}(\alpha_k), \varphi^{k+1}(a_{k+1})\big), \\ \qquad \text{all } k=1,\ldots,(p-1), \quad \text{all } \alpha_k \in \{a_1,\ldots,a_k\}, \\ \varphi^p(a) = a, \quad \text{all } a \in A. \end{cases} \qquad (5)$$

The sophisticated outcome of the overall mechanism is simply $\varphi^1(a_1) = S(\boldsymbol{u})$.

Monotonicity of S is obtained by an induction on p, the cardinality of A. Suppose that the claim holds true when $|A| \leq p-1$ and consider the case $|A| = p$. By (5) we have

$$S(\boldsymbol{u}) = \varphi^1(a_1) = ma\big(\varphi^2(a_1), \varphi^2(a_2)\big).$$

Observe that for $i=1,2$, $\varphi^2(a_i)$ is the s.c.f. sophisticatedly implemented by voting by sequential elimination on $A_i = \{a_i, a_3,\ldots,a_p\}$.

By the induction assumption, $\varphi^2(a_i)$ is monotonic viewed as a s.c.f. on A_i. Now if $a = S(\boldsymbol{u}) = \varphi^2(a_i)$ for both $i=1,2$, and $\boldsymbol{v}$ is obtained from $\boldsymbol{u}$ by improving upon the position of a, monotonicity of $\varphi^2(a_i)$ implies $a = \varphi^2(a_i)$ for profile $\boldsymbol{v}$ as well, hence $a = S(\boldsymbol{v})$.

Suppose finally that $a = \varphi^2(a_i) \neq \varphi^2(a_j)\{i,j\} = \{1,2\}$. Then we claim that $a = a_i$. Therefore $\boldsymbol{u}$ and $\boldsymbol{v}$ coincide on A_j hence $\varphi^2(a_j)$ is unaffected by the switch from $\boldsymbol{u}$ to $\boldsymbol{v}$, so that equality $\varphi^2(a_i) = ma(\varphi^2(a_1), \varphi^2(a_2))$ is unaffected as well.

It remains to prove $a = \varphi^2(a_i)$. We prove that for all $k = 2,\ldots,p$:

$$\forall \alpha, \beta \in \{a_1,\ldots,a_k\}\big(S(\boldsymbol{u}) = \varphi^k(\alpha) \neq \varphi^k(\beta)\big) \Rightarrow (S(\boldsymbol{u}) = \alpha).$$

This implication is obvious for $k = p$. Suppose it holds for $k+1,\ldots,p$ and consider any $\alpha, \beta \in \{a_1,\ldots,a_k\}$ such that $a = S(\boldsymbol{u}) = \varphi^k(\alpha) \neq \varphi^k(\beta)$. Twice applying (5) we get

$$a = ma\big(\varphi^{k+1}(\alpha), \varphi^{k+1}(a_{k+1})\big)$$

#

$$\varphi^k(\beta) = ma\big(\varphi^{k+1}(\beta), \varphi^{k+1}(a_{k+1})\big).$$

If $a = \varphi^{k+1}(\alpha)$, then the above system implies $a \neq \varphi^{k+1}(\beta)$ and we may use the induction assumption to (α, β) at order $(k+1)$. If $a \neq \varphi^{k+1}(\alpha)$ then we deduce $a = \varphi^{k+1}(a_{k+1})$ and $a \neq \varphi^{k+1}(\beta)$ so that we use the induction assumption to $\{a_{k+1}, \beta\}$ at order $(k+1)$. This concludes the proof of monotonicity of S.

The next step is to establish that S is efficient.

We prove now that outcome $a = \varphi^1(a_1)$ given by (5) is not Pareto dominated at $\boldsymbol{u}$. We fix an integer k, $1 \leq k \leq p$, and we prove that a_k is not Pareto superior to a by distinguishing two cases.

Case 1. $\varphi^k(a_k) = a_k$.

From (5) it follows that there exists some i, $1 \leq i \leq k-1$, such that $a = \varphi^{k-1}(a_i)$. From (5) again we have next:

$$a = ma\big(\varphi^k(a_i), \varphi^k(a_k)\big) = ma\big(\varphi^k(a_i), a_k\big).$$

Hence, a either is a_k or is strictly preferred to a_k by a strict majority of agents, which in particular implies that a_k is not Pareto superior to a.

Case 2. $\varphi^k(a_k) \neq a_k$.

In view of $\varphi^p(a_k) = a_k$ there exists an integer ℓ, $k \leq \ell \leq p-1$, such that

$$\varphi^\ell(a_k) \neq a_k \quad \text{and} \quad \varphi^{\ell+1}(a_k) = a_k$$

We set $b = \varphi^{\ell+1}(a_{\ell+1})$ and deduce from (5):

$$\varphi^\ell(a_k) = ma\big(\varphi^{\ell+1}(a_k); \quad \varphi^{\ell+1}(a_{\ell+1})\big) = ma(a_k, b).$$

Since $\varphi^\ell(a_k) \neq a_k$, this equality implies $b \neq a_k$ and $b = ma(a_k, b)$. Hence, by definition of ma:

$$|\{i \in N / u_i(b) > u_i(a_k)\}| > n/2. \qquad (6)$$

Next, there exists i, $1 \leq i \leq \ell$, such that $a = \varphi^\ell(a_i)$ implying, by (5) again:

$$a = \varphi^\ell(a_i) = ma(\varphi^{\ell+1}(a_i), b).$$

Therefore either $a = b$ and by (6) we conclude that a_k does not Pareto dominate a, or we have $a = ma(a, b)$; hence, by definition of ma:

$$|\{i \in N / u_i(a) > u_i(b)\}| \geq n/2. \tag{7}$$

If a_k Pareto dominates a, we derive from (6) and (7) a contradiction. This concludes the proof of theorem 2. ∎

In problem 13 we explore more properties of the sophisticated s.c.f.s implemented by successive amendments and by sequential elimination.

Problem 13: Comparing voting by successive amendments (VSA) and by sequential elimination (VSE) (Miller, 1977; Moulin, 1979). We use the notations of the above proof. Throughout the problem we fix a profile $u \in L(A)^N$

(1) Prove that the outcome b of sophisticated voting in VSA, when the outcomes of A are ranked $\{a_1, \ldots, a_p\}$, is given by the following algorithm:

$$\begin{cases} \beta_p = a_p, \\ \beta_k = ma(\beta_{k+1}, a_k), & k = 1, \ldots, (p-1), \\ b = \beta_1. \end{cases}$$

Prove that b is the outcome risk-aversedly implemented (see problem 12) by VSE if the ordering of A is $\{a_p, a_{p-1}, \ldots, a_1\}$.

(2) An earlier ranking is desirable in sophisticated VSA, whereas the reverse is true for sophisticated VSE. To prove this claim, consider two orderings of A:

$$\sigma = \{a_1, \ldots, a_{k-1}, a_k, a_{k+1}, a_{k+2}, \ldots, a_p\},$$

$$\sigma' = \{a_1, \ldots, a_{k-1}, a_{k+1}, a_k, a_{k+2}, \ldots, a_p\}.$$

Next show that if a_{k+1} is elected by sophisticated VSA according to σ, it is still chosen when σ is changed to σ'. Similarly, if a_{k+1} is elected by sophisticated VSE according to σ', show that it is still elected when σ replaces σ'.

(3) Show that the outcome b of sophisticated VSA belongs to the Condorcet top cycle $A_c(u)$ (see problem 3, Chapter 2) whatever the ordering σ of A. Show that b reaches every outcome of $A_c(u)$ for at least one ordering σ.

Show that the outcome a of sophisticated VSE belongs to Miller's uncovered set $A_c^*(u)$ (see problem 4, Chapter 2) and that the mapping $\sigma \to a$ is onto $A_c^*(u)$.

Problem 14: A procedure where risk-averse voting and sophisticated voting yield the same outcome. We assume that $n = |N|$ is odd and $A = \{a, b, c\}$ contains three distinct outcomes.

1*st round*: One outcome among a, b is selected and denoted α.
2*nd round*: One among α, c is selected and denoted β.
3*rd round*: Either β is elected *for good* or we go to the
4*th round*: This vote chooses a or b as the finally elected outcome.

All votes are taken by simple majority.

Prove that this game form implements the same s.c.f. whether the agents are all risk averse (see problem 12) or all sophisticated.

It is an open problem to decide on the existence of a voting by binary choices sharing the same properties when the cardinality of A is at least 4.

4. A necessary condition

A sophisticated social choice function is one that is sophisticatedly implemented by some finite dominance solvable game form (requiring finiteness of the message space is consistent with our assumption, throughout this chapter, that A and N are both finite). Thus, it is a s.c.f. that results from the non-cooperative behaviour of completely informed agents in some procedure. Optimally we would like to characterize the set $\mathcal{S}$ of sophisticated s.c.f.s. This would indeed explain much of the collective implications of non-cooperation. Actually, we will state only a few facts about $\mathcal{S}$: it is very big (theorem 3), but many familiar s.c.f.s are outside $\mathcal{S}$ (corollary of theorem 4). Meanwhile we establish a necessary condition for an s.c.f. to be sophisticated.

The family of voting by binary choices can be generalized by considering any finite tree (not necessarily a binary one) and assigning to each non-terminal node m a strategy-proof game form bearing on the successors of m. Formally, a finite tree is a pair $\Gamma = (M, \sigma)$, where M is the finite set of nodes and σ associates to each node its nearby predecessor. We require that σ satisfy the following properties:

(a) There is a unique node m_0 subject to $\sigma(m_0) = m_0$. It is the origin of Γ.
(b) There is an integer ℓ subject to $\sigma^\ell(m) = m_0$ for all $m \in M$.
(c) The smallest such integer is the *length* of Γ.

A node m subject to $\sigma^{-1}(m) = \emptyset$ is called a terminal node of Γ, and their set is denoted Z. For a non-terminal node m, we call $\sigma^{-1}(m)$ the set of successors of m.

Given a set A of outcomes, we construct a game form on A by assigning to each terminal node an element of A and to each non-terminal node a game form bearing on its successor nodes. Formally, let θ be a mapping from Z onto A, and for all $m \in M \setminus Z$, let $g_m = (X_i^m, i \in N; \pi^m)$ be a game form on $\sigma^{-1}(m)$. (Thus, $\pi^m \prod_{i \in N} X_i^m = \sigma^{-1}(m)$.) Then the game form associated with (M, σ, θ, g) is described as follows:

- A strategy x_i of agent i associates to each non-terminal node $m \in M \setminus Z$ an element x_i^m of X_i^m. Their set in denoted X_i.
- For each strategy N-tuple $x = (x_i, i \in N)$ we define $\pi(x) = \theta(m_T)$, where m_T is the first terminal node of the sequence

$$\begin{cases} m_0, m_1 = \pi^{m_0}(x^{m_0}), \ldots, m_{t+1} = \pi^{m_t}(x^{m_t}), \ldots, \\ \text{where } x^m = (x_i^m, i \in N). \end{cases}$$

Figure 5.7 visualizes a typical game form associated to a finite tree: σ associates to each node the nearby upper node; at nodes m_0 and n a

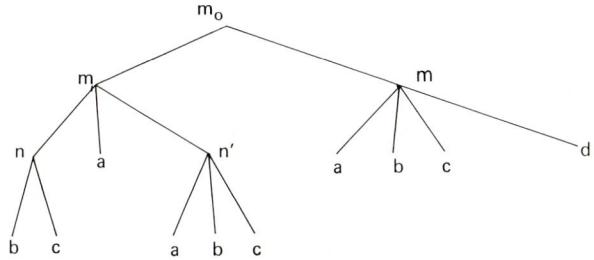

Fig. 5.7.

majority vote is taken to pick one successor; and at m (resp. at m', n') agent 1 (resp. agent 2) selects dictatorially the successor node.

Theorem 3 (Moulin, 1979). Under the above notations and assumptions suppose that for each non-terminal node m, the game form g_m is strategy-proof. Then the game form associated with (Γ, θ, g) is dominance-solvable.

Proof. This theorem is a straightforward generalization of theorem 1 above. Its proof is quite similar, and therefore constructive. Given a profile $u \in L(A)^N$ we display an algorithm $(M, \sigma, \theta) \to (M^1, \sigma^1, \theta^1) \to \cdots \to (M^t, \sigma^t, \theta^t) \to \cdots$ that strictly reduces the length of our tree at each step. Thus $(M^\ell, \sigma^\ell, \theta^\ell)$ is a 0-length tree and outcome $\theta^\ell(m_0)$ is the sophisticated outcome associated with u.

Let $Z^1 = \{m \in M \setminus Z / \sigma^{-1}(m) \subset Z\}$. For each node $m \in Z^1$, and each agent i, we denote by $x_i^m(u_i)$ a dominating strategy of i in g_m if the utility of i over $\sigma^{-1}(m)$ is given by $\tilde{u}_i(m') = u_i(\theta(m'))$. Next the reduced tree (M^1, σ^1) has terminal nodes $Z^1 \cup \{Z \setminus Z^0\}$, where $Z^0 = \{m \in Z / \sigma(m) \in Z^1\}$ and the mapping σ^1 is the restriction of σ to M^1. Finally, the mapping θ^1 is given by

$$\theta^1(m) = \begin{cases} \theta(m), & \text{if } m \in Z \setminus Z^0, \\ \theta(\pi^m(x_i^m(u_i), i \in N)), & \text{if } m \in Z^1. \end{cases}$$

As in theorem 1 we observe that if a strategy x_i of agent i is not dominated at u in the global game form, then for all $m \in Z^1$, x_i^m is a dominating strategy of i in g_m (corresponding to $\tilde{u}_i$). Now the robustness result (lemma 2) states essentially that if a "lazy" process of successive elimination of dominated strategies (i.e. eliminating only some dominated strategies at each step) eventually captures a single outcome, then our game form is dominance-solvable at this profile with the same associated sophisticated outcome. This concludes the proof of theorem 2.

In view of the Gibbard–Satterthwaite theorem, if the game form g_m is strategy-proof, then either g_m is binary, i.e. m has at most one successor, or g_m is dictatorial. Therefore the two main examples of dominance-solvable game forms derived from theorem 2 are the voting by binary choices at one extreme and the "voting by dictatorial choices" at the other extreme. Let us illustrate this last family by a voting rule of fundamental importance.

Example 5: Voting by successive veto. Let A and N be fixed with respective cardinalities p and n. Furthermore, let $p_1,\ldots,p_n$ be n non-negative integers such that

$$p_1 + \cdots + p_n = p - 1.$$

The voting rule is as follows: the agents are ordered, say $N = \{1,2,\ldots,n\}$. Agent 1 freely vetoes p_1 outcomes among A, say A_1. Next agent 2 vetoes p_2 outcomes among $A \setminus A_1$, say A_2. And so on, until a single outcome is left, after agent n has vetoed p_n outcomes among $A \setminus \{A_1 \cup \cdots \cup A_{n-1}\}$.

Clearly, this voting rule derives from a tree where at each node one agent dictatorially selects one successor. By theorem 1 it is therefore dominance-solvable. The whole of Chapter 6 is devoted to the remarkable strategical properties of this procedure and its variants.

The next example differs from the voting by binary choice methods presented in section 3, although it derives from a binary tree.

Example 6: Voting by unanimous approval. Let A be fixed with cardinality p and let $A = \{a_1,\ldots,a_p\}$ be an ordering of A. The agents vote first to elect a_1 or reject it. Unanimity is required to enforce a_1. If at least one agent's vote is against a_1 we go to the second round of voting where a_2 is on the floor, unanimity being needed to enforce a_2, and so on.

This procedure is pictured as a binary tree (identical to the tree of voting by successive amendments) where to each node is attached a non-neutral strategy-proof game form. As an exercise the reader may check that the sophisticatedly implemented s.c.f. is as follows.

We set $p_0 = p$, $p_1 = \sup\{k \in \{1,\ldots,p\}/a_k$ is Pareto superior to $a_p\},\ldots,$ $p_{t+1} = \sup\{k \in \{1,\ldots,p_t\}/a_{p_{t+1}}$ is Pareto superior to $a_{p_t}\}$. Then $S(\boldsymbol{u}) = a_{p_t}$, where p_t is the first integer such that no p_{t+1} exists. In particular $S(\boldsymbol{u})$ is an efficient, anonymous and monotonic s.c.f.

A basic feature of game forms derived from trees is the lack of symmetry they introduce among outcomes and/or among agents. If anonymity and neutrality are in order we can achieve anonymity at the cost of neutrality (see all voting by binary choices methods) or neutrality at the cost of anonymity (see the voting by veto method (example 5)). However, it can happen that a d-solvable game form lacks anonymity, whereas the associated sophisticated s.c.f. is anonymous. This point will be illustrated in Chapter 6 where an efficient anonymous and neutral sophisticated s.c.f. is constructed in this way (see problem 19). Nevertheless, the general comment remains, namely that dominance-solvability via a game tree induces a structural discrimination on the outcomes and/or the agents. No example is known, when $|A| \geq 3$, of a neutral anonymous and d-solvable game form.

Notation. Given a utility $u \in L(A)$ and a coalition $T \subset N$, we denote by $\bar{u}$ the *reverse* of u: $u(a) < u(b)$ iff $\bar{u}(b) < \bar{u}(a)$, and by $[u]_T \in L(A)^T$ the profile of coalition T of which every coordinate is u.

Definition 2. Let A, N and a s.c.f. S be given. We will say that S is *coalitionally easy* (in short C.E.) if the following property holds:

$$\forall u \in L(A), \forall T \subset N: u(S(v_T, [\bar{u}]_{T^c})) \leq u(S([u]_T, [\bar{u}]_{T^c}))$$

$$\leq u(S([u]_T, v_{T^c}))$$

$$\text{all } v_T \in L(A)^T, \quad \text{all } v_{T^c} \in L(A)^{T^c}. \quad (8)$$

Property (8) means that for those profiles for which society splits into two homogeneous and antagonistic coalitions (members of T all having utility u, members of T^c all having utility $\bar{u}$) then the sincere messages $[u]_T$, $[\bar{u}]_{T^c}$ form a saddle-point of the two-person zero sum game where T and its complement T^c are the two players with respective utilities u and $\bar{u}$. Hence, for this very peculiar sort of profile, truth is an optimal strategy for each coalition. It is a "maximin" strategy as well:

$$u(S([u]_T, [\bar{u}]_{T^c})) = \inf_{v_{T^c}} u(S([u]_T, v_{T^c})) = \sup_{v_T} \inf_{v_{T^c}} u(S(v_T, v_{T^c})). \quad (9)$$

These equations are an easy consequence of (8): it is well known that in the two-person zero sum games where a saddle point does exist, optimal strategies and maximin (prudent) strategies do coincide. Notice that it does not follow from (8) that the truth is a dominating strategy of either T or T^c.

Further interpretations of the C.E. condition will be drawn in Chapter 7 (section 3). There it is shown that (8) implies that the allocation of veto power among coalitions is maximal (see theorem 2), a necessary condition for cooperative implementation as well.

Theorem 4. Given A and N both finite, a sophisticated social choice function necessarily is coalitionally easy:

$$\{S \in \tilde{\mathcal{S}}\} \Rightarrow \{S \text{ satisfy C.E.}\}.$$

Proof. We fix S, a sophisticated s.c.f. implemented by the (finite) game form $g = (X_i, i \in N; \pi)$. We also fix a coalition T and a utility $u \in L(A)$.

Let us consider the *two*-person game form $g^1 = (X_T, X_{T^c}, \pi)$ where coalitions T and T^c are viewed as two single agents. It follows from lemma 3 below that g^1 is dominance-solvable. Therefore given the profile $(u, \bar{u}) \in L(A)^2$, a sophisticated equilibrium strategy exists in the game $(X_T, X_{T^c}, u \circ \pi, \bar{u} \circ \pi)$. Such a strategy 2-tuple is in particular a Nash equilibrium (this result can be checked by the reader as an exercise), and therefore is a saddle-point of $u \circ \pi$. Thus, we have

$$\sup_{x_T} \inf_{x_{T^c}} u \circ \pi(x_T, x_{T^c}) = \inf_{x_{T^c}} \sup_{x_T} u \circ \pi(x_T, x_{T^c}). \tag{10}$$

We consider next the $(n - t + 1)$-person game form (where $t = |T|$), $g^2 = (X_T, X_j, j \in T^c, \pi)$. By lemma 3 again, g^2 is dominance-solvable. Thus, for every profile $v_{T^c} \in L(A)^{T^c}$ the game derived from g^2 where agent T's utility is u and for all $j \in T^c$, agent j's utility is v_j, has at least one sophisticated equilibrium that we denote by $y = (y_T, y_j, j \in T^c)$. It follows from lemma 3 below that the sophisticated outcome $\pi(y)$ of g^2 at (u, v_{T^c}) equals the sophisticated outcome of g at profile $([u]_T, v_{T^c})$. Since g implements S this implies

$$\pi(y) = S([u]_T, v_{T^c}). \tag{11}$$

Since y is in particular a Nash equilibrium of g^2 at (u, v_{T^c}) we have

$$u \circ \pi(y) = \sup_{x_T \in X_T} u \circ \pi(x_T, y_{T^c}) \geq \inf_{x_{T^c}} \sup_{x_T} u \circ \pi(x_T, x_{T^c}). \tag{12}$$

Let us denote by $\mathrm{val}_T(u)$ the value of the two-person zero sum game g^1 at $([u]_T, [\bar{u}]_{T^c})$, i.e. the utility level (10). From (10) to (12) we deduce:

$$u(S([u]_T, v_{T^c})) \geq \mathrm{val}_T(u). \tag{13}$$

Since the above inequality holds for arbitrary u, T and v_{T^c}, it holds true for $\bar{u}$, T^c and some $v_T \in X_T$:

$$\bar{u}(S(v_T, [\bar{u}]_{T^c})) \geq \mathrm{val}_{T^c}(\bar{u}). \tag{14}$$

Notice that

$$\operatorname{val}_{T^c}(\bar{u}) = \inf_{x_T} \sup_{x_{T^c}} \bar{u} \circ \pi(x_T, x_{T^c}) = \sup_{x_{T^c}} \inf_{x_T} \bar{u} \circ \pi(x_T, x_{T^c}). \tag{15}$$

Comparing (15) and (10) we conclude that (14) can be rewritten as

$$u(S(v_T, [\bar{u}]_{T^c})) \leq \operatorname{val}_T(u). \tag{16}$$

Inequalities (14) and (16) together mean that $([u]_T, [\bar{u}]_{T^c})$ is a saddle-point of game g^1 at $(u, \bar{u})$, which is the desired conclusion.

Lemma 3. Let $g = (X_i, i \in N; \pi)$ be a finite dominance-solvable game form and $N = \bigcup_{k \in L} N_k$ be a partition of N with cardinality $|L| = \ell$. Then the ℓ-person game form $g^* = (X_{N_k}, k \in L, \pi)$ is dominance-solvable. Moreover, its sophisticated outcome at profile $u = (u_k, k \in L) \in L(A)^L$ equals the sophisticated outcome of g at the following profile v:

$$v = (v_i)_{i \in N}, \quad \text{where } v_i = u_k, \quad \text{if } i \in N_k. \tag{17}$$

Proof. We fix a profile $u = (u_k, k \in L) \in L(A)^L$ and consider the corresponding profile $v \in L(A)^N$ given by (17). As in the proof of lemma 2 we denote by X_i^1 the subset of agent i undominated strategies in g at profile v. Similarly, $X_{N_k}^1$ is agent N_k's subset of undominated strategies in g^* at profile u.

Observe that neither of the inclusions $X_{N_k}^1 \supset \prod_{i \in N_k} X_i^1$ or $\prod_{i \in N_k} X_i^1 \supset X_{N_k}^1$ is true in general. However, if we set $A_k = \prod_{i \in N_k} X_i^1, k \in L, A = \prod_{k \in L} A_k$, we will prove that

$$A \cap \left(\prod_{k \in L} X_{N_k}^1 \right) \to \prod_{k \in L} X_{N_k}^1, \tag{18}$$

where $B \to C$ is the notation introduced in the proof of theorem 1 and refers to game g^*.

To prove (18) we pick $k \in L$ and $x_{N_k} \in X_{N_k}^1$. Fix any $i \in N_k$: if $x_i \notin X_i^1$ by the finiteness of X_i, there exists $y_i \in X_i^1$ such that

$$u_k \circ \pi(x_i, y_{\hat{\imath}}) \leq u_k \circ \pi(y_i, x_{\hat{\imath}}), \quad \text{all } y_{\hat{\imath}} \in X_{\hat{\imath}}.$$

Therefore

$$y_{N_k} = (y_i, x_{N_k \setminus \{i\}})$$

is such that

$$u_k \circ \pi(x_{N_k}, z_{\hat{k}}) \leq u_k \circ \pi(y_{N_k}, z_{\hat{k}}), \quad \text{all } z_{\hat{k}} \in \prod_{k' \in L - \{k\}} X_{N_{k'}}. \tag{19}$$

Since x_{N_k} is undominated in g^*, this inequality actually is an equality. Repeating the argument we obtain:

$$y'_{N_k} = (y_i, y'_{i'}, x_{N_k \setminus \{i, i'\}}),$$

where $y_{i'} \in X^1_{i'}$ whereas x_{N_k} and y_{N_k} are indiscernible in g^*. After $|L|$ iterations of this argument, we obtain the existence of an

$$\bar{y}_{N_k} \in \prod_{i \in N_k} X^1_i = A_k,$$

such that

$$u_k \circ \pi(x_{N_k}, z_{\hat{k}}) = u_k \circ \pi(\bar{y}_{N_k}, z_{\hat{k}}), \quad \text{all } z_{\hat{k}} \in \prod_{k \in L - \{k\}} X_{N_k},$$

which in turn proves (18).

We establish now a result quite similar to lemma 2 above. We shall use the same notations with the following additional one: $C \xrightarrow{A} B$ means $C \subset B \subset A$ and for all i and all $x_i \in B_i$, there exists $y_i \in C_i$ such that

$$u_i \circ \pi(x_i, x_{\hat{i}}) = u_i \circ \pi(y_i, x_{\hat{i}}), \quad \text{all } x_{\hat{i}} \in A_{\hat{i}}.$$

In the statement of lemma 2-bis, we use L and k to denote the society L with current agent k instead of N and i.

Lemma 2-bis. Let $g^* = (Y_k, k \in L, \pi)$ be any finite game form and $u \in L(A)^L$ be any fixed profile. For every k, let A_k be a subset of Y_k such that

$$A \cap Y^1 \xrightarrow{Y} Y^1, \quad \text{where } A = \prod_{k \in L} A_k. \tag{20}$$

Then $g^*(Y)$ is dominance-solvable at u if and only if $g^*(A) = (A_k, k \in L, \pi)$ is dominance-solvable at u. In that case, their sophisticated outcomes coincide.

Applying lemma 2-bis for $Y_k = X_{N_k}$ and $A_k = \prod_{i \in N_k} X_i^1$, we deduce lemma 3 by an obvious induction argument. Now to the proof of lemma 2-bis.

First (20) implies

$$A^1 \cap Y^1 \underset{A}{\to} A^1. \tag{21}$$

Namely fix k and $x_k \in A_k^1 \setminus Y_k^1$. By the finiteness of Y_k there exists $y_k \in Y_k^1$ such that

$$u_k \circ \pi(x_k, x_{\hat{k}}) \leq u_k \circ \pi(y_k, x_{\hat{k}}), \quad \text{all } x_{\hat{k}} \in Y_{\hat{k}}.$$

Suppose $y_k \in A_k$. Since $x_k \in A_k^1$, the above inequality is an equality on $A_{\hat{k}}$ and $y_k \in A_k^1$ as well. If $y_k \notin A_k$, there exists by (20) some $z_k \in A_k \cap Y_k^1$ such that

$$u_k \circ \pi(y_k, x_{\hat{k}}) = u_k \circ \pi(z_k, x_{\hat{k}}), \quad \text{all } x_{\hat{k}} \in Y_{\hat{k}}.$$

The above two properties imply in particular:

$$u_k \circ \pi(x_k, x_{\hat{k}}) \leq u_k \circ \pi(z_k, x_{\hat{k}}), \quad \text{all } x_{\hat{k}} \in A_{\hat{k}}.$$

Since $x_k \in A_k^1$, this inequality actually is an equality and $z_k \in A_k^1$, which was to be proved.

We now set

$$A_* = A^1 \cap Y^1; \quad Y_* = A \cap Y^1,$$

and we prove that

$$A_* \cap Y_*^1 \underset{Y_*}{\to} Y_*^1. \tag{22}$$

That is, let $x_k \in Y_{*k}^1$. If $x_k \in A_k^1$, we are done. Otherwise we can choose $y_k \in A_k^1$ such that

$$u_k \circ \pi(x_k, x_{\hat{k}}) \leq u_k \circ \pi(y_k, x_{\hat{k}}), \quad \text{all } x_{\hat{k}} \in A_{\hat{k}}.$$

If $y_k \notin Y_k^1$, we can choose $z_k \in A_k^1 \cap Y_k^1$ (by (21)) such that

$$u_k \circ \pi(y_k, x_{\hat{k}}) = u_k \circ \pi(z_k, x_{\hat{k}}), \quad \text{all } x_{\hat{k}} \in A_{\hat{k}}.$$

Thus, there always exists $z_k \in A_{*k} \subset Y_{*k}$ such that

$$u_k \circ \pi(x_k, x_{\hat{k}}) \leq u_k \circ \pi(z_k, x_{\hat{k}}), \quad \text{all } x_{\hat{k}} \in A_{\hat{k}} \tag{23}$$

(if $y_k \in Y_k^1$ we simply take $z_k = y_k$).

Observe that $z_k \in Y_{*k}$, $x_k \in Y_{*k}^1$ and the above inequality holds true in particular for all $x_{\hat{k}} \in Y_{*\hat{k}} \subset A_{\hat{k}}$. Therefore $z_k \in Y_{*k}^1$ and (23) is an equality on $Y_{*\hat{k}}$. Which concludes the proof of (22).

We now prove lemma 2-bis by an induction argument. Assume it holds for all g^*, where $|Y| \leq r$ and that $|Y| \geq r+1$. If Y_* has cardinality $r+1$, then $A = Y$ and there is nothing to prove. Suppose, on the contrary, $|Y_*| \leq r$. By the induction assumption and (22) we have that $g^*(Y_*)$ is d-solvable iff $g^*(A_*)$ is with the same sophisticated outcome. Next, by (21) and step 1 of lemma 2, $g^*(A_*) = g^*(A^1 \cap Y^1)$ is d-solvable iff $g^*(A^1)$ is, hence iff $g^*(A)$ is, with the same sophisticated outcome. Furthermore, by (20) and step 1 of lemma 2 again, $g^*(Y_*) = g^*(A \cap Y^1)$ is d-solvable iff $g^*(Y^1)$ is, hence iff $g^*(Y)$ is, with the same sophisticated outcome. This concludes the proof of lemma 2-bis and theorem 4.

As a consequence of theorem 4, we obtain that several familiar s.c.f.s are *not* sophisticatedly implementable.

We call S a *scoring social choice function* if S is a single-valued selection of some scoring correspondence S_s (see example 1, Chapter 2). In particular S is a *Borda* scoring s.c.f. if s is given by

$$\bar{s}_1 = p - 1, \ldots, \quad \bar{s}_k = p - k, \ldots, \quad \bar{s}_p = 0.$$

Given for every agent $i \in N$ a weight $\lambda_i > 0$, we denote by R_λ the following *Rawlsian* social choice correspondence:

$$a \in R_\lambda(u), \quad \text{iff } \varphi(b) = \min_{i \in N}\{\lambda_i \tau(u_i, b)\} \text{ is maximal at } a \text{ over } A,$$

where $\tau(u_i, b)$ is the Borda score of outcome b at u_i.

A *Rawlsian social choice function* is any selection of a Rawlsian s.c.c. R_λ.

Corollary of theorem 4. We fix A with cardinality $p \geq 3$. Let s be a scoring vector such that

$$s_1 > s_2 > \cdots > s_p.$$

Then for $n = |N|$ large enough, no corresponding scoring s.c.f. is sophisticatedly implementable. For instance, no Borda scoring s.c.f. is sophisticated for $n \geq 7$.

We next fix N with cardinality $n \geq 3$. Let λ be a weighting vector on N. Then for $p = |A|$ large enough, no corresponding Rawlsian s.c.f. is sophisticatedly implementable. For instance, if $\lambda_i = 1$, all i, $p \geq 5$ is enough.

Proof. We give a complete proof for the Borda scoring s.c.f. and let the reader derive a similar proof for the general case.

Let A and N be fixed with respective cardinalities p and n, and let S be a Borda scoring s.c.f.

For all profile $\boldsymbol{u} \in L(A)^N$ we denote by $B(\boldsymbol{u})$ the set of Borda winners at $\boldsymbol{u}$. Thus, we have

$$\begin{cases} a \in B(\boldsymbol{u}), & \text{iff } \sum_{i \in N} \tau(u_i, b) \text{ is maximal at } a \text{ over } A, \\ S(\boldsymbol{u}) \in B(\boldsymbol{u}). \end{cases}$$

Suppose first that n is odd: $n = 2n' - 1 \geq 3$.

We pick a coalition T with cardinality n', and a utility u with top candidate a. One checks that $B([u]_T, [\bar{u}]_{T^c}) = \{a\}$. Hence, if property (8) holds true we must have

$$S([u]_T, u_{T^c}) = a, \quad \text{all } u_{T^c} \in L(A)^{T^c} \tag{24}$$

Now denote b the candidate ranked second by u and pick a utility v, where b is ranked first and a is ranked last. The Borda score of a with respect to $([u]_T, [v]_{T^c})$ is $n'(p-1)$ and that of b is $n'(p-2) + (n'-1)(p-1)$. Therefore if $n'/(n'-1) < p - 1$, the score of b strictly exceeds that of a, a contradiction of (24). Clearly $n'/(n'-1) < p - 1$ holds for $p \geq 4$ or $\{p = 3$ and $n \geq 5\}$.

Suppose now that n is even: $n = 2, n' \geq 2$.

Let T be a coalition with cardinality n'. We fix an element u of $L(A)$ such that $u(A) = \{0, \ldots, p-1\}$ (thus $u(a) = \tau(u, a)$) and we construct v as

$$\begin{cases} v(a) = p - 1 - u(a), & \text{if } u(a) \geq 2, \\ v(a_1) = p - 1, & \text{where } u(a_1) = 1, \\ v(a_0) = p - 2, & \text{where } u(a_0) = 0. \end{cases}$$

One checks that a_1 is the unique Borda winner of profile $([u]_T, [v]_{T^c})$, therefore $S([u]_T, [v]_{T^c}) = a_1$. By (8) this implies $u(S([u]_T, [\bar{u}]_{T^c})) \leq u(S([u]_T, [v]_{T^c})) = 1$. A symmetrical argument yields $\bar{u}(S([u]_T, [\bar{u}]_{T^c})) \leq 1$, hence a contradiction for $p \geq 4$.

It remains only to check the case $p = 3$, n even, $n = 2n'$.

Choosing a coalition T with cardinality $n' + 1$ one shows as above (case n odd) that T is dictatorial: property (24) holds. However, using the same pair u, v (where the top candidate of v is ranked second by u, and its bottom candidate is ranked first by u) we get the same contradiction if $(n'+1)(p-1)$ is strictly less than $(n'+1)(p-2)+(n'-1)(p-1)$. Since $p = 3$ this yields $n' \geq 4$, i.e. $n \geq 8$.

In each case we have derived a contradiction from (8), i.e. the assumption that S satisfies C.E. Hence, S does not belong to $\tilde{S}$.

We consider next a Rawlsian scoring s.c.f. S corresponding to the uniform weighting $\lambda_i = 1$. We assume that S satisfies C.E. and we fix a coalition T, $T \neq N$.

Suppose first $p = 2$, $p' + 1$ is odd. We again fix a utility u such that $u(A) = \{0, \ldots, (p-1)\}$. One checks that

$$R([u]_T, [\bar{u}]_{T^c}) = \{a\}, \quad \text{where } \tau(u, a) = p'.$$

Therefore if we set, for all T, u:

$$v_T(u) = u(S([u]_T, [\bar{u}]_{T^c})),$$

we obtain $v_T(u) = p'$ for *every* proper coalition T. If n is greater than or equal to 3, there exist three disjoint non-empty coalitions, T_i, $i = 1, 2, 3$, such that $v_{T_i}(u_i) = p'$ for all $i = 1, 2, 3$ and all u_i such that $u_i(A) = \{0, \ldots, (p-1)\}$.

In view of the assumption (8) we have

$$p' = v_{T_i}(u_i) = \inf_{u_{T_i^c}} u_i\left(S([u_i]_{T_i}, u_{T_i^c})\right). \tag{25}$$

This quantity will be interpreted in Chapter 7 as the *veto power* of coalition T_i. That is, consider any subset A_i of A with cardinality $\leq p'$ and such that $u_i(A_i) \subset \{0, \ldots, (p'-1)\}$.

Then by (25) we have

$$S([u_i]_{T_i}, u_{T_i^c}) \notin A_i, \quad \text{all } u_{T_i^c} \in L(A)^{T_i^c}. \tag{26}$$

Thus, coalition T_i vetoes A_i by sending the message $[u_i]_{T_i}$. Having this interpretation in mind, we observe that for $p \geq 3$ we have $p' \geq 1$, hence $3p' \geq p$. Therefore we can choose a partition A_i, $i = 1, 2, 3$, of A such that $|A_i| \leq p'$. Picking for all $i = 1, 2, 3$ a utility u_i such that $u_i(A) = \{0, \ldots, (p-1)\}$ and $u_i(A_i) \subset \{0, \ldots, (p'-1)\}$, we derive from (26):

$$S([u_1]_{T_1}, [u_2]_{T_2}, [u_3]_{T_3}) \notin A_i, \quad \text{all } i = 1, 2, 3.$$

This is the desired contradiction. Hence, for p odd, $p \geq 3$, the equal-weight Rawlsian s.c.f. is not sophisticated. A similar argument applies for p even, $p = 2p'$. Namely, for all u such that $u(A) = \{0, \ldots, (p-1)\}$ we get

$$R([u]_T, [\bar{u}]_{T^c}) = \{a, b\},$$

where $u(a) = p'$ and $u(b) = p' - 1$.

Therefore $v_T(u) \geq p' - 1$ for all proper non-empty coalition T. For $p \geq 6$ we can find A_i, $i = 1, 2, 3$, of A, where $|A_i| \leq p' - 1$ and derive an analogous contradiction.

By way of an exercise the reader may attempt to prove the general case of a Rawlsian scoring s.c.f with any associated weights $\lambda = (\lambda_i)_{i \in N}$. ∎

Problem 15: A sophisticated efficient anonymous and neutral s.c.f. (Kim and Roush, 1982). We suppose $|A| = p = 3$ and $|N| = n = 5$. We denote by σ an arbitrary ordering of A, written as a one-to-one mapping from $\{1, 2, 3\}$ into A. Next G_σ denotes the voting by successive amendments corresponding to σ (fig. 5.8).

For all $i \in N$, let H_i be the following voting rule: agent i picks one among the four other agents – say j – then agent j chooses an ordering σ of A, finally G_σ is played.

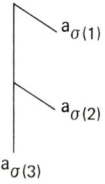

Fig. 5.8.

The overall procedure is any voting by binary choices over $H_1,\ldots,H_5$. Prove that this procedure is d-solvable and implements the plurality with a run-off s.c.f. (see example 1, Chapter 3), and hence an efficient anonymous and neutral s.c.f.

More examples of a non-anonymous game form that actually implements an anonymous s.c.f. will be given in Chapter 7.

References

Farquharson, R., 1969, Theory of voting, Yale University Press.
Gretlein, R., 1980a, "Dominance solvable voting schemes: A comment", forthcoming in Econometrica.
Gretlein, R., 1980b, Dominance elimination procedures on finite alternative games, School of Urban and Public Affairs, Carnegie Mellon University, Pittsburgh.
Kim, K.H. and F. Roush, 1982, "Dominance solvable games and trees", Mathematical Social Sciences, 2, 245–256.
McKelvey, R.D. and R.G. Niemi, 1978, "A multistage game representation of sophisticated voting for binary procedures", Journal of Economic Theory 18, 1–22.
Miller, N., 1977, "Graph-theoretical approaches to the theory of voting", American Journal of Political Science 21, 769–803.
Moulin, H., 1979, "Dominance solvable voting schemes", Econometrica 47, 1337–1351.
Owen, G., 1971, Game theory, Saunders, Philadelphia.
Rochet, J.C., 1980, Selection of a unique equilibrium pay-off for extensive games with perfect information, D.P. CEREMADE, Université Paris IX.

CHAPTER 6

VOTING BY VETO

1. Summary of the results

Sophisticated voting requires both complete information (each individual agent being aware of the whole profile) and non-cooperation. When the agents are few and the committee is to work repeatedly, these two requirements lack realism: mutual knowledge makes clear the profitable coalitional moves, and repetition of the voting mechanism enforces agreements by bilateral threats.[1]

It is the purpose of Chapters 6 and 7 to explore systematically the consequences of cooperative behaviour by the agents in voting mechanisms. In Chapter 6 we do not attack this question in the most abstract framework of game forms (this is the subject of Chapter 7). Rather, we focus on the particular class of voting by veto methods which share remarkable stability properties both with respect to cooperative and non-cooperative behaviour of the agents. The key of these methods is that individual agents or coalitions cannot force the election of one particular candidate but can *veto* certain subsets of candidates that they regard as detestable.

In section 2 we introduce the "minority principle", the ethical argument that supports the voting by veto methods: it suggests that any minority of agents should be given a right to veto a number of outcomes (candidates) roughly proportional to its size. This principle is viewed as a natural alternative to the Condorcet majority principle.

In section 3 we characterize the proportional veto function as the unique anonymous and neutral distribution of coalitional power optimally guaranteeing cooperative stability (theorem 1). This means that when the veto

---

[1] In the framework of repeated games, the "folk theorem" says that every utility vector of an outcome in the β-core of the original game is a strong equilibrium utility vector of the corresponding supergame (Rubinstein, 1979). In other words coalitional agreements can be enforced by repetition.

power is allocated to coalitions proportionally to their size, an outcome stable with respect to cooperative voting always exists and the set of stable outcomes is as small as possible. Section 4 is devoted to the (long) proof of theorem 1.

In the final two sections we explore the strategic features of voting by veto methods, namely game forms where the agents successively eliminate some of the existing outcomes until a single one is left. Section 5 is devoted to the voting by integer veto methods, where each agent is endowed with the right to veto an integer number of alternatives. There cooperative and non-cooperative behaviour of the agents prove to be consistent with each other (theorem 4): the outcome of either sophisticated or prudent voting always belong to the core of the associated cooperative game.

Finally, section 6 presents the general voting by veto methods where the veto power of coalitions can be fractional: it is shown that most of the above results still hold.

Both the simplicity of the voting rule and the depth of its strategic features strongly recommend the use of voting by veto methods for committees where the number of agents is small so that complete information and cooperation can be expected.

However, voting by veto methods are highly sensitive to the particular choice of the candidates' set and the electoral body. Because A and N are both exogenously fixed in our analysis this drawback is not apparent in the subsequent results.

The basic references on the current chapter are Moulin (1980, 1981a, 1981b) and Moulin and Peleg (1982).

2. The minority principle

Given a set A of possible outcomes, and a society N where cooperative behaviour prevails, the collective decision-making problem can be stated as follows. How can we allocate the decision power among individual agents and coalitions of agents so as to meet the two following conflicting goals:

(i) there always exists at least one stable outcome (i.e. a decision that cannot be objected to by any agent or coalition of agents), and

(ii) the set of stable outcomes is as small as possible (optimally unique)?

The first answer to these questions was proposed by Condorcet as early as 1785, namely the *majority principle*: society should select a Condorcet winner in the case there is one. As we have seen (theorem 3, Chapter 4) this principle is justified by deep strategic arguments: selecting the Condorcet winner is indeed a strategy proof s.c.f. and is also robust against manipulations by coalitions of agents (see remark 3, Chapter 4). The main objection to the majority principle is of course the Condorcet paradox (lemma 2, Chapter 2): a Condorcet winner may fail to exist. The paradox is readily interpretable in terms of cooperative instability: given that a coalition has full power if it is a strict majority (and zero power otherwise), to say that there is no Condorcet winner amounts to saying that against every outcome at least one coalition has a profitable objection, henceforth no outcome is stable with respect to coalitional power.

The essential instability implied by the majority principle results from the very sharp underlying distribution of power: any coalition has either full or zero power. In particular, a 49% minority can be exploited to death by the opposing 51% majority. To avoid this instability, we use a more flexible allocation of coalitional power where a coalition T can block up to $v(T)$ outcomes, $v(T)$ being an integer between 0 and $(p-1)$. Here v is a given function, increasing with T. The choice of v allows us to smooth the distribution of power among coalitions ($v(T) = p/2$ can be interpreted as: coalition T holds half of the decision power). By seeking to endow all coalitions (whether they are a majority or not) with as much power as possible, as long as the stability of at least one outcome is guaranteed for all profiles, we are led to the following *minority principle*: a coalition should be given the power to veto any subset of outcomes up to an upper bound which is nearly proportional to its size. The rigorous formulation of this principle is given in example 2 below. For the time being we give the intuition of it in the following example.

Suppose (as in the discussion of property (8), Chapter 5) that society N splits into two homogeneous and antagonistic coalitions, T and T^c, with respective utility u and $\bar{u}$. As usual we denote by p the cardinality of A and we order the outcomes in such a way that

$$u(a_1) > u(a_2) > \cdots > u(a_p).$$

Thus, t agents have utility u, whereas $(n-t)$ agents have the reverse utility.

The majority principle suggests the following s.c.f.: select a_1 if $t > n - t$ (because in that case a_1 is the Condorcet winner) or a_p if $t < n - t$ (because a_p is then the Condorcet winner). Therefore in most cases an extremist outcome is the solution as the majority crushes the antagonistic minority.

The minority principle suggests on the contrary that coalition T has the right to veto any subset B of A containing strictly less than $p(t/n)$ outcomes (i.e. as long as the ratio of $|B|$ to $|A|$ remains inferior to the ratio of

$|T|$ to $|N|$). Denoting by p_1 the greatest integer strictly less than $p(t/n)$, coalition T will actually block the following subset B of A:

$$B = \{a_p, a_{p-1}, \ldots, a_{p-p_1+1}\}.$$

Similarly, coalition T^c can veto any subset C of A whose cardinality is smaller than $p[(n-t)/n]$. Denoting by p_2 the greatest such integer, we obtain that T^c will block the following subset:

$$C = \{a_1, a_2, \ldots, a_{p_2}\}.$$

Observe finally that $p_1 + p_2$ is either $p-1$ or $p-2$ so that one or two outcomes are left in $A \setminus \{B \cup C\}$. This outcome(s) is the solution recommended by the minority principle (using the terminology of section 4, it is the core of the proportional veto function for that particular profile). This solution compromises between the antagonistic opinions by guaranteeing that a coalition with, say, 20% of the agents can prevent the election of (almost) its 20% most detestable outcomes. Thus, a basic feature of the minority principle is that non-zero minorities enjoy a non-zero security level when their members' utility coincide.

The next definition formally describes an anonymous distribution of coalitional power.

Definition 1. Let A and N be given with respective cardinalities n and p.

Let v be a mapping from $\{1,\ldots,n\}$ into $\{0,1,\ldots,(p-1)\}$. We say that v is an *anonymous veto function* if v is superadditive:

$$\forall t_1, t_2 \in \{1,\ldots,n\}[t_1 + t_2 \leq n] \Rightarrow [v(t_1) + v(t_2) \leq v(t_1 + t_2)].$$

We denote by V the set of anonymous veto functions.[2]

The interpretation of an element $v \in V$ is clear: any coalition T with cardinality t has a right to veto any subset B of A with cardinality $v(t)$, that is to say the agents of T can guarantee that the final outcome will not belong to B. In particular, if $v(t) = p-1$, then every coalition T with t agents is *winning*, that is to say the agents of T can enforce the choice of any outcome they wish to. Notice that a veto function (like a simple game) does not describe an explicit decision process in strategic form (such a complete description is a game form – definition 1, Chapter 4).

---

[2] By analogy with the characteristic function of cooperative games, the terminology *symmetric veto function* might seem appropriate. However, *anonymous* is more familiar in the social choice and voting theory literature.

The superadditivity assumption says that merging coalitions do not lose power: "l'union fait la force". It implies in particular that for all $t_1,\ldots,t_m$:

$$[t_1 + \cdots + t_m \leqslant n] \Rightarrow [v(t_1) + v(t_2) + \cdots + v(t_m) \leqslant p - 1]. \tag{1}$$

This property is needed if we want all coalition structures to be feasible. Namely if (1) fails for some $t_1,\ldots,t_m$, then a coalition structure $T_1,\ldots,T_m$ such that $|T_1| = t_1,\ldots,|T_m| = t_m$ could prevent any outcome from being chosen...

Simple games (where a coalition has either full veto power $p-1$ or zero power) provide a first example or anonymous veto functions, in the spirit of the majority principle.

Example 1: Majority games with quota $q(n/2 < q \leqslant n)$. Making $v(t) = 0$ or $p - 1$ for all t and taking into account the superadditivity assumption (which implies that w is non-decreasing) we deduce the existence of an integer quota q, $n/2 < q \leqslant n$, such that

$$v_q(t) = p - 1, \quad \text{if } q \leqslant t,$$
$$v_q(t) = 0, \quad \text{if } t < q.$$

Our next example captures the minority principle.

Example 2: Proportional veto. For every real number x we denote by $\lceil x \rceil$ the smallest integer greater than or equal to x and by $\lfloor x \rfloor$ the greatest integer smaller than or equal to x. The following veto function $\bar{v}_{n,p}$ is called the *proportional veto function*.

$$\forall t = 1,\ldots,n : \bar{v}_{n,p}(t) = \left\lceil p \cdot \frac{t}{n} \right\rceil - 1. \tag{2}$$

Thus, $\bar{v}_{n,p}(t)$ is *the greatest integer strictly less than* $p \cdot (t/n)$.

The superadditivity of $\bar{v}_{n,p}$ is easily deduced from the inequalities $\lceil x \rceil - 1 < x \leqslant \lceil x \rceil$ and the fact that $\lceil x \rceil$ is an integer.

Clearly, $\bar{v}_{n,p}(t)$ is roughly proportional to t. That is to say the inequalities $x \leqslant \lceil x \rceil < x + 1$ imply

$$\forall t = 1,\ldots,n : p \cdot \frac{t}{n} - 1 \leqslant \bar{v}_{n,p}(t) < p \cdot \frac{t}{n}.$$

In section 6 we define appropriate game forms which endow any coalition T with exactly the corresponding proportional veto $v(t)$ (see problem 19). Other examples of anonymous veto functions will be given in Chapter 7, where we compute the veto power associated with several familiar voting methods, like the Borda scoring correspondence.

3. The proportional veto core

For every fixed veto function $v \in V$ and every profile $\boldsymbol{u} \in L(A)^N$, the agents face a cooperative game (the structure of which is rather more complex than an ordinary simple game) where stability is axiomatized by a variant of the usual "core": we call unstable an outcome that some coalition can veto while guaranteeing a benefit to all its members.

Definition 2. Fix an anonymous veto function $v \in V$ and a profile $\boldsymbol{u} \in L(A)^N$. The *core* of v associated with $\boldsymbol{u}$ is the following (possibly empty) subset $C_v(\boldsymbol{u})$ of A:

$$a \in C_v(\boldsymbol{u}) \underset{\text{def.}}{\leftrightarrow} \text{No} \begin{cases} \exists T \subset N : |T| = t \\ \exists B \subset A : |B| = p - v(t) \end{cases} \text{ and}$$

$$\begin{cases} \forall i \in T: \\ \forall b \in A: \end{cases} u_i(b) > u_i(a). \tag{3}$$

By definition 2 an outcome a is not stable if some coalition T can find a subset B of A such that:

(i) a coalition T can force the final outcome in B by vetoing its complement B^c, which by assumption has cardinality $v(t)$; and

(ii) all members of coalition T have an advantage to do so because every agent within T strictly prefers *every* outcome in B to a.

Definition 3. We say that an anonymous veto function $v \in V$ is *stable* if for every profile $\boldsymbol{u} \in L(A)^N$ the associated core is non-empty:

$$\forall \boldsymbol{u} \in L(A)^N : C_v(u) \neq \emptyset.$$

Theorem 1 (Moulin, 1981b). For all n, p:

(i) the proportional veto function $\bar{v}_{n,p}$ is stable; for every profile $\boldsymbol{u}$ the associated core is called the *proportional veto core* associated with $\boldsymbol{u}$ and denoted by $C_{n,p}(\boldsymbol{u})$; and

(ii) an anonymous veto function is stable if and only if it is bounded above by the proportional veto function:

$$\forall v \in V \{v \text{ stable}\} \leftrightarrow \{\forall t = 1, \ldots, n : v(t) \leq \bar{v}_{n,p}(t)\}.$$

The proof of theorem 1 is given in section 4.

This result solves completely the problem raised in section 2: it says that the proportional veto function $\bar{v}_{n,p}$ is the optimal anonymous allocation of power if one wants:

(a) to guarantee the stability of at least one outcome (to avoid the Condorcet paradox); or

(b) to make the set of stable outcomes as small as possible (in order to reduce the indeterminacy of the final outcome).

That is to say, theorem 1 says that every stable anonymous veto function v is bounded above by $\bar{v}_{n,p}$ ($v(t) \leq \bar{v}_{n,p}(t)$ for all $t = 1,\ldots,n$). This implies that the core of v contains the veto core for all profiles:

$$C_{n,p}(\boldsymbol{u}) \subset C_v(\boldsymbol{u}).$$

Combining eq. (2) and definition 2 we get that the proportional veto core can be written as follows. For every profile $\boldsymbol{u} \in L(A)^N$:

$$\{a \in C_{n,p}(\boldsymbol{u})\} \Leftrightarrow \begin{cases} \forall T \subset N \\ \forall B \subset A \end{cases} [\forall i \in T, \forall b \in B: u_i(a) < u_i(b)]$$

$$\Rightarrow \left[|B| \leq \left\lfloor p\frac{n-t}{n} \right\rfloor\right].$$

Namely, by definition 2 an outcome a is in the veto core if and only if for all T and B such that every agent of T prefers every outcome of B to a, we have

$$|B| < p - \bar{v}_{n,p}(t) = p - \left\lceil \frac{pt}{n} \right\rceil + 1 = \left\lfloor p\frac{(n-t)}{n} \right\rfloor + 1.$$

Another equivalent reading of the theorem is the following. Any anonymous distribution of the veto power assigning to some coalitions a veto power more than proportional to their size will inevitably lead to an irreducible instability of the decision process for some profile of preferences: "more than proportional veto power implies a Condorcet paradox":

$$\forall v \in V \left\{ \exists t: v(t) \geq \left\lceil \frac{pt}{n} \right\rceil \right\} \Leftrightarrow \{\exists \boldsymbol{u} \in L(A)^N: C_v(\boldsymbol{u}) \neq \emptyset\}.$$

As a corollary of theorem 1, let us seek those integers $q, n/2 < q \leq n$, such that the majority game with quota q (example 1) is stable. By (ii) of theorem 1 this is equivalent to:

$$\forall t = 1,\ldots,n: v_q(t) \leqslant \bar{v}_{n,p}(t).$$

By the monotonicity of $\bar{v}_{n,p}$ this amounts to saying $\bar{v}_{n,p}(q) = p-1$, hence by (2):

$$\left\lceil \frac{pq}{n} \right\rceil = p \Leftrightarrow \frac{pq}{n} > p-1 \Leftrightarrow q > n - \frac{n}{p}.$$

This condition is quite restrictive: for instance, with $p = 10$, only coalitions with more than 90% of the agents are likely to win.

The above inequality is a particular case of Nakamura's (1975) theorem characterizing the stable simple games: see Chapter 7, section 3. For anonymous (symmetric) simple games, stability is equivalent to the latter inequality.

In the following examples we emphasize the difference between the proportional veto core and the Condorcet winner.

Some examples of the proportional veto core

Let $n = 3$ and $p = 4$ so that the proportional veto is simply $\bar{v}_{3,4}(t) = t, 1 \leqslant t \leqslant 3$. Consider the following profile:

u_1	u_2	u_3
d	a	a
c	d	c
b	b	b
a	c	d

Here a is the Condorcet winner, whereas the proportional veto core is $C_{3,4}(u) = \{b\}$ since outcomes a, c and d are blocked respectively by agents 1, 2 and 3. In words, b is the only candidate that no voter regards as extremist.

Suppose now $n = p = 5$, so that the proportional veto is $\bar{v}_{5,5}(t) = t - 1$, $1 \leq t \leq 5$. We consider the following profile:

u_1, u_5	u_2	u_3	u_4
a	e	d	c
b	a	e	d
c	b	a	e
d	c	b	a
e	d	c	b

Here there is no Condorcet winner. However, the veto core shrinks to a single outcome: $C_{5,5}(u) = \{a\}$. Namely, outcome e could not be the final decision, since coalition $\{1,5\}$ with veto power 1 would veto it. Similarly, outcome d gives rise to the coalition $\{1,5,2\}$ vetoing $\{e, d\}$. Likewise, c gives rise to coalition $\{1,5,2,3\}$ vetoing $\{e, d, c\}$. Finally, b is Pareto dominated by a so the grand coalition (endowed with full veto power) would object to the election of b by vetoing $\{e, d, c, b\}$.

In our final example $n = 5$ and $p = 6$ so that the proportional veto function is $\bar{v}(t) = t$, $1 \leq t \leq 5$.

Consider the following profile:

a	a	a	f
b	c	d	e
c	d	e	d
d	e	b	c
e	b	c	b
f	f	f	a
u_1	u_2	u_3	u_4, u_5

Here a is a Condorcet winner since it is the top candidate of a majority coalition $\{1,2,3\}$. The minority coalition $\{4,5\}$, however, has a veto power of 2 that it can use to prevent the election of both a and b. On the other hand, the majority $\{1,2,3\}$ although endowed with a right to veto any three outcomes will not use it since the agents in $\{1,2,3\}$ (although they agree on their top candidate a and their bottom candidate f) disagree on the ranking of the middle candidates (b, c, d, e). Only candidate f is therefore vetoed (by any single agent 1, 2 or 3) and the veto core is then $C_{5,6}(u) = \{c, d, e\}$.

From theorem 1, the proportional veto core emerges as a social choice correspondence of primary importance. It is an efficient, anonymous and neutral s.c.c. On the normative side its principal appeal is that it eliminates those issues that a significant minority feels are extremist. On the positive side it endows every coalition with as much power as possible so as to guarantee for every profile the existence of at least one outcome stable with respect to coalitional strategic manipulations. Last, but not least, the proportional veto core correspondence is strongly monotonic (see problem 17, section 5), a property that proves of crucial relevance to the implementation problem (Chapter 7).

4. Proof of theorem 1

Although the content of theorem 1 is very intuitive, its proof is very long and involves significant arithmetical technicalities. The non-technical reader can jump directly to section 5.

During the proof of theorem 1 two equivalent formulations of the proportional veto function are needed; these we present first. Throughout the proof we fix n and p and we denote by α the greatest common divisor of n and p. We denote simply by $\bar{v}$ the proportional veto function $\bar{v}_{n,p}$.

Lemma 1. Let us denote by $R(n, p)$ the set of those pairs (r, c) of positive integers such that

$$r \cdot n = c \cdot p - \alpha.$$

Then $R(n, p)$ is non-empty, and actually infinite: if (r, c) belongs to $R(n, p)$, then for every non-negative integer λ, $(r + \lambda p, c + \lambda n)$ belongs to $R(n, p)$ as well.

Moreover, for all $(r, c) \in R(n, p)$ such that $c > \alpha n$, we have

$$\bar{v}(t) = \left\lfloor \frac{rt}{c} \right\rfloor.$$

The proof of this Lemma is a straightforward application of the classical Bezout identity. It is left as an exercise to the reader.

Lemma 2. Let d be the integer quotient of n by p and s its remainder:

$$n = p \cdot d + s, \quad 0 \leq s < p; \quad 0 \leq d.$$

We consider the following non-decreasing sequence $(\theta_1,\ldots,\theta_p)$ of positive integers:

$$\forall k = 1,\ldots,p: \theta_k = k \cdot d + \left\lfloor \frac{sk}{p} \right\rfloor.$$

Then for every non-decreasing function v from $\{1,\ldots,n\}$ into $\{0,\ldots,(p-1)\}$ we have

$$[\forall k = 1,\ldots,p: v(\theta_k) \leq k-1] \Leftrightarrow [\forall t = 1,\ldots,n: v(t) \leq \bar{v}(t)]. \quad (4)$$

The proof of $\Leftarrow$ is immediate: for every $k = 1,\ldots,p$ we have $\theta_k \leq kd + sk/p$; hence,

$$\bar{v}(\theta_k) = \left\lceil \frac{p\theta_k}{n} \right\rceil - 1 \leq \left\lceil \frac{p\left(kd + \frac{sk}{p}\right)}{n} \right\rceil - 1 = k - 1.$$

In order to prove $\Rightarrow$, we reformulate the function $\bar{v}$ as follows. Set $\theta_0 = 0$. Then for all $k = 1,\ldots,p$:

$$\{\theta_{k-1} < t \leq \theta_k\} \Rightarrow \{\bar{v}(t) = k - 1\}. \quad (5)$$

We have already seen that $\bar{v}(\theta_k) \leq k - 1$. By the monotonicity of $\bar{v}$, property (5) is proved if we only establish

$$\theta_{k-1} < t \Rightarrow \bar{v}(t) \geq k - 1. \quad (6)$$

By definition of θ_k we have

$$\theta_{k-1} + 1 = (k-1)d + \left\lfloor \frac{s(k-1)}{p} \right\rfloor + 1 > (k-1)d + \frac{s(k-1)}{p}. \quad (7)$$

Notice that the latter formula is true if $k = 1$ as well. Pick any integer t, $1 \leq t \leq n$, such that $\theta_{k-1} < t$; that is to say, $\theta_{k-1} + 1 \leq t$. From (7) we deduce:

$$k - 1 = \frac{p\left\{(k-1)d + \frac{s(k-1)}{p}\right\}}{n} < \frac{p(\theta_{k-1}+1)}{n}$$

$$\leq \frac{pt}{n} \leq \left\lceil \frac{pt}{n} \right\rceil = \bar{v}(t) + 1.$$

This in turn implies $\bar{v}(t) \geq k - 1$, and concludes the proof of (6).

Now property (5) implies the ⇒ part of (4). Namely, if v is non-decreasing and satisfies

$$v(\theta_k) \leq k-1, \quad k = 1,\ldots,p,$$

then we have for all $t = 1,\ldots,n$:

$$v(t) \leq \inf\{j / \text{all integer } j \text{ such that } \theta_{j+1} \geq t\}.$$

From (5) it follows that the right-hand term in the latter inequality is nothing else but $\bar{v}(t)$.

Step 1: $\bar{v}$ is stable for all n, p.
We fix (n, p) and a pair $(r, c) \in R(n, p)$ such that $c > \alpha n$, so that (lemma 1) the function v is given by

$$\bar{v}(t) = \left\lfloor \frac{rt}{c} \right\rfloor, \quad \text{for all } t = 1,\ldots,n.$$

We also fix a profile $u \in L(A)^N$ and will construct an element a in $C_{\bar{v}}(u)$, the core of $\bar{v}$ associated with u. We set $\tilde{A} = \{1,\ldots,c\} \times A$ and extend straightforwardly the utility functions u_i to $\tilde{A}$:

$$\forall (\gamma, a) \in \tilde{A}: \tilde{u}_i(\gamma, a) = u_i(a).$$

The set $\tilde{A}$ is made up of c replicas of A and every agent is indifferent between two replicas of the same original outcome. Notice that $\tilde{u}_i$ is not a one-to-one utility on $\tilde{A}$.

For every subset X with cardinality at least r, we say that $Y \subset X$ is an *r-tail* of X according to $\tilde{u}_i$ if

$$|Y| = r \quad \text{and} \quad \forall x \in X \setminus Y, \forall y \in Y: \tilde{u}_i(y) \leq \tilde{u}_i(x).$$

Now we define inductively a finite sequence $\tilde{A}_1,\ldots,\tilde{A}_i,\ldots,\tilde{A}_n$ of disjoint subsets of $\tilde{A}$:

$\tilde{A}_1$ is an r-tail of $\tilde{A}$ according to $\tilde{u}_1$,

$\vdots$

$\tilde{A}_i$ is an r-tail of $\tilde{A} \setminus (\tilde{A}_1 \cup \cdots \cup \tilde{A}_{i-1})$ according to $\tilde{u}_i$, (8)

$\vdots$

$\tilde{A}_n$ is an r-tail of $\tilde{A} \setminus (\tilde{A}_1 \cup \cdots \cup \tilde{A}_{n-1})$ according to $\tilde{u}_n$.

By (8) the $\tilde{A}_i$ are disjoint and contain r elements each. Thus, $\Omega = \tilde{A} \setminus (\tilde{A}_1 \cup \cdots \cup \tilde{A}_n)$ contains $cp - rn = \alpha \geq 1$ elements. Let (γ, a) be one of these. We prove now that a belongs to $C_{\bar{v}}(u)$.

For if a does not belong to $C_{\bar{v}}(u)$ there exists a coalition $T \subset \{1, \ldots, n\}$ with cardinality t and a partition $A = B \cup B^c$ of A such that

$$|B^c| = \bar{v}(t) = \left\lfloor \frac{rt}{c} \right\rfloor,$$

$$\forall i \in T, \forall b \in B: u_i(a) < u_i(b). \tag{9}$$

Let $\tilde{B}^c = \{1, \ldots, c\} \times B^c \subset \tilde{A}$ be made up of the replicas of the elements of B^c. From (9) and the fact that the $\tilde{A}_i$ are all disjoint we deduce:

$$|B^c| \leq \frac{rt}{c} \Rightarrow |\tilde{B}^c| = c|B^c| \leq rt = \sum_{i \in T} |\tilde{A}_i| = \left| \bigcup_{i \in T} \tilde{A}_i \right|. \tag{10}$$

By (9) again we have $a \in B^c$, hence $\{1, \ldots, c\} \times \{a\} \subset \tilde{B}^c$. On the other hand, at least one $(\gamma, a)(1 \leq \gamma \leq c)$ belongs to Ω so that

$$(\gamma, a) \in \tilde{B}^c: (\gamma, a) \notin \bigcup_{i \in T} \tilde{A}_i. \tag{11}$$

From (10) and (11) we deduce the existence of at least one element (γ', a') of $\tilde{A}$ such that

$$(\gamma', a') \notin \tilde{B}^c: (\gamma', a') \in \bigcup_{i \in T} \tilde{A}_i.$$

Accordingly we have

$$\exists i \in T: (\gamma', a') \in \tilde{A}_i,$$

$$a' \in B \Rightarrow u_i(a) < u_i(a') \quad \text{(same as (i) above)}.$$

However, by definition (8), $\tilde{A}_i$ is an r-tail of $\tilde{C}_i = \tilde{A} \setminus (\tilde{A}_1 \cup \cdots \cup \tilde{A}_{i-1})$ according to $\tilde{u}_i$. We have just seen that $(\gamma', a') \in \tilde{A}_i$; moreover $(\gamma, a) \in \tilde{C}_i \setminus \tilde{A}_i$.

Hence, by definition of an r-tail we must have

$$u_i(a') = \tilde{u}_i(\gamma', a') \leq u_i(\gamma, a) = u_i(a).$$

This is the desired contradiction.

Step 2: We prove statement (ii) of theorem 1.

Since the stability of $\bar{v}$ is known (step 1) the "if" part in statement (ii) is true. For it is a priori evident that if two veto functions, v_1 and v_2, are such that $v_1(t) \leq v_2(t)$ for all $t = 1, \ldots, n$, then $C_{v_2}(u) \subset C_{v_1}(u)$ (whether these sets are empty or not). The greater the veto function the smaller the corresponding core.

In order to prove the "only if" statement we will show the following:

$$\forall v \in V : \{v \text{ stable}\} \Rightarrow \{\forall k = 1, \ldots, p \quad v(\theta_k) \leq k - 1\}. \tag{12}$$

In view of lemma 2 this completes the proof of statement (ii).

We prove (12) per absurdum. Let $v \in V$ be a stable veto function, we assume that for some k, $1 \leq k \leq p - 1$, we have $v(\theta_k) \geq k$. We then construct a profile u with an associated empty core $C_{\bar{v}}(u) = \varnothing$. Let us order the elements of A as $A = \{a_1, \ldots, a_p\}$ and denote by σ the following bijection of A onto itself:

$$\left. \begin{array}{l} \sigma(a_j) = a_{j+1} \\ \sigma(a_p) = a_1 \end{array} \right\}, \quad \text{for all } j = 1, \ldots, p - 1.$$

We now fix a particular utility function $u_0 \in L(A)$ and consider the following related utility functions:

$$\pi(j) = u_0 \circ \sigma^{j-1} \in L(A), \quad \text{for } j = 1, \ldots, p.$$

The profile u that we shall construct below (of which the associated core $C_v(u)$ is empty) is made up entirely of the utility functions $\pi(j)$. The key of the proof amounts to choosing properly the allocation of these p utility functions to the n agents. The following auxiliary result is needed.

Lemma 3. A subset I of $\{1, \ldots, p\}$ is called a *circular interval starting at a* if it is of the form $\{a, a+1, \ldots, b\}$ for some a and b such that $a \leq b$ or of the form $\{1, \ldots, (b-1), b\} \cup \{a, (a+1), \ldots, p\}$ for some a and b such that $b < a$. The *length* of I is respectively $(b - a)$ or $(p + b - a)$. Notice that the length of $I = \{a\}$ is zero and that of $I = \{1, \ldots, p\}$ is $(p - 1)$.

Suppose that r is an integer such that $1 \leq r \leq s$ and $rp \leq ks$. Then there exists a subset Ω of $\{1, \ldots, p\}$ with cardinality s such that every circular interval I with length at least $(k - 1)$ contains at least r elements of Ω.

Step 3 below is devoted to the proof of lemma 3.

Let us apply lemma 3 for $r = \lfloor sk/p \rfloor$ and choose accordingly a subset Ω of $\{1, \ldots, p\}$.

Now, we construct the desired profile $\boldsymbol{u} = (u_1, \ldots, u_n)$:

$$
\begin{aligned}
&u_i = \pi(1), && \text{for } 1 \leq i \leq d, \\
&u_i = \pi(2), && \text{for } d+1 \leq i \leq 2d, \\
&\vdots && \\
&u_i = \pi(j), && \text{for } (j-1)d + 1 \leq i \leq jd, \\
&\vdots && \\
&u_i = \pi(p), && \text{for } (p-1)d + 1 \leq i \leq pd, \\
&u_i = \pi(\tau(i)), && \text{for } pd + 1 \leq i \leq pd + s = n, \text{ where } \tau \text{ is a} \\
& && \text{bijection from } \{pd+1, \ldots, pd+s\} \text{ onto } \Omega.
\end{aligned} \tag{13}
$$

We prove that $C_v(\boldsymbol{u})$ is empty. Fix any $a \in A$. We set:

$$B = \{\sigma(a), \sigma^2(a), \ldots, \sigma^{p-k}(a)\} \subset A$$

and

$$I = \{j \in \{1, \ldots, p\} / \pi(j)(a) \leq k\}.$$

Then we remark that

$$\forall j', 1 \leq j' \leq p - k : \pi(j)(\sigma^{j'}(a)) = u_0\left[\sigma^{j+j'-1}(a)\right]$$
$$= u_0\left[\sigma^{j'}(\sigma^{j-1}(a))\right]. \tag{14}$$

If j belongs to I, then $b = \sigma^{j-1}(a)$ is such that $u_0(b) \leq k$. Hence, by the very definition of σ and the fact that the range of u_0 is $\{1, \ldots, p\}$, we get:

$$u_0(\sigma(b)) = u_0(b) + 1, \ldots, u_0(\sigma^{j'}(b)) = u_0(b) + j', \ldots, u_0(\sigma^{p-k}(b))$$
$$= u_0(b) + p - k. \tag{15}$$

From (14) and (15) we deduce:

$$\forall j \in I, \forall j' : 1 \leq j' \leq p - k : \pi(j)(\sigma^{j'}(a))$$
$$= u_0(\sigma^{j'}(b)) > u_0(b) = u_0(\sigma^{j-1}(a)) = \pi(j)(a).$$

In view of the definition of B, this can be rewritten as

$$\forall j \in I, \forall b \in B: \pi(j)(b) > \pi(j)(a).$$

We estimate now how many agents in the profile u have the utility function $\pi(j)$ for some $j \in I$. By (13) every agent i such that $(j-1)d + 1 \leqslant i \leqslant jd$ has utility $\pi(j)$. Thus, among the agents $\{1,\ldots,pd\}$, exactly kd have utility $\pi(j)$, for some $j \in I$, since I has cardinality k. In fact, we check immediately that I is a circular interval of $\{1,\ldots,p\}$ with length $(k-1)$. Therefore by our choice of Ω it must contain at least r elements of Ω, and from (13) it follows that at least r agents in $\{pd+1,\ldots,n\}$ have utility $\pi(j)$ for some $j \in I$. Gathering the above results we have proved the existence of a coalition $T \subset \{1,\ldots,n\}$ such that

$$\begin{cases} |T| \geqslant kd + r, \\ \forall i \in T, \forall b \in B: u_i(b) > u_i(a). \end{cases}$$

Notice that B has cardinality $p - k$. On the other hand, $kd + r = kd + \lfloor sk/p \rfloor = \theta_k$; hence, $v(|T|) \geqslant v(\theta_k) \geqslant k$. Therefore coalition T has a right to veto any subset of A with cardinality k, in particular the complement B^c of B. This proves that a cannot belong to the core of v associated to u and thus completes step 2.

Step 3: We prove lemma 3.

We prove by induction on p the following statement. For all integers (p, s, k, r) such that

$$1 \leqslant s < p, \quad 1 \leqslant k < p, \quad 1 \leqslant r \leqslant s \quad \text{and} \quad rp \leqslant ks, \tag{16}$$

there exists a subset Ω of $\{1,\ldots,p\}$ with cardinality s such that for every circular interval I of $\{1,\ldots,p\}$ with length $(k-1)$ we have

$$|I \cap \Omega| \geqslant r.$$

Strictly speaking lemma 3 is stated for $k = p$ as well: it is obvious in this case since any circular interval of length $(k-1)$ is $I = \{1,\ldots,p\}$.

For $p \leqslant 3$ the above statement is clear. Suppose now that it holds true until $(p-1)$ and consider some (p, s, k, r) satisfying (16). Let us divide p by s: the quotient q is non-zero since $s \leqslant p$:

$$p = qs + s', \quad 0 \leqslant s' < s, \quad 1 \leqslant q.$$

We set $\beta = \lceil rs'/s \rceil$ and remark:

$$k \geq \frac{rp}{s} = rq + \frac{rs'}{s} \Rightarrow k \geq rq + \beta. \tag{17}$$

We wish to apply the induction assumption to $(s, s', s - r, s' - \beta)$. This is possible if:

$$\begin{aligned} &1 \leq s' < s, && \text{i.e. } s' \text{ is non-zero,} \\ &1 \leq s - r \leq s, && \text{i.e. } s \text{ is different from } r, \\ &1 \leq s' - \beta \leq s', && \text{i.e. } s' \text{ is different from } \beta \\ &&& \text{(since (16) implies } \beta \leq s') \end{aligned} \tag{18}$$

$$(s' - \beta)s \leq (s - r)s', \quad \text{i.e. } \frac{rs'}{s} \leq \beta.$$

If (18) holds true, the induction assumption applies and we get:

There exists a subset H of $\{1,\ldots,s\}$ with cardinality s' such that every circular interval J of $\{1,\ldots,s\}$ with length $(s - r - 1)$ contains at least $(s' - \beta)$ elements of H. (19)

If (18) does not hold true, property (19) does hold true with our usual convention that the empty set is a circular interval with length -1. We then remark that $(s' = 0)$ $(s = r)$ and $(s' = \beta)$ all imply $(s' - \beta = 0)$ so that statement (19) is empty.

Thus (19) holds true in all cases. We consider the following subset Ω of $\{1,\ldots,p\}$ with cardinality s: $\Omega = \{j_1,\ldots,j_s\}$, where the sequence $j_1,\ldots,j_s$ is defined inductively:

$$j_1 = \begin{cases} q, & \text{if } 1 \notin H, \\ q+1, & \text{if } 1 \in H; \end{cases}$$

$$j_i = \begin{cases} j_{i-1} + q, & \text{if } i \notin H, \\ j_{i-1} + q + 1, & \text{if } i \in H; \end{cases} \tag{20}$$

$$j_s = \begin{cases} j_{s-1} + q, & \text{if } s \notin H, \\ j_{s-1} + q + 1, & \text{if } s \in H. \end{cases}$$

Since H has cardinality s', exactly s' integers j_i are such that $j_i = j_{i-1} + q + 1$, and $(s - s')$ are such that $j_i = j_{i-1} + q$. Therefore

$$j_s = sq + s' = p,$$

so that (20) actually defines a subset of $\{1,\ldots,p\}$. We prove now that Ω has the property claim at the beginning of step 3. Fix a circular interval I of $\{1,\ldots,p\}$ with length $(k-1)$, and starting at $j \in \{1,\ldots,p\}$. Next define

$$I' = \{i \in \{1,\ldots,s\} / j_i \in I\}.$$

Clearly I' is a circular interval of $\{1,\ldots,s\}$ starting at some $\bar{i} \in \{1,\ldots,s\}$. Let J be the circular interval of $\{1,\ldots,s\}$ with length $(r-1)$ and starting at $\bar{i}$:

$$\begin{aligned}J &= \{\bar{i}, \bar{i}+1, \ldots, \bar{i}+r-1\}, & \text{if } \bar{i} \leq s-r+1, \\ J &= \{1,\ldots,(\bar{i}+r-1-s)\} \cup \{\bar{i},\ldots,s\}, & \text{if } \bar{i} \geq s-r+2.\end{aligned} \quad (21)$$

Then the complement $J^c = \{1,\ldots,s\} \setminus J$ of J is a circular interval of $\{1,\ldots,s\}$ as well, with length $(s-r-1)$ (namely, J has cardinality r, and therefore J^c has cardinality $(s-r)$). By (19), J^c contains at least $(s'-\beta)$ elements of H. Since H has cardinality s', it follows that J contains *at most* β elements of H.

We consider now the circular interval $\tilde{J}$ of $\{1,\ldots,p\}$ starting at $j_{\bar{i}}$ and ending at $j_{\bar{\bar{i}}}$, where $\bar{\bar{i}}$ is the last element of J (in view of (21) we have then $\bar{\bar{i}} = \bar{i}+r-1$ if $\bar{i} \leq s-r+1$, $\bar{\bar{i}} = \bar{i}+r-1-s$ otherwise). By (20) we can compute an upper bound of the length of $\tilde{J}$:

$$\begin{aligned}\tilde{J} &= \{j_{\bar{i}}, j_{\bar{i}}+1, \ldots, j_{\bar{i}+1}, j_{\bar{i}+1}+1, \ldots, j_{\bar{\bar{i}}}\}, & \text{if } \bar{i} \leq s-r+1, \\ \tilde{J} &= \{1,\ldots,j_{\bar{\bar{i}}}\} \cup \{j_{\bar{i}}, j_{\bar{i}}+1, \ldots, p\}, & \text{otherwise.}\end{aligned}$$

That is to say, the length of the circular interval $\{j_i, j_i+1, \ldots, j_{i+1}\}$ (respectively $\{1,\ldots,j_1\} \cup \{j_s\}$) is q if $(i+1)$ (respectively 1) is not in H and $q+1$ otherwise. Since J has cardinality r and contains at most β elements of H, we get:

$$\begin{aligned}\text{length}(\tilde{J}) &= \begin{cases} j_{\bar{\bar{i}}} - j_{\bar{i}}, & \text{if } \bar{i} \leq s-r+1 \\ p + j_{\bar{\bar{i}}} - j_{\bar{i}}, & \text{if } \bar{i} \geq s-r+2 \end{cases} \\ &\leq \begin{cases} (r-1)q + \beta, & \text{if } \bar{i} \notin H, \\ (r-1)q + \beta - 1, & \text{if } \bar{i} \in H. \end{cases}\end{aligned} \quad (22)$$

We compare now $\tilde{J}$ and the circular interval I. By construction I starts at $\bar{j} \in \{1,\ldots,p\}$ and $j_{\bar{i}}$ is the first integer greater than or equal to $\bar{i}$ and belonging to Ω:

$$j_{\bar{i}} \geq \bar{j}, \quad j_{\bar{i}} \in \Omega: \quad j_{\bar{i}} = \inf\{j/j \geq \bar{j}, j \in \Omega\}. \tag{23}$$

To prove this assertion, consider two cases. If $\bar{j} \leq (p-1+k)$, then $I = \{\bar{j}, \bar{j}+1,\ldots,(\bar{j}+k-1)\}$ and every j_i such that $j_i \in I$ (i.e. $i \in I'$) is such that $\bar{j} \leq j_i$. If, on the contrary, $\bar{j} \geq (p-k+2)$, then I takes the form

$$I = \{1,\ldots,(\bar{j}+k-1-p)\} \cup \{\bar{j},\ldots,p\}.$$

Since the set $\{j \in \Omega/j \geq \bar{j}\}$ is non-empty (it contains $j_s = p$) its infimum is $j_{\bar{i}}$ indeed. From (22) we deduce $j_{\bar{i}} \geq \bar{j}$, and from (20) it follows that

$$\begin{aligned} j_{\bar{i}} - \bar{j} &\leq q - 1, \quad \text{if } i \notin H, \\ j_{\bar{i}} - \bar{j} &\leq q, \quad \text{if } i \in H. \end{aligned} \tag{24}$$

Gathering (22), (23), and (24) we obtain the following upper bound for the length of the circular interval $\tilde{I}$ starting at $\bar{j}$ and ending at $j_{\bar{i}}$ (where $\tilde{J}$ ends):

$$\text{length}(\tilde{I}) \leq rq + \beta - 1.$$

Taking (17) into account we get:

$$\text{length}(\tilde{I}) \leq k - 1 = \text{length}(I).$$

Since $\tilde{I}$ and I are two circular intervals both starting at the same integer $\bar{i}$ we conclude that I contains $\tilde{I}$, and therefore contains $\tilde{J}$. Since $\tilde{J}$ contains exactly r elements of Ω we deduce that I contains at least r elements of Ω, which was to be proved.

5. Voting by integer veto

We generalize slightly the voting by successive veto methods introduced in example 5, Chapter 5. We fix A and N with respective cardinalities p and n. Let V_i, $i \in N$, be non-negative integers such that

$$\sum_{i \in N} V_i = p - 1. \tag{25}$$

We set $V = (V_i)_{i \in N}$ and we denote by $\Sigma(V)$ the set of those mappings σ from $\{1,\ldots,p-1\}$ into N such that

$$\forall i \in N: \sigma^{-1}(i) \text{ has cardinality } V_i.$$

An element $\sigma \in \Sigma(V)$ is a finite sequence with length $(p-1)$ and values in N which entirely specifies the elimination process. More precisely, to σ we associate the game form g_σ defined (in extensive form) as follows:

First, agent $\sigma(1)$ eliminates one outcome within A, say a_1.
Next, agent $\sigma(2)$ eliminates one outcome within $A\backslash\{a_1\}$, say a_2.
$\vdots$

At step k, agent $\sigma(k)$ eliminates one outcome within $A\backslash\{a_1,\ldots,$ $\qquad$ (26) $a_{k-1}\}$, say a_k.
$\vdots$

The finally elected outcome is the remaining element of $A\backslash\{a_1,\ldots,a_{p-1}\}$.

Suppose, for instance, that N is ordered as $\{1,2,\ldots,n\}$ and $\sigma(1) = \cdots = \sigma(V_1) = 1$, $\sigma(V_1 + 1) = \cdots = \sigma(V_1 + V_2) = 2$, and so on. This means that first agent 1 is given the opportunity to veto p_1 outcomes within A, next agent 2 has to veto p_2 outcomes within the remaining outcomes, and so on. This is exactly the voting by successive veto method of example 5 in Chapter 5. However, our game form g_σ allows for more flexibility in the vetoing sequence. For example, suppose $V_1 = V_2 = (p-1)/2$ (p is odd) so that $V_j = 0$ for all $j \geq 3$, then we can choose σ so that agents 1 and 2 alternatively veto one outcome after the other:

$$\sigma(1) = 1, \quad \sigma(2) = 2,\ldots,\sigma(2k-1) = 1, \quad \sigma(2k) = 2,\ldots.$$

This voting method, termed "by alternative veto", is the subject of problem 17.

One common feature of all game forms g_σ is *neutrality* with respect to the outcomes in A. However, no g_σ is anonymous: even when the veto power V_i of agent i does not depend on i (which is only possible when p is congruent to 1 modulo n), the specific elimination ordering given by σ induces a dissymmetry among the agents which is reflected in the computation of the sophisticated equilibrium given below (theorem 2). Notice also that for $p \leq n$, some agents are endowed with zero veto power ($V_i = 0$): these agents are dummies, who do not influence *at all* the decision process.

Our aim in the current section is to compute both the non-cooperative (theorem 2) and the cooperative (theorem 3) behaviour of the agents facing g_σ. Next we show that these two behaviours are remarkably consistent in a sense to be made precise by theorem 4.

5.1. Non-cooperative behaviour

Two different non-cooperative behaviours can be explicitly computed for the game form g_σ. At one extreme the *sincere* (risk-averse) strategy is used by an agent who has no information on the other agents' preferences and is only aware of his or her own preference ordering. Thus, if at step k agent i must eliminate one outcome among $A \setminus \{a_1, \ldots, a_{k-1}\}$ he or she will eliminate his or her worst outcome. Hence, if $\boldsymbol{u} \in L(A)^N$ is a given profile and every agent plays sincerely, the elected outcome, denoted by $\sin(\sigma, \boldsymbol{u})$, is given by the following algorithm:

a_1 is the worst outcome of $u_{\sigma(1)}$ among A,
a_2 is the worst outcome of $u_{\sigma(2)}$ among $A \setminus \{a_1\}$,
$\vdots$
a_k is the worst outcome of $u_{\sigma(k)}$ among $A \setminus \{a_1, \ldots, a_{k-1}\}$, \hfill (27)
$\vdots$
a_{p-1} is the worst outcome of $u_{\sigma(p-1)}$ among $A \setminus \{a_1, \ldots, a_{p-2}\}$,
$\sin(\sigma, \boldsymbol{u}) = A \setminus \{a_1, \ldots, a_{p-1}\}$.

Exercise

Show that the sincere strategy of an agent i is risk-averse: using the notations of problem 12, Chapter 5, it belongs to the set $P_i(u_i)$.

Prove that in general the game form g_σ risk-aversedly implements a correspondence, not a function:

$$\sin(\sigma, \boldsymbol{u}) \in \pi_\sigma(P_1(u_1) \times \cdots \times P_n(u_n)),$$

where the right-hand term is not a singleton for some $\boldsymbol{u}$. Prove, however, that g_σ risk-aversedly implements a social choice *function* if and only if the following property holds:

$\forall i \in N: \sigma^{-1}(i)$ is an interval of $\{1, \ldots, (p-1)\}$.

At the other extreme sophisticated behaviour can be expected from non-cooperative agents completely informed of the overall profile. As we already noticed in example 5, Chapter 5, the game form g_σ derives from a tree where at each node one agent dictatorially selects a successor. Hence, by theorem 3, Chapter 5, g_σ is dominance-solvable. Let us denote by $\text{sop}(\sigma, \boldsymbol{u})$ the outcome elected by the sophisticated equilibrium of g_σ at profile $\boldsymbol{u}$. Our next theorem says that the sophisticated equilibrium strategies as well as the sophisticated outcome $\text{sop}(\sigma, \boldsymbol{u})$ can be computed by an algorithm quite similar to (28).

Theorem 2 (Mueller, 1978; Moulin, 1981a). For any element σ of $\Sigma(V)$ let us denote by $\bar{\sigma}$ the symmetrical mapping of σ:

$$\forall k = 1, \ldots, p-1: \bar{\sigma}(k) = \sigma(p-k).$$

Then we have

$$\forall \boldsymbol{u} \in L(A)^N: \text{sop}(\sigma, \boldsymbol{u}) = \sin(\bar{\sigma}, \boldsymbol{u}).$$

In other words, $\text{sop}(\sigma, \boldsymbol{u})$ is computed by the following algorithm:

b_1 is the worst outcome of $u_{\sigma(p-1)}$ among A,
b_2 is the worst outcome of $u_{\sigma(p-2)}$ among $A \setminus \{b_1\}$,
$\vdots$
b_k is the worst outcome of $u_{\sigma(p-k)}$ among $A \setminus \{b_1, \ldots, b_{k-1}\}$, (28)
$\vdots$
b_{p-1} is the worst outcome of $u_{\sigma(1)}$ among $A \setminus \{b_1, \ldots, b_{p-2}\}$,
$\text{sop}(\sigma, \boldsymbol{u}) = A \setminus \{b_1, \ldots, b_{p-1}\}.$

Notice that the above algorithm also gives the sophisticated equilibrium strategy of every agent. For instance, agent $\sigma(1)$ must perform the entire computation of $b_1, \ldots, b_{p-2}$ in order to obtain that outcome b_{p-1} that he is to eliminate at the first step.

Proof of theorem 2. We fix $\sigma \in \Sigma(V)$ and denote by N^* the corresponding set of active players in g_σ:

$$i \in N^* \Leftrightarrow \sigma^{-1}(i) \neq \emptyset \Leftrightarrow V_i \geq 1.$$

Next we denote by g_e the canonical voting by integer veto among society $\{1, \ldots, p-1\}$, where for all $k = 1, \ldots, p-1$ we take $e(k) = k$.

Voting by veto

To any profile $u \in L(A)^{N^*}$ we can associate the following profile v on $\{1,\ldots,p-1\}$:

$$v_k = u_{\sigma(k)}, \quad \text{all } k = 1,\ldots,p-1.$$

Since g_e is dominance-solvable it follows from lemma 3, Chapter 5, that the sophisticated outcome of g_e at v equals that of g_σ at u.

Accordingly, it is enough to prove theorem 2 when society N has $(p-1)$ agents, each $V_i = 1$ and the agents are ordered $N = \{1, 2, \ldots, (p-1)\}$ in such a way that agent k is active at step k.

For such a game form and any fixed profile u, we must show that the sophisticated outcome b is given by the following algorithm (where w.o. stands for worst outcome of):

b_1: w.o. of u_{p-1} among A,

$\vdots$

b_k: w.o. of u_{p-k} among $A \setminus \{b_1, \ldots, b_{k-1}\}$,

$\vdots$

b_{p-1}: w.o. of u_1 among $A \setminus \{b_1, \ldots, b_{p-2}\}$,

$b = A \setminus \{b_1, \ldots, b_{p-1}\}$.

The proof goes by induction on p. The theorem is obvious when $p = 2$: then g_σ is dictatorial and a dominating strategy of the dictator is to eliminate his worst candidate. Assume it holds when $|A| \leq p - 1$, choose a set A such that $|A| = p$, a profile $u \in L(A)^N$ and consider the decision problem of agent 1, at step 1.

Suppose that 1 eliminates a in step 1. Then the remaining agents will face a voting by integer veto game on $A \setminus \{a\}$. By the induction assumption, the corresponding outcome $\alpha(a)$ is given by the following algorithm:

a_1: w.o. of u_{p-1} among $A \setminus \{a\}$,

$\vdots$

a_k: w.o. of u_{p-k} among $A \setminus \{a, a_1, \ldots, a_{k-1}\}$, \hfill (30)

$\vdots$

a_{p-2}: w.o. of u_2 among $A \setminus \{a, a_1, \ldots, a_{p-3}\}$,

$\alpha(a) = A \setminus \{a, a_1, \ldots, a_{p-2}\}$.

We remark that $\alpha(b_{p-1}) = b$. Namely, we have:

$$b_{p-1} \neq b_1 \Rightarrow b_1 = \text{w.o. of } u_{p-1} \text{ among } A \setminus \{b_{p-1}\},$$

$$\vdots$$

$$b_{p-1} \notin \{b_1, \ldots, b_{k-1}\} \Rightarrow b_k$$
$$= \text{w.o. of } u_{p-k} \text{ among } A \setminus \{b_{p-1}, b_1, \ldots, b_{k-1}\},$$

$$\vdots$$

$$b_{p-1} \notin \{b_1, \ldots, b_{p-3}\} \Rightarrow b_{p-2}$$
$$= \text{w.o. of } u_2 \text{ among } A \setminus \{b_{p-1}, b_1, \ldots, b_{p-3}\}$$
$$\Rightarrow \alpha(b_{p-1}) = A \setminus \{b_{p-1}, b_1, \ldots, b_{p-2}\} = b.$$

It remains to prove that for all a, the outcome anticipated after agent 1 has eliminated a is not preferred to b by this very agent:

$$u_1(\alpha(a)) \leq u_1(b), \quad \text{all } a \in A$$

Comparing the definition of a_1 and b_1 we obtain first

$$b_1 \in \{a, a_1\} \Rightarrow A \setminus \{a, a_1\} \subset A \setminus \{b_1\}.$$

Therefore,

$$b_2 \in \{a, a_1, a_2\} \Rightarrow A \setminus \{a, a_1, a_2\} \subset A \setminus \{b_1, b_2\}.$$

An inductive argument arises:

$$A \setminus \{a, a_1, \ldots, a_k\} \subset A \setminus \{b_1, \ldots, b_k\} \Rightarrow b_{k+1} \in \{a, a_1, \ldots, a_{k+1}\}$$
$$\Rightarrow A \setminus \{a, a_1, \ldots, a_{k+1}\} \subset A \setminus \{b_1, \ldots, b_{k+1}\}.$$

After $(p-1)$ iterations of this argument we get:

$$\{\alpha(a)\} = A \setminus \{a, a_1, \ldots, a_{p-2}\} \subset A \setminus \{b_1, \ldots, b_{p-2}\} = \{b, b_{p-1}\}.$$

By definition of b_{p-1} we have $u_1(b_{p-1}) < u_1(b)$, henceforth $u_1(\alpha(a)) \leq u_1(b)$, which was to be proved. This concludes the proof of theorem 2.

As an immediate corollary of theorem 2, observe that if $\sigma = \bar{\sigma}$ then both the unanimously sophisticated behaviour of the agents and their unanimously sincere behaviour yield the election of the *same* outcome for all profile. There are plenty of such mappings σ, as the reader can easily verify: if p is even and $n = 2$, voting by alternating veto is an example.

Problem 16: Voting by alternating veto. Society contains two agents $N = \{1, 2\}$ who alternately eliminate one among the existing outcomes. For a given cardinality p of A, two voting by veto methods are in order:

$$\sigma_1: \sigma_1(1) = 1, \qquad \sigma_1(2) = 2, \ldots, \sigma_1(2k-1) = 1, \qquad \sigma_1(2k) = 2, \ldots,$$

where agent 1 starts the eliminating process, and

$$\sigma_2: \sigma_2(1) = 2, \qquad \sigma_2(2) = 1, \ldots, \sigma_2(2k-1) = 2, \qquad \sigma_2(2k) = 1, \ldots,$$

where agent 2 starts the eliminating process.

(1) For any given $p \geqslant 2$, find an example of a profile $\boldsymbol{u} \in L(A)^2$ such that

$$\text{sop}(\sigma_1, \boldsymbol{u}) \neq \text{sop}(\sigma_2, \boldsymbol{u}).$$

(2) Prove that, when sophisticated voting is in order, it is always an advantage to start to eliminate first:

$$\text{setting } a_i = \text{sop}(\sigma_i, \boldsymbol{u}): u_i(a_i) \geqslant u_i(a_j), \quad \text{for } \{i, j\} = \{1, 2\}.$$

When sincere voting is in order, is it an advantage or a disadvantage to start first?

(3) Prove that the outcomes of sophisticated voting a_i, $i = 1, 2$, either coincide or are two consecutive Pareto optima. There is no outcome c such that

$$u_1(a_2) < u_1(c) < u_1(a_1)$$

and

$$u_2(a_1) < u_2(c) < u_2(a_2).$$

5.2. Cooperative behaviour

Fix an element $\sigma \in \Sigma(V)$ and a profile $\boldsymbol{u} \in L(A)^N$. Suppose that in the normal form game $(g_\sigma, \boldsymbol{u})$, players can freely enter coalitions and sign binding agreements. Then the most demanding equilibrium concept is that of a strong equilibrium.

Definition 4. Given a game form $g = (X_i, i \in N; \pi)$ and a profile $u \in L(A)^N$ we shall say that $x = (x_i)_{i \in N}$ is a *strong equilibrium* if the following holds:

$$\forall T \subset N, \forall y_T \in X_T: \text{No}\{\forall i \in T: u_i \circ \pi(y_T, x_{T^c}) > u_i \circ \pi(x)\}. \tag{31}$$

In words, x is a strong equilibrium if no coalition of players can jointly deviate, this deviation being profitable if the players outside the coalition do not react. This passive behaviour from the non-deviating players must be seen as a threat successfully deterring the complement coalition. The fact that this threat is merely "no move" makes it particularly easy to carry out. Let us remark finally that a strong equilibrium must be in particular a Nash equilibrium and a Pareto optimum (as follows from (31) when T is a singleton coalition or is the grand coalition).

Most of Chapter 7 is devoted to implementation by strong equilibrium: what social choice correspondences can result from the strong equilibrium behaviour of the agents in some voting method? Here we simply characterize the strong equilibrium outcomes in voting by veto methods, and compare it to sincere and sophisticated equilibrium outcomes. This hopefully allows the reader quickly to capture the cooperative nature of the strong equilibrium concept.

To a given vector $V = (V_i)_{i \in N}$ of integer veto power we can associate a (*non*-anonymous) veto function:

$$\forall T \subset N: V(T) = \sum_{i \in T} V_i.$$

Clearly in the game g_σ (for any $\sigma \in \Sigma(V)$) coalition T has the power to veto any subset B whose cardinality is at most $V(T)$. Intuition suggests, and theorem 3 below confirms, that an outcome a can possibly be stable with respect to cooperative behaviour in (g_σ, u) only if

$$\text{No}\begin{cases} \exists T \subset N \\ \exists B \subset A \end{cases} : |B| = p - V(T) \quad \text{and} \quad \begin{cases} \forall i \in T \\ \forall b \in A \end{cases} : u_i(b) > u_i(a).$$

The above property defines the *veto core* $C_V(u)$ of V associated with u, of which the interpretation is the same as in the anonymous case (definition 2).

The following notation will be useful:

for all $t \subset N, a \in A, \boldsymbol{u} \in L(A)^N: \Pr(T, a, \boldsymbol{u})$

$= \{b \in A / \forall i \in T: u_i(a) < u_i(b)\}.$

Thus, the veto core $C_V(\boldsymbol{u})$ is equivalently defined by

$$C_V(\boldsymbol{u}) = \left\{ a \in A / \forall T \subset N : |\Pr(T, a, \boldsymbol{u})| \leq p - V(T) - 1 = \sum_{i \notin T} V_i \right\}.$$

(32)

Theorem 3. Given V and a profile $\boldsymbol{u} \in L(A)^N$, the set of strong equilibrium outcomes of the game $(g_\sigma, \boldsymbol{u})$ is non-empty and does not depend on the particular choice of σ within $\Sigma(V)$. It coincides with the veto core $C_V(\boldsymbol{u})$ defined by (32):

$\forall a \in A \{a \in C_V(\boldsymbol{u})\}$

$\Leftrightarrow \{$a strong equilibrium x of $(g_\sigma, \boldsymbol{u})$ exists, s.t. $a = \pi(x)\}.$ (33)

Theorem 3 is proved immediately after theorem 4.

Notice that we have not made explicit the strategy sets X_i and the decision rule π of the game form g_σ. Namely, working with the extensive form (26) will make all proofs more readable. The results of Chapter 7, that generalize theorem 3, are on the contrary stated and proved for abstract game forms.

Theorem 4 (Moulin and Peleg, 1982). Given V and a profile $\boldsymbol{u} \in L(A)^N$ the associated veto core $C_V(\boldsymbol{u})$ equals the set of sophisticated equilibrium (resp. sincere) outcomes when σ varies over $\Sigma(V)$:

$C_V(\boldsymbol{u}) = \{\text{sop}(\sigma, \boldsymbol{u}) / \sigma \in \Sigma(V)\} = \{\text{sin}(\sigma, \boldsymbol{u}) / \sigma \in \Sigma(V)\}.$

Theorems 3 and 4 provide two different characterizations of the veto core $C_V(\boldsymbol{u})$. On the one hand it is the set of strong equilibrium outcomes of every game form g_σ (provided that $\sigma \in \Sigma(V)$): as is apparent from the proof of theorem 3 below, one can describe explicitly a strong equilibrium strategy n-tuple to "implement" any given element of $C_V(\boldsymbol{u})$. In addition problem 17 below and theorem 7, Chapter 7 shows that other game forms can be constructed to implement $C_V(u)$ by means of the strong equilibrium concept.

On the other hand, by theorem 4, the computation of $C_V(u)$ is made by an easy algorithm: choosing any $\sigma \in \Sigma(V)$ the corresponding algorithm (27) or equivalently (28) yields an outcome of $C_V(u)$. Moreover, when σ varies, the outcomes $\sin(\sigma, u)$ (as well as $\text{sop}(\sigma, u)$) cover the veto core $C_V(u)$.

Theorem 4 also raises a remarkable property of the voting by veto method: the non-cooperative outcome always is coalitionally stable as well. This is *not* to say that a sincere (resp. sophisticated) strategy n-tuple is immune against coalitional manipulation – which would indeed contradict the Gibbard–Satterthwaite theorem! More modestly we say that any *outcome* that results from the sincere (resp. sophisticated) strategy n-tuple also results from a strong equilibrium (in general different) strategy n-tuple. This *consistency* property was first introduced by Peleg (in a slightly different context, though). We shall say more about this in Chapter 7.

Proof of theorem 4. Throughout the proof, V and a profile u are fixed. From theorem 2 it is clear that

$$\{\text{sop}(\sigma, u)/\sigma \in \Sigma(V)\} = \{\sin(\bar{\sigma}, u)/\sigma \in \Sigma(V)\}$$
$$= \{\sin(\sigma, u)/\sigma \in \Sigma(V)\}.$$

We now fix $\sigma \in \Sigma(V)$ and prove that $a = \sin(\sigma, u)$ belongs to $C_V(u)$. The proof is essentially the same as step 1 of theorem 1, and in fact simpler: let $a_1, \ldots, a_{p-1}$ be the sequence constructed by (27), so that

$$a = A \setminus \{a_1, \ldots, a_{p-1}\}.$$

Suppose a does not belong to $C_V(u)$. Then for some coalition T we have

$$|\Pr(T, a, u)| \geq p - V(T).$$

For all $k \in \{1, \ldots, p-1\}$, such that $\sigma(k) \in T$, we have $u_{\sigma(k)}(a_k) < u_{\sigma(k)}(a)$, henceforth $a_k \notin \Pr(T, a, u)$. There are $\sum_{i \in T} V_i = V(T)$ for such a_k and they all differ from a. Therefore $\{a\}$, $\Pr(T, a, u)$ and $\{a_k/\sigma(k) \in T\}$ are all disjoint, whereas their cardinalities sum up above p. This is the desired contradiction.

To prove the converse argument, we observe that it is enough to prove the inclusion

$$C_{V^*}(u) \subset \{\sin(\sigma, u)/\sigma \in \Sigma(V^*)\} \qquad (34)$$

for those pairs A and N such that $n = p - 1$ and the particular egalitarian allocation of veto power $V_i^* = 1$, all $i \in N$.

That is to say, to any fixed A, N, V and $\boldsymbol{u}$ we associate A, N^* and $\boldsymbol{u}^*$ in the following way:

$$N^* = \{(i,t) / i \in N, 1 \leq t \leq V_i, t \text{ integer}\},$$

$$u^*_{(i,t)} = u_i, \quad \text{all } t, 1 \leq t \leq V_i.$$

Clearly, $C_V(\boldsymbol{u})$ equals the veto core of A, N^* and $\boldsymbol{u}^*$ associated with the veto function V^*. Moreover, to every one-to-one mapping σ^*: $\{1,\ldots,p-1\} \to N^*$ corresponds an element $\sigma \in \Sigma(V)$:

$$\sigma^*(k) = (\sigma(k), t(k)),$$

such that

$$\sin(\sigma^*, \boldsymbol{u}^*) = \sin(\sigma, \boldsymbol{u}).$$

Thus, it remains to prove (34) when $n = p - 1$ and $V_i^* = 1$, all i. In this case the definition of $C_{V^*}(\boldsymbol{u})$ can be written as follows:

$$a \in C_{V^*}(\boldsymbol{u}) \Leftrightarrow \forall T \subset N : |\Pr(T, a, \boldsymbol{u})| \leq p - |T| - 1. \tag{35}$$

Setting

$$X(T, a, \boldsymbol{u}) = \{b \in A / \exists i \in T : u_i(b) < u_i(a)\}$$

for all T, a and $\boldsymbol{u}$, we observe that $X(T, a, \boldsymbol{u})$, $\{a\}$, $\Pr(T, a, \boldsymbol{u})$ partition A so that (35) can be written as

$$a \in C_{V^*}(\boldsymbol{u}) \Leftrightarrow \forall T \subset N : |T| \leq X(T, a, \boldsymbol{u}). \tag{36}$$

At this point we need the following auxiliary result, which is a variant of the well-known marriage lemma.

Lemma 4. Let n be a positive integer, and X and N be two sets with cardinality n. For all $i \in N$, let X_i be a subset of X such that

$$\forall T \subset N : |T| \leq \left| \bigcup_{i \in T} X_i \right|. \tag{37}$$

Then there exists an $i_1 \in N$ such that

$$\forall T \subset N \setminus \{i_1\} : \left\{ \left| \bigcup_{i \in T} X_i \right| = |T| \right\} \Rightarrow \left\{ X_{i_1} \cap \left[\bigcup_{i \in T} X_i \right] = \emptyset \right\}. \tag{38}$$

The proof of lemma 4 is reviewed below.

Returning to the proof of inclusion (34) we choose an outcome $a \in C_{V^*}(\boldsymbol{u})$. Next we observe that $X_i = X(\{i\}, a, \boldsymbol{u})$ is a subset of $X = A \setminus \{a\}$ such that

$$\forall T \subset N : \bigcup_{i \in T} X_i = X(T, a, \boldsymbol{u}).$$

Therefore, by (36) lemma 4 implies that there exists $i_1 \in N$ such that (38) holds. By (37), X_{i_1} is non-empty. Let a_1 be the worst outcome of u_{i_1} among A. By definition of X_{i_1} we have $a_1 \in X_{i_1}$.

We claim that a belongs to the veto core $C[\hat{i}_1 \hat{a}_1]$ corresponding to outcome space $A \setminus \{a_1\}$, society $N \setminus \{i_1\}$, profile $u_{N \setminus \{i_1\}}$, and veto power 1 to every agent.

That is to say, suppose the claim fails to be true and let $T \subset N \setminus \{i_1\}$ be a coalition objecting against a within $A \setminus \{a_1\}$. Setting $B = \{b \in A \setminus \{a_1\} / \forall i \in T : u_i(a) < u_i(b)\}$ we have $|B| \geq (p-1) - |T|$.

Observe that $B \cup \{a\}$ and $X(T, a, \boldsymbol{u})$ are disjoint (in A) so that

$$|X(T, a, \boldsymbol{u})| \leq p - (|B| + 1) \leq |T|. \tag{39}$$

Comparing this inequality with (36) we get

$$|X(T, a, \boldsymbol{u})| = |T|. \tag{40}$$

Henceforth, by (38),

$$X_{i_1} \cap X(T, a, \boldsymbol{u}) = \emptyset.$$

Thus, $a_1 \notin X(T, a, \boldsymbol{u})$. Since $a_1 \neq a$, we deduce $a_1 \in \Pr(T, a, \boldsymbol{u})$. In view of the definition of B we get

$$\Pr(T, a, \boldsymbol{u}) = B \cup \{a_1\}.$$

From (39) and (40) we now have

$$|\Pr(T, a, \boldsymbol{u})| = |B| + 1 = p - |T|,$$

a contradiction of our assumption $a \in C_{V^*}(\boldsymbol{u})$.

The claim allows us to construct inductively the (one-to-one) mapping σ such that $a = \sin(\sigma, \boldsymbol{u})$. Namely, set $\sigma(1) = i_1$. By construction a_1 is the worst outcome of u_{i_1} on A. Since $a \in C[\hat{i}_1 \hat{a}_1]$ we can repeat the argument and select $i_2 \in N\setminus\{i_1\}$, a_2 the worst outcome of u_{i_2} among $A\setminus\{a_1\}$ in such a way that a belongs to the veto core $C[\widehat{i_1 i_2 a_1 a_2}]$ corresponding to outcome space $A\setminus\{a_1 a_2\}$, society $N\setminus\{i_1, i_2\}$, profile $u_{n\setminus\{i_1 i_2\}}$ and veto power 1 to every agent. Then we set $\sigma(2) = i_2$ and so on.

Sketch of the proof of lemma 4. For every coalition T we set $X(T) = \bigcup_{i \in T} X_i$ and

$$\mathcal{T} = \{T \subset N / |X(T)| = |T|\}.$$

For any two T_1 and $T_2 \in \mathcal{T}$ one deduces easily from (37) that only two cases may arise:

either $T_1 \cap T_2 \neq \emptyset$ and $T_1 \cap T_2 \in \mathcal{T}$,

or $T_1 \cap T_2 = \emptyset$ and $X(T_1) \cap X(T_2) = \emptyset$. (41)

Next, lemma 4 is proved by induction on n. For a given n, choose a $T \in \mathcal{T}$ minimal with respect to inclusion in $\mathcal{T}$. If $T = N$, then any $i_1 \in N$ satisfies (38) for there is no $T \subset N\setminus\{i_1\}$ such that $|X(T)| = |T|$. If $T \subsetneq N$ then, by the induction assumption, we may apply lemma 4 to $X(T)$, T and the subsets $(X_i)_{i \in T}$ of $X(T)$. We check finally that any i_1 satisfying (38) for $X(T)$ and T does so for X and N as well: this follows from inclusion minimality of T and property (41).

Proof of theorem 3. Throughout the proof, V and a profile u are fixed. Theorem 4 implies in particular non-emptyness of $C_V(u)$. Hence, we have only to prove equivalence (33).

Suppose first that x is a strong equilibrium of (g_σ, u) such that $a = \pi(x)$. Then a belongs to $C_V(u)$. For otherwise there exists a coalition T such that

$$|\Pr(T, a, u)| \geq p - V(T).$$

Therefore we can construct for all $i \in T$ a subset B_i of A with cardinality V_i such that all B_i are disjoint and, moreover,

$$A \setminus \left\{ \bigcup_{i \in T} B_i \right\} \subset \Pr(T, a, u).$$

Let y_i be a strategy where player i, whenever he has the move, eliminates an outcome of B_i as long as all outcomes in B_i are not eliminated. It is clear that $\pi(y_T, x_{T^c}) \notin \bigcup_{i \in T} B_i$, henceforth

$$\forall i \in T: u_i \circ \pi(y_T, x_{T^c}) > u_i(a) = u_i \circ \pi(x),$$

thus contradicting the strong equilibrium property of x.

Conversely, we select any outcome a in $C_V(u)$ and must construct a strong equilibrium strategy n-tuple x such that $\pi(x) = a$. By theorem 4 there exists $\sigma \in \Sigma(V)$ such that $a = \sin(\sigma, u)$. Let us denote by $a_1, \ldots, a_{p-1}$ the corresponding elimination sequence given by (27). Now let x_i be a strategy of player i, where i eliminates a_k at any step k such that $\sigma(k) = i$ unless a_k has previously been eliminated (notice that x_i need not be specified more precisely). Clearly, $\pi(x) = a$. It remains to check that x is a strong equilibrium. Take any coalition T and strategy T-tuple y_T. By definition of x_{T^c}, $b = \pi(y_T, x_{T^c})$ cannot be any of the a_k for which $\sigma(k) \in T^c$. Therefore b either is a or some a_k where $\sigma(k) \in T$. By (27) we have

$$u_{\sigma(k)}(a_k) < u_{\sigma(k)}(a), \quad \text{all } k;$$

henceforth b either is a or is less preferred than a by some $\sigma(k)$ of T. In both cases we conclude that condition (31) of definition 4 holds true. This concludes the proof of theorem 3.

Problem 17: The social choice correspondence C_V. Given A, N and some V such that (25) holds, we can speak of the s.c.c. C_V since $C_V(u)$ is non-empty for all u (theorem 3). Clearly, C_V is efficient and neutral.

(1) Prove (with the help of theorem 4) that C_V is inclusion minimal strongly monotonic (problem 7, Chapter 3).

(2) Consider any s.c. *function* S, a single-valued selection of C_V:

$$\forall u \in L(A)^N : S(u) \in C_V(u).$$

To S, associate the canonical game form g_S of which the message space is $L(A)$ and the decision rule is S. Prove that S implements C_V by means of the strong equilibrium notion:

$$\forall a \in A\{a \in C_V(u)\} \Leftrightarrow \{\text{a strong equilibrium } x \text{ of } (g_S, u)$$

$$\text{exists s.t. } a = \pi(x)\}.$$

(3) Prove that the proportional veto core $C_{n,p}$ is a strongly monotonic s.c.c. but is not in general inclusion minimal strongly monotonic.

6. General voting by veto

The remarkable strategic properties of voting by integer veto (the consistency of non-cooperative and cooperative behaviour) can be combined with the main ethical feature of proportional veto (no minority could possibly be crushed by the opposing majority: this goal being optimally achieved by a proportional allocation of veto power).

For that purpose we propose a more general class of voting methods where the outcomes are replicated and each agent is endowed with an integer veto power on the replica set. Thus, the distribution of veto power can be viewed as "fractional". Particular members of this class are voting by integer veto and the proportional veto voting methods (see problem 19 below).

We fix A and N with respective cardinalities p and n. Let μ_i, $i \in N$, and λ_a, $a \in A$, be some non-negative integers such that

$$1 + \sum_{i \in N} \mu_i = \sum_{a \in A} \lambda_a. \tag{42}$$

Now consider a set A_λ made up of λ_a replicas of outcome a, for all $a \in A$. Formally:

$$A_\lambda = \{(a, z)/a \in A, 1 \leq z \leq \lambda_a, z \text{ integer}\}.$$

Next, let us denote by $\Sigma(\mu)$ the set of all finite sequences of N such that i appears exactly μ_i times for all i. Formally:

$$\Sigma(\mu) = \{\sigma : \{1, \ldots, \bar{\mu}\} \to N / |\sigma^{-1}(i)| = \mu_i\},$$

where $\bar{\mu} = \sum_{i \in N} \mu_i$.

To every particular element $\sigma \in \Sigma(\mu)$ we associate the following game form, denoted $g_{\sigma, \lambda}$:

First, agent $\sigma(1)$ eliminates one outcome within A_λ, say (a_1, t_1).

Next, agent $\sigma(2)$ eliminates one outcome within $A_\lambda \setminus \{(a_1, t_1)\}$, say (a_2, t_2).

⋮

At step k agent $\sigma(k)$ eliminates one outcome within

$A_\lambda \setminus \{(a_1, t_1) \cdots (a_{k-1}, t_{k-1})\}$, say (a_k, t_k).

⋮

After step $\bar{\mu}$ there remains exactly one non-eliminated outcome within A_λ, say (a, t): then a is the finally elected outcome.

The additional property of $g_{\sigma,\lambda}$, as compared with the voting by integer veto g_σ (see (26)), is that we are now able to adjust at will the resistance of the various outcomes of A to elimination: for if $\lambda_a > \lambda_b$ it is strictly easier for any agent or coalition of agents to eliminate b rather than a. Game forms $g_{\sigma,\lambda}$ are not neutral in general.

General voting by veto shares all the strategic properties of voting by integer veto. We shall state now the analogous results to theorems 2, 3 and 4 and *leave their proofs as an exercise for the reader*.

To define first the non-cooperative elimination algorithm let us extend straightforwardly the utility functions of some profile $u \in L(A)^N$ to A_λ by setting

$$\tilde{u}_i(a,t) = u_i(a), \quad \text{all } i \in N, \quad \text{all } (a,t) \in A_\lambda.$$

Notice that the extended utility function $\tilde{u}_i$ *does* involve some indifference.

Given a particular profile u we denote by $\sin(\sigma,\lambda;u)$ the outcome resulting from the *sincere* behaviour of the agents, henceforth defined by the following algorithm:

(a_1, t_1) is one of the w.a. of $\tilde{u}_{\sigma(1)}$ among A_λ.

$\vdots$

(a_k, t_k) is one of the w.a. of $\tilde{u}_{\sigma(k)}$ among

$A_\lambda \setminus \{(a_1, t_1), \ldots, (a_{k-1}, t_{k-1})\}$.

$\vdots$

Set $(a,t) = A_\lambda \setminus \{(a_1, t_1), \ldots, (a_{\bar{\mu}}, t_{\bar{\mu}})\}$, then $a = \sin(\sigma, \lambda; u)$.

In the above algorithm the particular choice of one replica does not affect the final outcome, $\sin(\sigma, \lambda, u)$.

Theorem 2-bis. Given λ, μ and a particular $\sigma \in \Sigma(\mu)$, the sophisticated outcome $\text{sop}(\sigma, \lambda; u)$ of game form $g_{\sigma, \lambda}$ at profile u is given by

$$\text{sop}(\sigma, \lambda; u) = \sin(\bar{\sigma}, \lambda; u), \quad \text{all } u \in L(A)^N,$$

where $\bar{\sigma}$ is the symmetrical of σ:

$$\forall k = 1, \ldots, \bar{\mu}: \bar{\sigma}(k) = \sigma(\bar{\mu} - k + 1).$$

Going now to the cooperative behaviour, we observe that given (λ, μ) the possibility for coalition T to veto the subset B of outcomes is no longer determined by the cardinality of B alone: the veto power of $g_{\sigma,\lambda}$ is not neutral in general.

Actually, we have that T can veto B if and only if

$$\sum_{i \in T} \mu_i = \mu(T) \geq \lambda(B) = \sum_{a \in B} \lambda_a.$$

In the particular case where n and p are relatively prime, it is indeed possible to make λ_a independent of $a \in A$ and μ_i independent of $i \in N$; in which case we are back to the proportional veto function. See problem 19 below.

We define now the veto core associated to a pair λ, μ and denoted $C_{\lambda,\mu}$:

$$C_{\lambda,\mu}(u) = \{a \in A / \forall T \subset N : \lambda(\Pr(T, a, u)) + \mu(T) \leq \bar{\mu}\}. \tag{43}$$

Theorem 3-bis. Given λ, μ and a profile $u \in L(A)^N$, the set of strong equilibrium outcomes of the game $(g_{\sigma,\lambda}, u)$ is non-empty and does not depend on the particular choice of σ within $\Sigma(\mu)$. It coincides with the veto core $C_{\lambda,\mu}(u)$ defined by (43).

Theorem 4-bis. Given λ, μ and a profile $u \in L(A)^N$, the associated veto core equals the set of sophisticated equilibrium (resp. sincere) outcomes when σ varies over $\Sigma(\mu)$:

$$C_{\lambda,\mu}(u) = \{\text{sop}(\sigma, \lambda; u) / \sigma \in \Sigma(\mu)\} = \{\text{sin}(\sigma, \lambda; u) / \sigma \in \Sigma(\mu)\}.$$

Problem 19: Nearly anonymous voting by veto (Moulin, 1980a). We assume that n and p are relatively prime and we choose a pair r, c as in lemma 1, that is to say such that the proportional veto function is written as

$$\bar{v}(t) = \left\lfloor \frac{rt}{c} \right\rfloor, \quad \text{all } t = 1, \ldots, n.$$

Next we choose $\bar{\mu}$: $\bar{\mu}_i = r$, all $i \in N$, and $\bar{\lambda}$: $\bar{\lambda}_a = c$, all $a \in A$. Finally, for any given τ, a bijection of $\{1, \ldots, n\}$ into N, we denote by σ_τ the following element of $\Sigma(\bar{\mu})$:

$$\sigma_\tau: \underbrace{\tau(1), \tau(2), \ldots, \tau(n)}_{1}, \underbrace{\tau(1), \ldots, \tau(n)}_{2}, \ldots, \underbrace{\tau(1), \ldots, \tau(n)}_{r},$$

i.e.

$$\sigma_\tau(kn + s) = \tau(s), \quad \text{for all } k, 0 \leq k \leq r - 1 \text{ and all } s, 1 \leq s \leq n.$$

Notice that the veto power of $g_{\sigma_\tau,\bar{\lambda}}$ is the proportional veto function. The aim of this problem is to show that for some n, p, r and c the sophisticated s.c.f. $S_\tau = \text{sop}(\sigma_\tau, \bar{\lambda}, \cdot)$ does not depend on τ: in which case it is an efficient anonymous and neutral s.c.f.

(1) Choosing $n = 2$ and $p \geq 3$ prove that for all r, c the s.c.f. S_τ does depend on τ (see problem 17)

(2) We fix now a profile $u \in L(A)^N$ and we set $a^* = S_\tau(u)$. For all subsets C of A and every outcome a not belonging to C we denote by n_a^C the cardinality of the following subset of N:

$$\left\{ i \in N / u_i(a) = \min_{b \in A \setminus C} u_i(b) \right\}.$$

Prove the existence of an ordering $a_1, \ldots, a_p$ of A such that $a_p = a^*$ and

$$\exists t_1, \ldots, t_p \geq 0, \alpha_1, \ldots, \alpha_p \in \mathbf{R} \text{ such that } |\alpha_j| \leq n/c$$

and

$$1 = t_1 n_{a_1} + \alpha_1,$$
$$1 = t_1 n_{a_2} + t_2 n_{a_2}^{a_1} + \alpha_2,$$
$$\vdots$$
$$1 = t_1 n_{a_j} + t_2 n_{a_j}^{a_1} + \cdots + t_j n_{a_j}^{a_1 \cdots a_{j-1}} + \alpha_j,$$
$$\vdots$$
$$1 = t_1 n_{a_p} + t_2 n_{a_p}^{a_1} + \cdots + t_{p-1} n_{a_p}^{a_1 \cdots a_{p-2}} + t_p n + \alpha_p.$$

(3) Suppose now that n is a prime integer, strictly greater than p. Prove that for r, c large enough, the s.c.f. S_τ does *not* depend on τ.

Hint: Making $\alpha_1 = \alpha_2 = \cdots = \alpha_p = 0$ in the above system, prove that the sequence $t_1 = t_{j_1} = t_{j_2} = t_{j_2}, \ldots$ of the non-zero element in $\{t_1, \ldots, t_p\}$ does not depend on the particular ordering $a_1, \ldots, a_p$. Next use the assumption that n is prime and greater than p to show that t_p cannot be zero.

Questions (2) and (3) parallel question (c) of problem 5, Chapter 3.

References

Moulin, H., 1981a, "Prudence versus sophistication in voting strategy", Journal of Economic Theory, 24, 398–412.
Moulin, H., 1980, "Implementing efficient, anonymous and neutral social choice functions", Journal of Mathematical Economics 7, 249–269.
Moulin, H., 1981b, "The proportional veto principle", Review of Economic Studies 48, 407–416.
Moulin, H. and B. Peleg, 1982, "Core of effectivity functions and implementation theory", Journal of Mathematical Economics 10, 115–145.
Mueller, D., 1978, "Voting by veto", Journal of Public Economics 10, 57–75.
Nakamura, K., 1975, "The core of a simple game with ordinal preferences", International Journal of Game Theory 4, 95–104.
Rubinstein, A., 1979, "Equilibrium in supergames with the overtaking criterion", Journal of Economic Theory 21, 1–9.

CHAPTER 7

COOPERATIVE VOTING

1. Summary of the results

Chapter 6 emphasized the strategic properties of the voting by veto methods. There, some veto power (either integer or fractional) is allocated to agents in such a way that when every individual agent has exhausted his or her veto "token" only one candidate, namely the elected candidate, remains. The aim of this chapter is to show that the analysis of cooperative voting in *any* voting method has much to do with the underlying allocation of veto power to individuals and coalitions. This becomes clear via the concept of the "effectivity function", a binary relation that says for each coalition T and each subset of outcomes B whether or not T can force the final outcome within B (or, equivalently, T can veto $B^c = A \setminus B$).

In section 2 we study effectivity functions for their own sake. To every social choice function (resp. game form) we can associate three (resp. two) possibly different effectivity functions. This is illustrated using several familiar voting methods.

In section 3 we focus on *maximal* effectivity functions that allocate as much veto power as possible to the various coalitions. We show that sophisticated voting always results in a maximal underlying effectivity function and that, conversely, all maximal and superadditive effectivity functions can be reached by sophisticated s.c.f.

Since an effectivity function describes a particular allocation of power among agents and coalitions of agents, its main strategic feature is *cooperative stability*. That is to say, does it exist for all profiles of a non-empty core of the corresponding cooperative game? Section 4 is devoted to stable effectivity functions, of which the main examples are the *additive* effectivity functions derived from the general voting by veto methods.

In section 5 the principal results on cooperative voting are stated and proved: we almost characterize the social choice correspondences that can be implemented by strong equilibrium, i.e. that result from cooperative voting behaviour in some game form. It turns out that these s.c.c. are all contained in the core correspondence of the associated effectivity functions. Conversely this core correspondence is implementable by strong equilibrium (theorem 7). Another necessary condition for implementability by strong equilibrium is the strong monotonicity of the s.c.c. (theorem 9). This implies that no s.c. *function* is strongly implementable: henceforth some indeterminancy in the choice set must follow from cooperative voting.

Finally, section 6 attacks the question of implementation by Nash equilibrium. There strong monotonicity of the s.c.c. is a necessary and almost sufficient condition for S to be implementable. In particular an inclusion minimal strongly monotonic s.c.c. is implementable by Nash equilibrium (theorem 11). The actual game form used in the constructive proof of this result shows that the Nash equilibrium behaviour of the agents is quite cooperative in spirit.

Contrary to the strategy-proofness requirement, the condition that a voting rule yields for every profile a non-empty set of cooperatively stable outcomes does not amount to dictatorship of one agent: both anonymity and neutrality of the social choice correspondence are compatible with this property, as illustrated by the proportional veto core correspondence (Chapter 6, section 3). Contrary to non-cooperative behaviour (as formalized by sophisticated voting) it is not possible to achieve single-valuedness of the outcome when cooperative voting is in order.

Let us emphasize finally that the proof of the main results of this chapter (theorems 7 and 11) are constructive. Explicit game forms are given to implement respectively the core correspondence of any particular effectivity function (in the sense of strong equilibrium) or any inclusion minimal strongly monotonic s.c.c.

The basic reference in this chapter is Moulin and Peleg (1982).

2. Effectivity functions

Throughout Chapter 7 we assume that A and N are both finite. All game forms are supposed to be finite as well.

An effectivity function is a model of the distribution of power among agents and coalitions. Given A the set of outcomes, and N the society, we say that coalition $T \subset N$ is effective for the subset B of A if T can force the final decision within B or, equivalently, can veto the subset $B^c = A \setminus B$ of A.

Definition 1. Given A and N an effectivity function is a binary relation defined on coalitions and subsets of outcomes (it is then a subset of $2^N \times 2^A$) denoted "eff" and satisfying the following properties.

(i) Monotonicity with respect to coalitions:

$$\{T \text{eff } B \text{ and } T \subset T'\} \Rightarrow \{T' \text{eff } B\}, \quad \text{for all } T, T' \text{ and } B.$$

(ii) Monotonicity with respect to subsets of outcomes:

$$\{T \text{eff } B \text{ and } B \subset B'\} \Rightarrow \{T \text{eff } B'\}, \quad \text{for all } T, B \text{ and } B'.$$

(iii) Boundary conditions:

$T \text{eff } A$, for all *non-empty* T, and No $\{\varnothing \text{ eff } A\}$,

$N \text{eff } B$, for all *non-empty* B, and No $\{N \text{eff } \varnothing\}$.

The above conditions imply in particular:

$$\{T \text{eff } B\} \Rightarrow \{T \neq \varnothing \text{ and } B \neq \varnothing\}.$$

Definition 2. An effectivity function eff is said to be superadditive if the following condition holds:

$$\{T_i \text{eff } B_i, i = 1, 2 \text{ and } T_1 \cap T_2 \neq \varnothing\} \Rightarrow \{T_1 \cup T_2 \text{eff } B_1 \cap B_2\},$$

for all $T_i, B_i,$ $i = 1, 2.$

Superadditivity means that merging coalitions do not loose power: "l'union fait la force". It implies the following:

$$T \text{eff } B \Rightarrow \text{No } \{T^c \text{eff } B^c\}.$$

Most effectivity functions deriving from social choice correspondences and game forms are superadditive, as will be seen below.

Example 1: Effectivity functions generalize simple games. A simple game on society N is given by a monotonic subset W of coalitions, called the winning coalitions:

$$W \subset 2^N, \varnothing \notin W, \{T \in W \text{ and } T \subset T'\} \Rightarrow \{T' \in W\}.$$

It will be identified with the following effectivity function:

$$T \text{ eff } B, \quad \text{iff} \begin{cases} T \in W \text{ and } B \neq \emptyset, \\ \text{or} \\ \emptyset \neq T \notin W \text{ and } B = A. \end{cases}$$

As we noticed in Chapter 6, section 2, simple games embody a very sharp distribution of power: a coalition either has full power (is winning) or zero power. Effectivity functions on the other hand allow us to smooth the distribution of coalitional power. Notice that a simple game, viewed as an effectivity function, is superadditive if and only if it is *proper*, namely

$$T \in W \Rightarrow T^c \notin W.$$

Example 2: Unanimity with status quo. Let $a_0 \in A$ be a fixed status quo outcome. The following effectivity function,

$$T \text{ eff } B, \quad \text{iff} \begin{cases} T \neq \emptyset \text{ and } a_0 \in B \neq \emptyset, \\ \text{or} \\ T = N \text{ and } B \neq \emptyset, \end{cases}$$

means that only unanimous agents can force an outcome different from a_0, whereas every single agent can force a_0 to be the final outcome. It is a superadditive effectivity function.

Example 3: Veto functions. An effectivity function is *neutral* if it does not discriminate among outcomes. Simple games (example 1) are neutral, whereas unanimity with status quo (example 2) is not. Formally, the effectivity function eff is neutral if

$$\{T \text{ eff } B, |B| = |B'|\} \Rightarrow \{T \text{ eff } B'\}.$$

This amounts to saying that eff is represented by an integer valued mapping $T \rightarrow e(T)$ in the following way:

$$T \text{ eff } B, \quad \text{iff} |B| \geq e(T),$$

where $e(T) \in \{1,\ldots,p\}$ for all $T \subset N$, $T \neq \emptyset$.

Assumption (i) implies that e is non-increasing with respect to inclusion.

Setting $v(T) = p - e(T)$ we obtain a *veto function*, i.e. a non-decreasing mapping from $2^N - \emptyset$ into $\langle 0,\ldots,p-1 \rangle$.

Conversely, to any non-decreasing mapping v from $2^N - \emptyset$ into $(0,\ldots, p-1\}$ we can associate the effectivity function

$$T \text{ eff } B, \quad \text{iff } v(T) \geq |B^c| = p - |B|. \tag{1}$$

The above effectivity function is superadditive if and only if v is superadditive in the usual sense, namely

$$T_1 \cap T_2 = \emptyset \Rightarrow v(T_1) + v(T_2) \leq v(T_1 \cup T_2).$$

(The proof of this claim is left as an exercise for the reader.)

When the additional requirement of anonymity is made, then $v(T)$ depends on $|T|$ only and we are back to definition 1, Chapter 6, except that the superadditivity property is now replaced by

$v: \{1,\ldots,n\} \to \{0,\ldots,p-1\}$ is non-decreasing.

To every effectivity function we can associate a simple game, made up of its winning coalitions:

$$T \text{ is winning for eff} \overset{\text{def}}{\Leftrightarrow} T \text{ eff } B, \quad \text{all } B \neq \emptyset. \tag{2}$$

Of course, the simple game associated with a given effectivity function carries much less information about the distribution of power among coalitions.

We shall say that a s.c.c. S satisfies *strong citizen sovereignty* if the following holds:

$$\forall a \in A, \exists u \in L(A)^N: S(u) = \{a\}. \tag{3}$$

This is a slight strengthening of the citizen-sovereignty condition introduced in Chapter 3 (relation (8)).

To any social choice correspondence (resp. game form) one can associate two possibly different effectivity functions.

Definition 3. Let A and N be given. Let S be a s.c.c. satisfying strong citizen sovereignty. Let $g = (X_i, i \in N, \pi)$ be a g.f. satisfying citizen sovereignty as well (Chapter 4, section 4). We denote by $\alpha\text{-eff}_S$ and $\alpha\text{-eff}_g$

the following effectivity functions. For all non-empty T and B:

$T\alpha\text{-eff}_S B \quad \text{iff } \exists u_T \in L(A)^T \; \forall u_{T^c} \in L(A)^{T^c} : S(u_T, u_{T^c}) \subset B,$

$T\alpha\text{-eff}_g B \quad \text{iff } \exists x_T \in X_T \; \forall x_{T^c} \in X_{T^c} : \pi(x_T, x_{T^c}) \in B.$

Similarly, we denote by $\beta\text{-eff}_S$ and $\beta\text{-eff}_g$ the following effectivity functions. For all non-empty T and B:

$T\beta\text{-eff}_S B \quad \text{iff } \forall u_{T^c} \in L(A)^{T^c} \; \exists u_T \in L(A)^T : S(u_T, u_{T^c}) \subset B,$

$T\beta\text{-eff}_g B \quad \text{iff } \forall x_{T^c} \in X_{T^c} \; \exists x_T \in X_T : \pi(x_T, x_{T^c}) \in B.$

We leave as an exercise for the reader to check that we have indeed defined four effectivity functions. The α-effectivity functions are always superadditive. As will be clear from the examples below, the β-effectivity functions are not necessarily superadditive (see problems 1 and 2).

The following implications always hold:

$T\alpha\text{-eff}_S B \Rightarrow T\beta\text{-eff}_S B,$

$T\alpha\text{-eff}_g B \Rightarrow T\beta\text{-eff}_g B.$
(4)

In order to be α-effective for B, coalition T must have a message that guarantees that the final outcome belongs to B no matter what is the message sent by the complement coalition. To be β-effective for B, coalition T needs only to possess a *reply* to any message sent by T^c that eventually forces the outcome within B.

The examples given below prove that the converse implications in (4) do not hold.

Definition 4. Given A and N, a s.c.c. S and a g.f. g, we say that S (resp. g) is *tight* if $\alpha\text{-eff}_S$ and $\beta\text{-eff}_S$ coincide (resp. $\alpha\text{-eff}_g = \beta\text{-eff}_g$).

We illustrate definitions 3 and 4 using the three main families of voting methods.

Example 4: Condorcet-type s.c.c. Recall that a s.c.c. is Condorcet-type if it coincides with the set of Condorcet winners whenever the later is non-empty. Suppose $n = |N|$ is odd. Then any Condorcet-type s.c.c. is *tight*, the associated effectivity function being simply the simple majority game

(N, W):

$$T \in W \Leftrightarrow |T| > n/2.$$

To check this, observe that any strict majority T enforces the election of any outcome b by sending a message u_T such that b is the top outcome of u_i, $i \in T$. Then b is the unique Condorcet winner of profile (u_T, u_{T^c}), all $u_{T^c} \in L(A)^{T^c}$.

Example 5: Borda scoring correspondence. The Borda scoring correspondence B, or any single valued selection of it, is not tight. To prove this we look first at its associated β-effectivity function. We claim that every strict majority T is winning for β-eff:

$$|T| > \frac{n}{2} \Rightarrow \{T \text{ is winning for } \beta\text{-eff}_B\}. \tag{5}$$

It is enough to prove that for any strict majority coalition T and any outcome a we have

$$\forall u_{T^c} \in L(A)^{T^c}, \exists u_T \in L(A)^T : B(u_T, u_{T^c}) = \{a\}.$$

Fix any u_{T^c}. Since $|T| \geqslant |T^c| + 1$ we can set $T = T_1 \cup T_2$, where σ is a one-to-one mapping from T_1 into T^c and T_2 is non-empty. Then we take u_T such that:

$$\begin{cases} \forall i \in T_1: & u_i = \bar{u}_{\sigma(i)} \\ & (\text{where } \bar{u} \text{ is the reverse ordering of } u), \\ \forall i \in T_2: & a = \text{top outcome of } u_1. \end{cases}$$

All outcomes in A get the same Borda score with respect to (u_{T_1}, u_{T^c}), therefore

$$B(u_{T_1}, u_{T_2}, u_{T^c}) = \{a\}.$$

Let us describe now the winning coalitions of the α-effectivity function associated with B. We will prove the following:

$$\{T \text{ is winning for } \alpha\text{-eff}_B\} \Rightarrow |T| > \frac{2p-2}{3p-2} \cdot n, \tag{6}$$

where $n = |N|$ and $p = |A|$. The above implication compared with (5) makes it clear that α-eff$_B$ and β-eff$_B$ differ. Let us prove (6).

Suppose T is a winning coalition for α-eff$_B$. Fix an outcome $a \in A$ and a profile u_T for coalition T. Denoting by $\sigma(b, u_T)$ the Borda score of outcome b at profile u_T (remember that the top outcome gets $(p-1)$ and the bottom outcome gets 0) we have

$$\sum_{b \in A \setminus \{a\}} \sigma(b, u_T) \geq |T| \frac{(p-1)(p-2)}{2};$$

henceforth, for at least one outcome b in $A \setminus \{a\}$:

$$\sigma(b, u_T) \geq |T| \left(\frac{p-2}{2} \right).$$

Consider now a profile u_{T^c} of coalition T^c such that

$\begin{Bmatrix} a \\ b \end{Bmatrix}$ is the $\begin{Bmatrix} \text{bottom} \\ \text{top} \end{Bmatrix}$ outcome of u_i, all $i \in T$.

Then we easily compute

$$\sigma(a, u_T, u_{T^c}) \leq |T|(p-1),$$

$$|T| \cdot \left(\frac{p-2}{2} \right) + (n-|T|)(p-1) \leq \sigma(b, u_T, u_{T^c}).$$
(7)

Since T is winning, there exists u_T such that for all u_{T^c}, $B(u_T, u_{T^c}) = \{a\}$. This implies in particular that

$$\sigma(b, u_T, u_{T^c}) < \sigma(a, u_T, u_{T^c}).$$

Taking (7) into account we conclude that T satisfies the right-hand inequality in (6).

For the sake of completeness we now prove a converse property of (6) that will be useful:

$$|T| > \frac{2n+1}{3} \Rightarrow \{T \text{ is winning for } \alpha\text{-eff}_B\}. \tag{8}$$

To prove (8) we pick a coalition T such that $|T| > (2n+1)/3$ and an outcome a. Next we construct a profile u_T such that

a is the top outcome of u_i, all $i \in T$,

$$\sigma(b, u_T) \leq \frac{t+1}{2}(p-1), \quad \text{all } b \neq a. \tag{9}$$

If $t = 2t'$ is even, this is done by matching pairwise the agents in such a way that the orderings of $A \setminus \{a\}$ are opposite to each other. If $t = 2t' + 1$, the last agent gets an arbitrary preference (as long as a is its top outcome).

Now (9) and the assumption $|T| > (2n+1)/3$ together imply, for all u_{T^c} and all $b \neq a$:

$$\sigma(b, u_T, u_{T^c}) \leq \frac{t+1}{2}(p-1) + (n-t)(p-1) < t(p-1)$$

$$\leq \sigma(a, u_T, u_{T^c}).$$

A more detailed analysis of the effectivity functions associated with the Borda scoring correspondence is developed in problem 1 below. It is shown in particular that β-eff$_B$ is not superadditive.

Our final example analyses the effectivity functions derived from the voting by veto methods studied in Chapter 6.

Definition 5. Given A and N and two probability distributions ℓ and m on A and N, respectively:

$$\ell = (\ell_a)_{a \in A}, \quad \ell_a > 0; \quad \sum_{a \in A} \ell_a = 1,$$

$$m = (m_i)_{i \in N}, \quad m_i > 0; \quad \sum_{i \in N} m_i = 1,$$

we denote by eff$_{\ell, m}$ the following effectivity function:

$$T \text{eff}_{\ell, m} B, \quad \text{iff } m(T) + \ell(B) > 1. \tag{10}$$

We say that an effectivity function is *additive* if it coincides with eff$_{\ell, m}$ for some probability distributions ℓ and m.

Since all ℓ_a and m_i are non-zero, eff$_{\ell, m}$ satisfies all the axioms of effectivity functions. Notice that additive effectivity functions are superadditive as well.

We show now that additive effectivity functions are exactly those derived from the general voting by veto game forms introduced in Chapter 6, section 6. In the sequel we denote by λ and μ, respectively, two integer-valued functions on A and N such that

$$\lambda = (\lambda_a), \quad \lambda_a \text{ positive integer,}$$

$$\mu = (\mu_i), \quad \mu_i \text{ non-negative integer,} \tag{11}$$

$$1 + \sum_{i \in N} \mu_i = \sum_{a \in A} \lambda_a.$$

Now every game form $g_{\sigma,\lambda}$ (where $\sigma \in \Sigma(\mu)$, notations as in Chapter 6, section 6) satisfies strong citizen sovereignty since all λ_a are positive. Moreover, $g_{\sigma,\lambda}$ is tight and its associated effectivity function is as follows. For every non-empty coalition T:

$$T \text{eff}_{\lambda,\mu} B, \quad \text{iff } \mu(T) + \lambda(B) \geq \lambda(A), \tag{12}$$

where $\lambda(B)$ stands for $\sum_{a \in B} \lambda_a$ and $\mu(T)$ for $\sum_{i \in T} \mu_i$.
This follows easily from the definition of $g_{\sigma,\lambda}$.

Lemma 1. Every effectivity function associated to a voting by veto method where λ_a is positive for all a is an additive effectivity function.

Proof. We choose a pair λ and μ such that (11) holds and assume first that μ_i is non-zero for all i. Next we define two probability measures, ℓ and m, by

$$\ell_a = \frac{\lambda_a}{\lambda(A)}; \quad m_i = \frac{\mu_i}{\mu(N)}. \tag{13}$$

We claim that for all non-empty T and B:

$$\mu(T) + \lambda(B) \geq \lambda(A) \Leftrightarrow m(T) + \lambda(B) > 1. \tag{14}$$

The $\Rightarrow$ implication is clear, since

$$m(T) + \ell(B) > \frac{\mu(T)}{\lambda(A)} + \frac{\lambda(B)}{\lambda(A)} \geq 1.$$

Strict inequality follows from our assumption that μ_i is non-zero for all i. To prove the $\Leftarrow$ implication, suppose that T and B are given such that

$$\mu(T) + \lambda(B) < \lambda(A).$$

Since μ and λ are integer valued, this yields

$$\mu(T) \leqslant \lambda(B^c) - 1;$$

henceforth

$$\lambda(A)\mu(T) \leqslant \lambda(A)\lambda(B^c) - \lambda(A) = \mu(A)\lambda(B^c) + \lambda(B^c) - \lambda(A)$$

$$\leqslant \mu(A)\lambda(B^c)$$

and therefore

$$m(T) = \frac{\mu(T)}{\mu(A)} \leqslant \frac{\lambda(B^c)}{\lambda(A)} = \ell(B^c),$$

which is the desired conclusion.

It remains to prove the lemma when some of the μ_i are zero. More precisely we set

$$T_0 = \{i \in N / \mu_i > 0\}.$$

The above argument shows that the probability distributions ℓ and m defined by (13) satisfy, for all non-empty T and B,

$$T \subset T_0 \Rightarrow \{\mu(T) + \lambda(B) \geqslant \lambda(A) \Leftrightarrow m(T) + l(B) > 1\}.$$

Observe that when T and B are non-empty and T is a subset of T_0, the equality

$$m(T) + \ell(B) = 1$$

is impossible. Namely, it would imply

$$\frac{\mu(T)}{\mu(A)} = \frac{\lambda(B^c)}{\mu(A) + 1} \Rightarrow \mu(T) = \mu(A)[\lambda(B^c) - \mu(T)].$$

Since $1 \leq \mu(T) \leq \mu(A)$ this implies $\mu(T) = \mu(A)$ and $\lambda(B^c) = \mu(A)+1 = \lambda(A)$; henceforth $B^c = A$, a contradiction

Thus, if the probability distribution m' is close enough to m, we will have

$$m(T) + \ell(B) > 1 \Leftrightarrow m'(T) + \ell(B) > 1, \quad \text{all non-empty } T \text{ and } B.$$

In particular we can choose m' such that $m'_i > 0$ for all i, which completes the proof of lemma 1.

The converse property of lemma 1 is not true: see lemma 4 below.

As an exercise the reader can check that the social choice functions sop$(\sigma, \lambda; \cdot)$ and sin$(\sigma, \lambda; \cdot)$ are tight and their associated effectivity function is eff$_{\lambda, \mu}$ (of course one has to assume that all λ_a are non-zero so that these s.c.f.s satisfy citizen sovereignty).

As a conclusion to section 2 we prove that every superadditive effectivity function is the α-effectivity function of some game form satisfying citizen sovereignty. The proof is constructive and exhibits a "universal" game form that will be useful in the sequel.

Lemma 2. Let eff be a superadditive effectivity function on A and N. Let T_k and B_k, $k+1,\ldots,K$, be respectively a finite sequence of coalitions and a finite sequence of subsets of A such that

$$\begin{cases} T_k \cap T_{k'} = \varnothing, & \text{all } k, k': \text{coalitions } T_k \text{ are pairwise disjoint}, \\ T_k \text{eff } B_k, & \text{all } k. \end{cases}$$

Then coalition $T = \cup_{k=1}^{K} T_k$ is effective for $B = \cap_{k=1}^{K} B_k$. In particular, B is non-empty.

Proof. Straightforward.

Theorem 1. Given an effectivity function eff on A and N, the two following statements are equivalent:
  (i) eff is superadditive, and
  (ii) there exists a game form g such that α-eff$_g$ = eff.

Proof. The (ii) $\Rightarrow$ (i) being clear, we prove only (i) $\Rightarrow$ (ii).

For every agent i we denote $\mathcal{T}_i$ the set of coalitions T to which i belongs.

From now on a superadditive effectivity function eff is given. For any $i \in N$, we denote by X_i the set of mappings x_i that associate to every coalition T in $\mathcal{T}_i$ a subset $x_i(T)$ for which T is effective:

$$x_i \in X_i: \mathcal{T}_i \ni T \to x_i(T): T \text{ eff } x_i(T). \tag{15}$$

Given a strategy n-tuple $x \in \prod_{i \in N} X_i = X_N$ and a coalition $T \subset N$ we denote by $\mathcal{P}(x, T)$ the coarsest partition $\{T_1, \ldots, T_K\}$ of T such that

$$\forall k = 1, \ldots, K, \forall i, j \in T_k: x_i(T) = x_j(T).$$

Next we associate to x the following sequence of increasingly fine partitions of N:

$$\mathcal{P}_0 = \{N\},$$
$$\mathcal{P}_1 = \mathcal{P}(x, N) = \{T_1^1, \ldots, T_{K_1}^1\},$$
$$\mathcal{P}_2 = \{P(x, T_1^1), P(x, T_2^1), \ldots, \mathcal{P}(x, T_{K_1}^1)\} = \{T_1^2, \ldots, T_{K_2}^2\},$$
$$\vdots$$
$$\mathcal{P}_t = \{\mathcal{P}(x, T_1^{t-1}), \ldots, \mathcal{P}(x, T_{K_{t-1}}^{t-1})\} = \{T_1^t, \ldots, T_{K_t}^t\},$$
$$\mathcal{P}_{t+1} = \{P(x, T_1^t), \ldots, \mathcal{P}(x, T_{K_t}^t)\} = \{T_1^{t+1}, \ldots, T_{K_{t+1}}^{t+1}\},$$
$$\vdots$$

Since N is finite this sequence is constant after finitely many steps. Its limit is denoted

$$\mathcal{P}_\infty(x) = \{T_1, \ldots, T_K\}.$$

By construction $x_i(T_k)$ does not depend on $i \in T_k$ so that it can be denoted as $x(T_k)$. Finally, we denote

$$G(x) = \bigcap_{T \in \mathcal{P}_\infty(x)} x(T) = \bigcap_{k=1}^{K} x(T_k).$$

By construction of $\mathcal{P}_\infty(x)$, coalition T_k is effective for $x(T_k)$. Hence, by lemma 2, $G(x)$ is non-empty for all $x \in X_N$.

A universal game form associated with the effectivity function eff is any $g = (X_i, i \in N, \pi)$, where π is a single-valued selection of G:

$$\pi(x) \in G(x), \quad \text{all } x \in X_i. \tag{16}$$

The interpretation of g is that every agent proposes a feasible "veto" for every conceivable coalition to which he or she belongs. Next, agents are partitioned into coalitions where the same veto has been unanimously proposed, and the various vetos of these coalitions are taken into account.

The following implication holds true. For all non-empty T and B,

$$T \text{ eff } B \Rightarrow T\alpha\text{-eff}_g B. \tag{17}$$

Namely, for all $i \in T$, denote by $x_i \in X_i$ a strategy such that

$$\forall T': T \subset T' \Rightarrow x_i(T') = B.$$

(By monotonicity of eff, T' is indeed effective for B.)

We claim that for all $y \in X_N$:

$$\{\forall i \in T: y_i = x_i\} \Rightarrow \pi(y) \in B.$$

Namely, in all partitions $\mathcal{P}_0, \ldots, \mathcal{P}_t, \ldots$, associated with y, the agents of T never split:

$$\forall t = 1, 2, \ldots, \exists k = 1, \ldots, K_t: T \subset T_k^t$$

(this claim is clear by induction). Hence, there is an element T_k of $\mathcal{P}_\infty(x)$ that contains T. Thus we have

$$\pi(x) \in G(x) \subset x(T_k) = x(T) = B.$$

From our definition of g, which does not specify the single-valued selection π of G, the converse implication in (17) need not necessarily be true. In order to prove theorem 1 we must therefore choose π in such a way that no coalition gains any additional power from π. This can be done in several ways. Since this final specification is useless in the sequel, we simply propose one to the careful reader.

Exercise

Denote $A = \{a_0, \ldots, a_{p-1}\}$ and endow A with the addition modulo p (hence identifying A with the additive group Z/pZ).

For every subset B of A choose a mapping σ_B from A onto B. For any strategy $x_i \in X_i$, denote by $s(x_i)$ the highest ranked outcome of $x_i(N)$ according to the above ordering of A.

Now we define our particular selection π of the correspondence G in the following way:

$$\pi(x) = \sigma_{G(x)}\left[\sum_{i \in N} s(x_i)\right].$$

Prove that for the corresponding game form g, implication (17) actually is an equivalence.

Problem 19: The veto function of the Borda scoring correspondence (Moulin, 1982). The Borda scoring correspondence B (see example 1, Chapter 2) is neutral and anonymous. Hence its α- and β-effectivity functions are described by two veto functions, v_α and v_β (see example 3 above).

(1) Show that v_α is determined, with an error of at most one, by the following formulas:

$$v_\alpha(t) = 0, \qquad \text{if } t < \frac{n}{2},$$

$$2\left[\left(2 - \frac{n}{t}\right) \cdot (p-1) - \frac{1}{t}\right] \leq v_\alpha(t)$$

$$\leq \left[2\left(2 - \frac{n}{t}\right) \cdot (p-1)\right] + 1, \quad \text{if } \frac{n}{2} \leq t \leq \frac{2n}{3},$$

$$v_\alpha(t) = p - 1, \qquad \text{if } \frac{2n}{3} < t.$$

In particular, for large n and p we have the following approximation:

$$v(t) \simeq 2\left(2 - \frac{n}{t}\right) \cdot (p-1), \quad \text{if } \frac{n}{2} \leq t \leq \frac{2n}{3}.$$

Which coalitions are endowed by B with a veto power nearly proportional to their size?

(2) Give a similar approximation of v_β and prove it is not superadditive.

Problem 20: The *-effectivity function of a s.c.c. Given A and N and a social choice correspondence S we consider the following binary relation on all non-empty T and B:

$T *\text{-eff}_S B$, iff $\forall u \in L(A)^N$:

$\{\forall i \in T, \forall b \in B, \forall a \in B^c : u_i(a) < u_i(b)\} \Rightarrow \{S(u) \subset B\}$.

(1) Prove that *-eff$_S$ is *not* in general an effectivity function: choose for S the Kramer s.c.c. (Chapter 2, section 5).

(2) Prove that when S is the Copeland s.c.c. the Condorcet cycle, or Miller's uncovered set (Chapter 2, section 5), then *-eff$_S$ is an effectivity function and coincide with α-eff$_S$, i.e. the simple majority game.

(3) Given an integer valued vector (λ, μ) such that (11) holds, prove that every associated s.c.f. $S = \text{sop}(\sigma, \lambda, \cdot)$ is such that

$$\text{*-eff}_S = \text{eff}_{\lambda, \mu}.$$

(4) Prove that when B is the Borda scoring correspondence, *-eff$_S$ is an anonymous and neutral effectivity function.

Prove that T is a *-winning coalition if and only if

$$|T| > \left(\frac{p-1}{p}\right) n.$$

Give an approximation of the veto function v_* similar to that proposed in problem 1.

Problem 21: Social choice functions with zero veto power. The s.c. correspondence

$$S(u) = a, \quad \text{if } a = \text{top outcome of } u_i, \text{ for all } i \in N,$$

$$= A, \quad \text{otherwise,}$$

gives no veto power to any coalition, except the grand coalition N. It is a tight s.c.c. with associated (α- and β-) effectivity function:

$$T \text{ eff } B, \quad \text{iff} \begin{cases} B = A, \\ \text{or} \\ B \subsetneq A \text{ and } T = N. \end{cases} \quad (18)$$

The aim of the problem is to seek social choice *functions* with the same associated α-effectivity functions.

(1) Fix an ordering $A = \{a_0, \ldots, a_{p-1}\}$ of the outcomes and endow A with the addition modulo p (hence identifying A with the additive group Z/pZ). Then consider the following anonymous s.c.f. where $t(u)$ stands for top outcome of u:

$$S(u) = \sum_{i \in N} t(u_i),$$

Prove that its associated α-effectivity function is given by (18). What is its associated β-effectivity function?

(2) Assume that preference orderings $u \in L(A)$ are represented by fixed-scale utility functions:

$$u: A \to \{0, \ldots, p-1\}, \qquad u \text{ is one-to-one.}$$

Compute the α-effectivity function of the following neutral s.c.f. and prove that it coincides with (18) for some cardinalities of n and p:

$$S(u) = u_1^{-1}\left(\sum_{i \in N \setminus \{1\}} u_1(t(u_i))\right)$$

(again the addition is taken modulo p, in Z/pZ).

(3) When n has no prime factor less than or equal to p, the existence of an anonymous, neutral and efficient s.c.f. with associated α-effectivity function (18) is an open problem.

3. Maximal effectivity functions

For any game form g, the definition of α- and β-effectivity functions are related by

$$T\alpha\text{-eff}_g B \Leftrightarrow \text{No}\{T^c \beta\text{-eff}_g B^c\}. \tag{19}$$

This property follows immediately from the definition of α-eff$_g$ and β-eff$_g$. Notice that it holds true as well for the α- and β-effectivity functions associated with s.c. *functions* (since they can be viewed as game forms) but not with s.c. *correspondences*. This is clear from definition 3 or from the following trivial s.c.c.:

$$S(u) = A, \quad \text{all } u \in L(A)^N.$$

From (19) we get that the effectivity function associated with a tight game form satisfies the following maximality property.

Definition 6. An effectivity function eff on A and N is said to be *maximal* if it is such that

$$T \text{eff } B \Leftrightarrow \text{No}\{T^c \text{eff } B^c\}, \quad \text{all non-empty } T \text{ and } B. \tag{20}$$

Notice that the boundary assumptions – condition (iii) of definition 1 – yield No{N eff $\emptyset$} and No{$\emptyset$ eff A}, justifying the requirement that *both* T and B are non-empty in (20).

Lemma 3. Given a game form g on A and N, the three following statements are equivalent:
  (i) g is tight: α-eff$_g = \beta$-eff$_g$;
  (ii) α-eff$_g$ is maximal; and
  (iii) β-eff$_g$ is maximal.
As a corollary to theorem 1 we get:

Corollary of theorem 1. Given an effectivity function eff on A and N, the two following statements are equivalent:
  (i) eff is superadditive and maximal, and
  (ii) there exists a tight game form g such that α-eff$_g = \beta$-eff$_g =$ eff.

Proof. The (ii) $\Rightarrow$ (i) statement follows from lemma 3.

To prove (i) $\Rightarrow$ (ii) fix a superadditive and maximal effectivity function eff and consider an associated "universal" game form g as defined in the proof of theorem 1. Then implication (17) holds. Since eff is maximal, the converse implication holds as well. Namely, we have

$$\text{No}\{T \text{ eff } B\} \Rightarrow T^c \text{eff } B^c \Rightarrow T^c \alpha\text{-eff}_g B^c \Rightarrow \text{No}\{T \alpha\text{-eff}_g B\},$$

where the right-hand implication follows from the superadditivity of α-eff$_g$.

Therefore we do not need to specify our decision rule π more than (16) to guarantee that g represents the effectivity function eff.

A simple game (example 1) is a maximal effectivity function iff it is strong:

$$T \in W \Leftrightarrow T^c \notin W, \quad \text{all } T.$$

A veto function (example 3) is maximal iff it satisfies

$$v(T) + v(T^c) = p - 1, \quad \text{all } T.$$

This follows easily from (1).

Our next result characterizes those additive effectivity functions which are maximal. They all derive from the general voting by veto methods:

Lemma 4. An additive effectivity function is maximal if and only if it takes the form $\text{eff}_{\lambda,\mu}$ for some integer valued vectors (λ, μ) satisfying (11).

Proof. The effectivity function $\text{eff}_{\lambda,\mu}$ given by (12) is maximal. Namely, by (11) we have

$$\mu(T) + \lambda(B) \geq \lambda(A) \Leftrightarrow \mu(T^c) + \lambda(B^c) \leq \mu(N) = \lambda(A) - 1$$

$$\Leftrightarrow \mu(T^c) + \lambda(B^c) < \lambda(A)$$

$$\Leftrightarrow \text{No}\{\mu(T^c) + \lambda(B^c) \geq \lambda(A)\}.$$

Conversely, choose an additive effectivity function $\text{eff}_{m,\ell}$ (definition 5) and suppose that it is maximal:

$$m(T) + \ell(B) > 1 \Leftrightarrow m(T^c) + \ell(B^c) \leq 1, \quad \text{all non-empty } T \text{ and } B.$$

Since m and ℓ are probability distributions, this gives

$$m(T) + \ell(B) > 1 \Leftrightarrow m(T) + \ell(B) \geq 1. \tag{21}$$

Thus, $\text{eff}_{\ell,m}$ is maximal if and only if

$$m(T) + \ell(B) = 1, \quad \text{is impossible for non-empty } T \text{ and } B.$$

Setting

$$\varepsilon = \inf_{T \neq \emptyset, B \neq \emptyset} |m(T) + \ell(B) - 1|,$$

we can find integer valued vectors λ and μ such that (11) holds and, moreover,

$$\left| m(T) - \frac{\mu(T)}{\lambda(A)} \right| < \frac{\varepsilon}{2}, \quad \text{all non-empty } T,$$

$$\left| \ell(B) - \frac{\lambda(B)}{\lambda(A)} \right| < \frac{\varepsilon}{2}, \quad \text{all non-empty } B.$$

By the very definition of ε this implies

$$m(T)+\ell(B)>1 \Leftrightarrow \mu(T)+\lambda(B) \geq \lambda(A).$$

This is the desired conclusion.

The maximality property of an effectivity function implies an analogous property to the coalitional easiness of a s.c.f. Using the notation of definition 2, Chapter 5, we consider a profile $([u]_T,[\bar{u}]_{T^c})$, where society splits into two homogeneous antagonistic coalitions, T and T^c, with respective preference orderings u and $\bar{u}$. Let us assume that u is given by $u(a_1) < u(a_2) < \cdots < u(a_p)$ and let eff be a maximal effectivity function. Then for every $k, 1 \leq k \leq p$, either T is effective for $\{a_k, a_{k+1}, \ldots, a_p\}$ or T^c is effective for $\{a_1, \ldots, a_{k-1}\}$. Therefore if k^* is the largest integer k such that T is effective for $\{a_k, \ldots, a_p\}$, we have:

T is effective for $\{a_{k^*}, \ldots, a_p\}$,

T^c is effective for $\{a_1, \ldots, a_{k^*}\}$.

Hence, for every game form $g = (X_i, i \in N, \pi)$ with associated effectivity function eff, the two-person zero sum game $(X_T, X_{T^c}, u \circ \pi, \bar{u} \circ \pi)$ has a saddle-point and its value is $u(a_{k^*})$.

In the next result we characterize the effectivity functions that derive from some sophisticated s.c.f. and/or dominance-solvable game forms. As in Chapter 5, section 4, we denote by $\mathcal{S}$ the set of sophisticated s.c.f.s.

Theorem 2. Every dominance-solvable game form is tight. The sophisticated s.c.f. that it implements is tight also with the same effectivity function:

$$\forall S \in \mathcal{S}, \forall g \{g \text{ sophisticatedly implements } S\} \Rightarrow \alpha\text{-eff}_g = \beta\text{-eff}_g = \alpha\text{-eff}_S$$

$$= \alpha\text{-eff}_g.$$

Moreover, an effectivity function can be derived from some sophisticated s.c.f. if and only if it is superadditive and maximal. For any eff we then have

$\{\text{eff superadditive and maximal}\} \Leftrightarrow \{\exists S \in \mathcal{S}: \text{eff}_S = \text{eff}\}.$

Proof. Fix a dominance-solvable game form $g = (X_i, i \in N, \pi)$ and denote by $S \in \mathcal{S}$ the sophisticated s.c.f. it implements. Fix T and B, both non-empty, and choose a utility $u \in L(A)$ such that

$$\forall b \in B, \forall a \in B^c: u(a) < u(b).$$

Now we consider the two-person zero sum game $g^1(u) = (X_T, X_{T^c}, u \circ \pi, \bar{u} \circ \pi)$. From the proof of theorem 4, Chapter 5, it follows that this game has a value, val(u). Moreover, this is also the value of the two-person game:

$$\left(L(A)^T, L(A)^{T^c}, u \circ S, \bar{u} \circ S\right).$$

Setting $a_0 = S([u]_T, [\bar{u}]_{T^c})$ we then have

$$\forall x_T \in X_T, x_{T^c} \in X_{T^c}: u\pi(x_T, \bar{x}_{T^c}) \leq u(a_0) \leq u\pi(\bar{x}_T, x_{T^c}),$$

where $(\bar{x}_T, \bar{x}_{T^c})$ is any saddle-point of $g^1(u)$.
Similarly we have (relation (8), Chapter 5):

$$\forall u_T \in L(A)^T, u_{T^c} \in L(A)^{T^c}: uS(u_T, [\bar{u}]_{T^c}) \leq u(a_0) \leq uS([u]_T, u_{T^c}).$$

In view of the construction of u these two relations imply

$$a_0 \in B \Leftrightarrow T\alpha\text{-eff}_g B \quad \text{and} \quad T\alpha\text{-eff}_S B,$$

$$a_0 \in B^c \Leftrightarrow T^c\alpha\text{-eff}_g B^c \quad \text{and} \quad T^c\alpha\text{-eff}_S B^c.$$

This in turn proves the maximality of $\alpha\text{-eff}_g = \alpha\text{-eff}_S$, and hence by lemma 3 tightness of g and S.

Now to the second statement of theorem 2.

Given a maximal and superadditive effectivity function eff we denote by $g = (X_i, i \in N; \pi)$ an associated universal game form (see the proof of Theorem 1). We order arbitrarily the agents $N = \{1, 2, \ldots, n\}$ and consider the game form $\tilde{g}$ that describes in normal form the following voting rule: the agents $1, 2, \ldots, n$ choose successively a strategy in $X_1, X_2, \ldots, X_n$, agent i being informed when choosing x_i of the choices made by the agents $1, \ldots, (i-1)$.

By theorem 3, Chapter 5, $\tilde{g}$ is dominance-solvable with associated s.c.f. $\tilde{S}$. We let the reader check the following implication. For all T and B

non-empty:

$$T\alpha\text{-eff}_g B \Rightarrow T\alpha\text{-eff}_{\tilde{g}} B.$$

Now $\alpha\text{-eff}_g = \text{eff}$ (corollary of theorem 1) and since eff is maximal the above implication actually is an equivalence. Hence,

$$\text{eff} = \alpha\text{-eff}_{\tilde{g}} = \alpha\text{-eff}_{\tilde{S}},$$

which concludes the proof of theorem 2.

4. Stable effectivity functions

Notation. Given a coalition T, an outcome a, and a profile $\boldsymbol{u}$ we denote by $\Pr(T, a, \boldsymbol{u})$ the set of those outcomes that coalition T unanimously prefer to a:

$$\Pr(T, a, \boldsymbol{u}) = \{b \in A / \forall i \in T : u_i(a) < u_i(b)\}.$$

Definition 7. Given A and N, an effectivity function eff, and a profile $\boldsymbol{u} \in L(A)^N$ the *core* $C(\text{eff}, \boldsymbol{u})$ is the following – possibly empty – subset of A:

$$\forall a \in A\{a \in C(\text{eff}, \boldsymbol{u})\} \overset{\text{def}}{\Leftrightarrow} \{\forall T \subset N : \text{No}\{T \text{eff} \Pr(T, a, \boldsymbol{u})\}\}.$$

We shall say that eff is a *stable* effectivity function if the associated core is non-empty for all profiles:

$$\{\text{eff is stable}\} \overset{\text{def}}{\Leftrightarrow} \{\forall \boldsymbol{u} \in L(A)^N C(\text{eff}, \boldsymbol{u}) \neq \emptyset\}.$$

The core of an effectivity function at a particular profile is the set of cooperatively stable outcomes: an outcome a is unstable if a coalition T can force the final outcome within B, where all members of T strictly prefer every outcome in B to a. Since N is effective for any singleton, it follows that the core of any e.f. at any profile contains only Pareto optimal outcomes.

Consider, for instance, a simple game (N, W) (example 1). There the corresponding core can be simply written as

$$C(W, \boldsymbol{u}) = \{a \in A / \forall b \in A : \{i \in N / u_i(a) < u_i(b)\} \notin W\}.$$

In particular let W be the simple majority game:

$$T \in W \Leftrightarrow |T| > \frac{n}{2} = \frac{|N|}{2}.$$

Then the core at u is simply the set $CW(u)$ of Condorcet winners (definition 6, Chapter 2). Non-existence of Condorcet winners for some profiles (lemma 2, Chapter 2) is now interpreted as the essential cooperative instability of the simple majority game. Nakamura's theorem (theorem 6 below) provides a complete characterization of stable effectivity functions derived from simple games.

The additive effectivity functions are the main example of a stable e.f.

Theorem 3 (Moulin and Peleg, 1982). Every additive effectivity function is stable.

Proof. Let A and N and an additive e.f. $\text{eff}_{\ell,m}$ be given. Suppose first that $\text{eff}_{\ell,m}$ is maximal. Then by lemma 4 it takes the form $\text{eff}_{\lambda,\mu}$ for some integer valued vectors (λ, μ) satisfying (11).

For every profile $u \in L(A)^N$, the core of this latter e.f. is written as

$$C(\text{eff}_{\lambda,\mu}, u) = \{a \in A / \forall T \subset N : \text{No}\{\mu(T) + \lambda(\Pr(T, a, u)) \geq \lambda(A)\}\}$$

$$= \{a \in A / \forall T \subset N : \lambda(\Pr(T, a, u)) \leq \mu(T^c)\}.$$

Therefore it coincides with the set of strong equilibrium outcomes of any voting by veto game form $g_{\sigma,\mu}$, where $\sigma \in \Sigma(\mu)$, and it has been proved non-empty in Chapter 6 (theorem 3 and 3-bis).

Suppose now that $\text{eff}_{\ell,m}$ is not maximal. This amounts to saying that for some non-empty T and B:

$$m(T) + \ell(B) = 1.$$

We set

$$\varepsilon = \tfrac{1}{2} \inf |m(T) + \ell(B) - 1|, \tag{22}$$

where the infimum is taken on

$$\{T, B : m(T) + \ell(B) \neq 1\},$$

and choose an arbitrary maximal additive e.f. $\mathrm{eff}_{\ell_0, m_0}$. Now we define two probability distributions, ℓ_1 and m_1, on A and N, respectively, by

$$\ell_1 = (1-\varepsilon)\ell + \varepsilon\ell_0,$$

$$m_1 = (1-\varepsilon)m + \varepsilon m_0.$$

We claim first that $\mathrm{eff}_{\ell_1, m_1}$ is maximal. Namely, for any non-empty T and B, the equality

$$m_1(T) + \ell_1(B) = 1$$

can be written as

$$(1-\varepsilon)(m(T) + \ell(B) - 1) = \varepsilon(1 - m_0(T) - \ell_0(B)).$$

Since $m(T) + \ell(B) = 1$ would contradict the maximality of $\mathrm{eff}_{\ell_0, m_0}$, we have simultaneously

$$|(1-\varepsilon)(m(T) + \ell(B) - 1)| \geq 2\varepsilon(1-\varepsilon),$$

$$|\varepsilon(1 - m_0(T) - \ell_0(B))| \leq \varepsilon,$$

a contradiction of $\varepsilon < \tfrac{1}{2}$ which follows from the definition of ε.

Next we claim that for all non-empty T and B:

$$m(T) + \ell(B) > 1 \Rightarrow m_1(T) + \ell_1(B) > 1. \tag{23}$$

This results from a similar argument.

Now property (23) implies

$$C(\mathrm{eff}_{\ell_1, m_1}, \boldsymbol{u}) \subset C(\mathrm{eff}_{\ell, m}, \boldsymbol{u}), \quad \text{all } \boldsymbol{u} \in L(A)^N.$$

Since $\mathrm{eff}_{\ell_1, m_1}$ is a stable e.f. we have reached the desired conclusion. ∎

A full characterization of the stable effectivity functions is difficult (cf. problem 22 below). However, important particular cases can be explored fully. Suppose, for instance, that we want to focus on *anonymous* and *neutral* effectivity functions. They are represented by anonymous veto functions (see example 3 above):

v maps $\{1,\ldots,n\}$ into $\{0,\ldots,p-1\}$,

and for non-empty T and B:

$$\{T \operatorname{eff} B \Leftrightarrow v(|T|)+|B| \geq p\}.$$

The above definition yields an effectivity function if and only if v is non-decreasing. Notice that, contrary to definition 1, Chapter 6, we do not require superadditivity of v.

Theorem 1, Chapter 6 can be reformulated as follows.

Theorem 4. The proportional veto function

$$\bar{v}(t) = \left\lceil p\frac{t}{n} \right\rceil - 1, \quad t=1,\ldots,n,$$

yields a stable (additive) anonymous and neutral effectivity function.

A veto function v yields a stable anonymous and neutral effectivity function if and only if it is bounded above by the proportional veto function

$$v \text{ stable} \Leftrightarrow v(t) \leq \bar{v}(t), \quad \text{all } t=1,\ldots,n.$$

The effectivity function of the proportional veto function is additive: it coincides with $\operatorname{eff}_{\bar{\ell},\bar{m}}$, where $\bar{\ell}$ and $\bar{m}$ are the *uniform* probability distributions on A and N:

$$\bar{\ell}_a = \frac{1}{p}, \text{ all } a \in A; \quad \bar{m}_i = \frac{1}{n}, \text{ all } i \in N.$$

That is to say, for all non-empty T and B we have successively:

$$T \operatorname{eff}_{\bar{\ell},\bar{m}} B \Leftrightarrow p\frac{|T|}{n} + |B| > p,$$

$$v(|T|)+|B| \geq p \Leftrightarrow \left\lceil p\frac{|T|}{n} \right\rceil + |B| \geq p+1.$$

The right-hand side inequalities coincide by definition of $\lceil \ \rceil$.

Theorem 4 implies, for instance, that the α- and β-effectivity functions of the Borda scoring correspondence are *not* stable (see the computation of α- and β-winning coalitions in example 5 or the approximation formulae of problem 20). Exercise: Is the effectivity function *-eff_B (see problem 21) stable?

Stable and maximal effectivity functions play a central role in cooperative voting: see section 5 below. Accordingly, the next theorem gives a useful characterization.

Definition 8. An effectivity function is said to be *subadditive* if the following condition holds:

$$\{T_i \text{eff } B_i, i=1,2 \text{ and } B_1 \cap B_2 = \emptyset\} \Rightarrow \{T_1 \cap T_2 \text{eff } B_1 \cup B_2\},$$

$$\text{for all } T_i \text{ and } B_i, \quad i=1,2. \tag{24}$$

Subadditivity is analogous to superadditivity (definition 2) although its interpretation is less transparent. For instance, one checks easily that a neutral effectivity function, described by a veto function v – see example 3 – is subadditive if and only if

$$v(T_1) + v(T_2) \leq v(T_1 \cap T_2) + p, \quad \text{all } T_1 \text{ and } T_2 \tag{25}$$

(with the convention $v(\emptyset) = 0$).

Another equivalent formulation of subadditivity is analogous to lemma 2:

$$\left.\begin{array}{l} B_k \cap B_{k'} = \emptyset, \quad \text{all } k, k' \\ T_k \text{eff } B_k \end{array}\right\} \Rightarrow \bigcap_k T_k \text{eff } \bigcup_k B_k. \tag{26}$$

The above implication is true for all *finite* sequences T_k and B_k. In particular, (26) implies that $\bigcap_k T_k$ is non-empty.

We remark, finally, that an additive effectivity function is subadditive as well, thus avoiding any contradiction in our terminology. Namely, let $\text{eff}_{\ell, m}$ be an additive e.f. and T_i and B_i, $i = 1, 2$, be as in the premises of (24). Then we have

$$m(T_1 \cap T_2) = m(T_1) + m(T_2) - m(T_1 \cup T_2) \geq m(T_1) + m(T_2) - 1.$$

Therefore

$$m(T_1 \cap T_2) + \ell(B_1 \cup B_2) \geq m(T_1) + \ell(B_1) + m(T_2) + \ell(B_2) - 1 > 1.$$

Theorem 5 (Abdou, 1981). A stable and maximal effectivity function is superadditive and subadditive.

Corollary. If a veto function $v: 2^N \setminus \{\emptyset\} \to \{0, \ldots, p-1\}$ is stable and maximal, then we have

$$T_1 \cap T_2 = \emptyset \Rightarrow v(T_1) + v(T_2) \leq v(T_1 \cup T_2) \leq v(T_1) + v(T_2) + 1.$$

Proof of theorem 5. Let eff be a stable and maximal e.f. Let T_i and B_i, $i = 1, 2$, be such that

$$T_i \text{eff } B_i \quad \text{and} \quad T_1 \cap T_2 = \emptyset.$$

Suppose $T_1 \cup T_2 \text{eff } B_1 \cap B_2$ fails. Then by the maximality of eff we have

$$T_3 \text{eff } B_3, \quad \text{where } T_3 = [T_1 \cup T_2]^c \quad \text{and} \quad B_3 = [B_1 \cap B_2]^c.$$

We consider now the partition C_1, C_2, C_3 of A:

$$C_3 = B_1 \cap B_2,$$

$$C_2 = B_2^c,$$

$$C_1 = B_2 \cap B_1^c.$$

Clearly, $T_j \text{eff } C_j^c$ for $j = 1, 2, 3$ (since $C_j^c = B_j$ for $j = 2, 3$ and $C_1^c \supset B_1$). Since T_j, $j = 1, 2, 3$, partition N just as C_j, $j = 1, 2, 3$, partition A, we can find a profile $\boldsymbol{u} \in L(A)^N$ such that

$$\forall i \in T_j, \forall a \in C_j, \forall b \notin C_j : u_i(a) < u_i(b).$$

In other words C_j is the bottom of u_{T_j}.

Clearly, for all $a \in C_j$ we have

$$\Pr(T_j, a, \boldsymbol{u}) \supset C_j^c.$$

Since $T_j \text{eff } C_j^c$ it follows that a does not belong to $C(\text{eff}, \boldsymbol{u})$. Since C_j, $j = 1, 2, 3$, cover A, we get $C(\text{eff}, \boldsymbol{u}) = \emptyset$, contradicting the stability of eff.

We have proved superadditivity of eff. We now prove the subadditivity. Let T_i and B_i, $i = 1, 2$, be such that

$$T_i \text{eff } B_i \quad \text{and} \quad B_1 \cap B_2 = \emptyset.$$

Suppose $T_1 \cap T_2 \text{eff } B_1 \cup B_2$ fails. Then by the maximality of eff we have

$T_3 \text{eff } B_3$, where $T_3 = [T_1 \cap T_2]^c$ and $B_3 = [B_1 \cup B_2]^c$.

Setting

$$R_3 = T_1 \cap T_2,$$

$$R_2 = T_2^c,$$

$$R_1 = T_2 \cap T_1^c,$$

we have that R_1, R_2, R_3 partition N, and

$R_i \cup R_j \text{eff } B_k$, all $\{i, j, k\} = \{1, 2, 3\}$.

Now we choose a profile $\boldsymbol{u} \in L(A)^N$ such that

$\forall i \in R_1: u_i(B_1) < u_i(B_2) < u_i(B_3),$

$\forall i \in R_2: u_i(B_2) < u_i(B_3) < u_i(B_1),$

$\forall i \in R_3: u_i(B_3) < u_i(B_1) < u_i(B_2).$

For all $a \in B_1$ we have

$\Pr(R_1 \cup R_3, a, \boldsymbol{u}) \supset B_2 \Rightarrow a \notin C(\text{eff}, \boldsymbol{u}).$

Similarly:

$\forall a \in B_2: \Pr(R_1 \cup R_2, a, \boldsymbol{u}) \supset B_3 \Rightarrow a \notin C(\text{eff}, \boldsymbol{u}),$

$\forall a \in B_3: \Pr(R_2 \cup R_3, a, \boldsymbol{u}) \supset B_1 \Rightarrow a \notin C(\text{eff}, \boldsymbol{u}).$

Once again we have constructed a profile with an associated empty core.

Proof of the corollary. If v is a stable and maximal veto function, it is a subadditive effectivity function, so that (25) holds. Moreover, the maximality of v can be written as follows:

$$v(T) + v(T^c) = p - 1. \tag{27}$$

Combining (25) and (27) we have, for all T_1 and T_2:

$$(p-1-v(T_1))+(p-1-v(T_2)) = v(T_1^c)+v(T_2^c) \leqslant v(T_1^c \cap T_2^c)+p$$
$$= 2p-1-v(T_1 \cup T_2).$$

Henceforth:

$$v(T_1 \cup T_2) \leqslant v(T_1)+v(T_2)+1$$

holds for all T_1 and T_2. ∎

It results from Peleg (1982) that the converse of theorem 5 does hold: a maximal, superadditive and subadditive effectivity function is stable. The proof of this fact is too long to be included here.

The corollary of theorem 5 means that stable and maximal *neutral* e.f. have a nearly additive veto function. If we focus on *anonymous* and *neutral* e.f. (in short a.n.e.f.), theorem 4 has the following consequence.

Corollary of theorem 4. If n and p are relatively prime, the proportional veto function is the *unique* stable and maximal a.n.e.f.

If n and p are not relatively prime, there is no stable and maximal a.n.e.f.

Proof. We simply have to check that the proportional veto function $\bar{v}$ is maximal if and only if n and p are relatively prime:

$$n \cap p = 1 \Leftrightarrow \{\forall t \in \{1,\ldots,n\}: \bar{v}(t)+\bar{v}(n-t) = p-1\}.$$

Suppose $n \cap p = 1$ and choose $t \in \{1,\ldots,(n-1)\}$. Since $\bar{v}$ is superadditive we have

$$\bar{v}(t)+\bar{v}(n-t) \leqslant p-1.$$

Suppose now that

$$\bar{v}(t)+\bar{v}(n-t) < p-1,$$

i.e.

$$\left\lfloor p\frac{t}{n} \right\rfloor + \left\lfloor p\frac{(n-t)}{n} \right\rfloor \leqslant p. \qquad (28)$$

We remark that

$$\left[p\frac{t}{n}\right] \geq p\frac{t}{n},$$

$$\left[p\frac{(n-t)}{n}\right] \geq p\frac{(n-t)}{n}. \tag{29}$$

Comparing (28) and (29) we deduce that $p(t/n)$ is an integer, contradicting our assumptions $n \cap p = 1$ and $1 \leq t \leq n-1$.

We leave as an exercise for the reader to check the converse implication. ∎

To conclude section 4 we state and prove Nakamura's theorem, characterizing all stable effectivity functions derived from simple games.

Given a simple game (N, W) (example 1), its *Nakamura number* ν is the minimal number of winning coalitions with an empty intersection. Formally, ν is defined by

$$\nu = +\infty, \quad \text{if} \bigcap_{T \in W} T \neq \emptyset,$$

$$\nu = \inf\left\{|\mathcal{T}| / \mathcal{T} \subset W \quad \text{and} \bigcap_{T \in \mathcal{T}} T = \emptyset\right\}.$$

In particular, a simple game is proper ($T \in W \Rightarrow T^c \notin W^c$) if and only if its Nakamura number is at least 3. In that case its associated effectivity function on any A is superadditive.

Theorem 6 (Nakamura, 1975). Given A and N, and a simple game (N, W), the corresponding effectivity function is stable iff A contains less outcomes than the Nakamura number of (N, W):

$$\{(N, W) \text{ stable on } A\} \Leftrightarrow \{|A| < \nu\}.$$

Corollary. If A is a doubleton ($p = 2$), then every proper simple game yields a stable effectivity function on A.

If A contains at least three distinct outcomes ($p \geq 3$), then among the strong proper simple games (of which the associated e.f. on A is maximal)

$$T \in W \Leftrightarrow T^c \notin W^c,$$

only the dictatorial ones are stable:

$$\{(N,W) \text{ strong and stable on } A\} \Leftrightarrow \{(N,W) \text{ is dictatorial}\}.$$

Proof. Suppose $|A| < \nu$ and that (N,W) is not stable. There exists a profile $u \in L(A)^N$ such that the corresponding core is empty. Denoting for all distinct outcomes a and b:

$$T(a,b) = \{i \in N / u_i(a) < u_i(b)\}.$$

We then have

$$\forall a \in A, \exists b \in A : T(a,b) \in W.$$

By the finiteness of A we can find a sequence $a_1, \ldots, a_K, a_{K+1} = a_1$ such that

$$K \leq p = |A| \quad \text{and} \quad T(a_k, a_{k+1}) \in W, \quad \text{all } k = 1, \ldots, K.$$

Since $K < \nu$ there exists an agent i such that

$$i \in \bigcap_{k=1,\ldots,K} T(a_k, a_{k+1}).$$

This implies a contradiction:

$$u_i(a_1) < u_i(a_2) < u_i(a_3) < \cdots < u_i(a_K) < u_i(a_1).$$

Conversely, suppose that $\nu \leq |A|$.

Denoting $p = |A|$, we can find a sequence $T_1, \ldots, T_p$ of winning coalitions with an empty intersection:

$$T_k \in W, \quad \text{all} \quad k = 1, \ldots, p \quad \text{and} \quad \bigcap_{k=1,\ldots,p} T_k = \emptyset.$$

Since $\bigcup_{k=1,\ldots,p} T_k^c = N$ we can find a sequence $R_1, \ldots, R_p$ of pairwise disjoint (possibly empty) coalitions such that

$$R_k \subset T_k^c, \quad k = 1, \ldots, p \quad \text{and} \quad \bigcup_{k=1,\ldots,p} R_k = N.$$

Next, order arbitrarily the outcomes

$$A = \{b_1, \ldots, b_p\}.$$

Since T_k is winning $R_k^c = \bigcup_{k' \neq k} R_{k'}$ is winning as well, so that we have

$$R_k^c \mathrm{eff}\{b_k\}, \quad \text{all } k = 1,\ldots,p. \tag{30}$$

We now construct a profile u such that

on R_1: $b_1 < b_2 < \cdots < b_p$,
on R_2: $b_2 < b_3 < \cdots < b_p < b_1$,
$\vdots$
on R_k: $b_k < b_{k+1} < \cdots < b_p < b_1 < \cdots < b_{k-1}$,
on R_p: $b_p < b_1 < \cdots < b_{p-1}$.

We claim that the core of the effectivity function derived from (N, W) on A at the above profile is empty. Namely, in view of (30) we have

$$T(b_1, b_2) = R_2^c \Rightarrow b_1 \notin C(W, u),$$
$$\vdots$$
$$T(b_k, b_{k+1}) = R_{k+1}^c \Rightarrow b_k \notin C(W, u),$$
$$\vdots$$
$$T(b_p, b_1) = R_1^c \Rightarrow b_p \notin C(W, u).$$

This concludes the proof of theorem 6.

For any proper simple game (N, W) Nakamura's number ν is that at least 3. Hence, the first statement of the corollary.

Suppose now that the e.f. associated with (N, W) on A (where $|A| \geq 3$) is stable and maximal. Since this e.f. is neutral, the corollary of theorem 5 applies. This e.f. is represented by a veto function v such that

$$v(T_1 \cup T_2) \leq v(T_1) + v(T_2) + 1, \quad \text{all non-empty } T_1 \text{ and } T_2.$$

Choose an inclusion minimal winning coalition T and suppose that T is not a singleton: it can be written as $T = T_1 \cup T_2$, where both T_1 and T_2 are non-empty. Hence,

$$p - 1 = v(T) \leq v(T_1) + v(T_2) + 1 \Rightarrow 1 \leq p - 2 \leq v(T_1) + v(T_2).$$

Since a coalition outside W has zero veto power we conclude that either T_1 or T_2 is winning, a contradiction. Therefore T is a singleton so that (N,W) is dictatorial.

In problem 22 we propose examples of stable and maximal effectivity functions that are *not* additive, thus establishing that the converse of theorem 3 does not hold.

Problem 22: Non-additive stable and maximal effectivity functions.

(1) Suppose $N = \{1,2\}$, $A = \{a, b, c, d\}$ and consider the following (non-neutral, non-anonymous) effectivity function:

1 is effective for $\{a, b\}\{c, d\}\{b, c\}$ and every superset of these,

2 is effective for $\{a, c\}\{b, d\}\{b, c\}$ and every superset of these.

Prove that it is a stable maximal effectivity function which is not additive.

(2) When $|A| = 2$ prove that a proper simple game (N, W) yields an additive effectivity function if and only if it is a weighted majority game: there exist $\bar{m}_i > 0$, all $i \in N$, such that

$$T \in W \Leftrightarrow \bar{m}(T) > 1.$$

Give an example of a proper strong simple game that is not a weighted majority game. This gives a neutral stable and maximal effectivity function which is not additive.

(3) When $|N| = 2$ and A is an arbitrary finite set, prove that every maximal effectivity function on (A, N) is stable as well.

Denote by $\mathcal{E}$ a subset of $2^A \setminus \emptyset$ such that

$$\{B \in \mathcal{E}, B \subset B'\} \Rightarrow B' \in \mathcal{E}. \tag{31}$$

Prove that the mapping

$$\text{eff} \to \tau(\text{eff}) = \{B \subset A / \{1\} \text{eff } B\}$$

is a bijection from the set E of maximal (hence stable) effectivity functions on A, $N = \{1,2\}$, onto the set of subsets $\mathcal{E}$ of $2^A \setminus \emptyset$ satisfying (31).

Prove that an anonymous element eff of E is additive if and only if there exist $\bar{\ell}_a > 0$, all $a \in A$, such that

$$B \in \tau(\text{eff}) \Leftrightarrow \bar{\ell}(B) > 1.$$

Give an example of an anonymous maximal (hence stable) effectivity function that is not additive.

5. Implementation by strong equilibrium

Definition 9. Given A and N, a game form $g = (X_i, i \in N; \pi)$, and a profile $\boldsymbol{u} \in L(A)^N$, we say that an N-tuple $x \in X_N$ is a *strong equilibrium* of g at $\boldsymbol{u}$ if we have

$$\forall T \subset N, \forall y_T \in X_T: \pi(y_T, x_{T^c}) \notin \Pr(T, \pi(x), \boldsymbol{u}). \quad (32)$$

We denote by $\mathrm{SE}(g, \boldsymbol{u}) \subset X_N$ the (possibly empty) set of strong equilibriums of g at $\boldsymbol{u}$.

Given a social choice correspondence S, we say that g *strongly implements* S if we have

$$\forall \boldsymbol{u} \in L(A)^N: S(\boldsymbol{u}) = \pi(\mathrm{SE}(g, \boldsymbol{u})). \quad (33)$$

We say that S is *strongly implementable* if there exists a game form g that strongly implements S.

A strong equilibrium is in particular a Pareto optimum and a Nash equilibrium (see definition 10 below). It is actually much more than that. The underlying behavioural scenario is that of a cooperative agreement enforced by passive threats: the agents agree on outcome x and the mere fact that agents of T^c stick to their original strategies prevents coalition T from finding a profitable move (i.e. a move that would improve the utility of every agent in T). Observe that the passive behaviour by T^c might be very harmful to T^c itself, and/or there may exist, *given that coalition T plays y_T*, a better strategy y_{T^c} than x_{T^c}:

$$\pi(y_T, y_{T^c}) \in \Pr(T^c, \pi(y_T, x_{T^c}), \boldsymbol{u}).$$

But by the Pareto optimality of $\pi(x)$ we have

$$\pi(y_T, y_{T^c}) \in \Pr(T, \pi(x), \boldsymbol{u}) \Rightarrow \pi(y_T, y_{T^c}) \notin \Pr(T^c, \pi(x), \boldsymbol{u}).$$

Therefore if coalition T has an incentive to manipulate coalition T^c (by inducing a reaction y_{T^c} to y_T) it cannot be afterall profitable for T^c to comply: the passive behaviour by T^c deters T from moving and prevents T^c from being exploited.

Cooperative voting 189

The strong equilibrium is a very demanding concept that fails to exist in many usual normal form games. However, as was already apparent in Chapter 6 (sections 5 and 6) implementation by strong equilibrium is possible for a rich family of social choice correspondences. Indeed, we proved that the game form $g_{\sigma,\lambda}$ strongly implements the core correspondence of the (additive) effectivity function $\text{eff}_{\lambda,\mu}$ (theorems 3 and 3-bis). This result can be generalized as follows.

Theorem 7 (Moulin and Peleg, 1982). Let eff be a stable and maximal effectivity function on A and N. Then its core correspondence, namely the following s.c.c.

$$\forall u \in L(A)^N : S(u) = C(\text{eff}, u),$$

is strongly implementable. Any universal game form (as defined in the proof of theorem 1) does the job.

Proof. Let $g = (X_i, i \in N, \pi)$ be a universal game form associated with eff. Thus, X_i are defined by (15) and π satisfies (16). We must prove (33).

First we fix a profile u, an outcome a in $C(\text{eff}, u)$ and we construct a strong equilibrium x of g at u such that $\pi(x) = a$. By definition of the core and maximality of eff we have

$$\forall T \neq N : \text{No}\{T \text{eff Pr}(T, a, u)\} \Rightarrow \{T^c \text{eff Pr}(T, a, u)^c\}.$$

For all $i \in N$ define $x_i \in X_i$ as

$$\begin{cases} x_i(N) = \{a\}, \\ \forall T \in \mathcal{T}_i, T \neq N : x_i(T) = \Pr(T^c, a, u)^c. \end{cases}$$

Clearly, $\mathcal{P}_\infty(x) = \{N\}$ so that by (16)

$$\pi(x) = a.$$

To prove that $x \in \text{SE}(g, u)$ we remark first that a is Pareto optimal, hence (32) holds for $T = N$. Choose next a coalition $T \subsetneq N$ and a strategy y_T of T. Since all agents of T^c agree on all coalitions T' and $T^c \subset T'$, it follows that in partition $\mathcal{P}_\infty(y_T, x_{T^c})$ all agents of T belong to the same T_{k_0} and $T^c \subset T_{k_0}$. By (16) this implies

$$\pi(y_T, x_{T^c}) \in x(T_{k_0}) = \Pr(T_{k_0}^c, a, u)^c.$$

But $T_{k_0}^c \subset T$ implies $\Pr(T, a, \boldsymbol{u}) \subset \Pr(T_{k_0}^c, a, \boldsymbol{u})$; henceforth

$$\pi(y_T, x_{T^c}) \in \Pr(T, a, \boldsymbol{u})^c,$$

which was to be proved.

Conversely, we choose any $x \in SE(g, \boldsymbol{u})$ and prove that $\pi(x) = a$ is in $C(\text{eff}, \boldsymbol{u})$. For if it is not there exists a coalition T such that

$$T \text{ eff } \Pr(T, a, \boldsymbol{u}).$$

Then consider a strategy y_T of coalition T where for all $i \in T$ we have

$$\forall T' \in \mathcal{T}_i\{T \subset T'\} \Rightarrow \{y_i(T') = \Pr(T, a, \boldsymbol{u})\}.$$

By the same argument as above, we have that partition $\mathcal{P}_\infty(y_T, x_{T^c})$ does not discriminate the agents in T:

$$\exists k_0: T \subset T_{k_0} \quad \text{and} \quad T_{k_0} \in \mathcal{P}_\infty(y_T, x_{T^c}).$$

From (16) we deduce that

$$\pi(y_T, x_{T^c}) \in y(T_{k_0}) = \Pr(T, a, \boldsymbol{u}).$$

This contradicts the strong equilibrium property of x and concludes the proof of theorem 7.

The next two results give *necessary* conditions for an s.c.c. to be strongly implementable: stable and maximal effectivity functions are on stage again.

Throughout the rest of this chapter we assume that all s.c.c. (resp. g.f.) satisfy strong citizen sovereignty (3) (resp. citizen sovereignty).

Theorem 8 (Moulin and Peleg, 1982). Let g be a game form that strongly implements the s.c.c. S. Then g and S are tight with the same effectivity function denoted eff. Moreover, eff is stable and maximal and

$$\forall \boldsymbol{u} \in L(A)^N: \pi(\text{SE}(g, \boldsymbol{u})) = S(\boldsymbol{u}) \subset C(\text{eff}, \boldsymbol{u}). \tag{34}$$

Proof. The following notation will be useful. Given a coalition T, a profile u_T of coalition T and a subset B of outcomes, we say that B is *on top of* u_T iff the following holds true:

$$\forall i \in T, \forall b \in B, \forall a \in B^c: u_i(a) < u_i(b). \tag{35}$$

Let g be a game form that strongly implements the s.c.c. S. We choose any two non-empty T and B such that $T\beta$-eff$_g B$. Take any $u_T \in L(A)^T$ with B on top. We claim that

$$\forall u_{T^c} \in L(A)^{T^c} S(u_T, u_{T^c}) \subset B. \tag{36}$$

Suppose the claim fails for some u_{T^c}. Then there exists an outcome $a \in B^c$ and a strategy $x \in X_N$ such that

$$a = \pi(x) \in B^c \quad \text{and} \quad x \in \text{SE}(g,(u_T, u_{T^c})). \tag{37}$$

Because T is β-effective for B in g there exists $y_T \in X_T$ such that

$$\pi(y_T, x_{T^c}) \in B.$$

By our choice of u_T we have

$$\pi(y_T, x_{T^c}) \in \text{Pr}(T, a, (u_T, u_{T^c})),$$

contradicting (32). We have just proved

$$T\beta\text{-eff}_g B \Rightarrow T\alpha\text{-eff}_S B. \tag{38}$$

Similarly, we now prove

$$T\beta\text{-eff}_S B \Rightarrow T\alpha\text{-eff}_g B. \tag{39}$$

Choose any two non-empty T and B such that $T\beta$-eff$_S B$. Next choose $u_{T^c} \in L(A)^{T^c}$ with B^c on top. Since T is β-effective for B in S, there exists $u_T \in L(A)^T$ such that

$$S(u_T, u_{T^c}) \subset B.$$

Therefore there exists an outcome $b \in B$ and a strategy $x \in X_N$ such that

$$b = \pi(x) \in B \quad \text{and} \quad x \in \text{SE}(g,(u_T, u_{T^c})). \tag{40}$$

Now take any strategy y_{T^c} of coalition T^c.

By our choice of u_{T^c} a contradiction would follow from $\pi(x_T, y_{T^c}) \in B^c$ and (40). Therefore $\pi(x_T, y_{T^c}) \in B$ so that T is α-effective for B in g. This proves (39).

From (38), (39) and property (4) we conclude that g and S are tight with the same effectivity function eff. From the corollary of theorem 1 we have that eff is maximal. Thus, it remains only to prove the inclusion (34).

Fix a profile u and a strong equilibrium x of g at u. We must show that

$$\pi(x) \in C(\text{eff}, u).$$

Suppose this fails to be true. Then there exists a coalition T such that

$$T\alpha\text{-eff}_g \Pr(T, \pi(x), u).$$

Hence, there exists $y_T \in X_T$ such that

$$\pi(y_T, x_{T^c}) \in \Pr(T, \pi(x), u),$$

thus contradicting the strong equilibrium property of x. This concludes the proof of theorem 8. ∎

During the above proof we have shown the following property which is interesting by itself. Let S be a strongly implementable s.c.c. and eff be its associated e.f. Then for all non-empty T and B:

T eff B if and only if

$$\cdot \left[\forall u \in L(A)^N \{ B \text{ is on top of } u_T \} \Rightarrow \{ S(u_T, u_{T^c}) \subset B \} \right]. \quad (41)$$

In other words the effectivity function of S coincides with its *-eff_S (see problem 22 above).

The if statement is clear; the only if statement is property (36), taking into account that $\beta\text{-eff}_g = \text{eff}$.

Theorems 7 and 8 together characterize the strongly implementable s.c.c. that are inclusion maximal with respect to that property. Denote by $\mathcal{E}$ the set of strongly implementable s.c.c.s. Then for every $S \in \mathcal{E}$, the two following statements are equivalent:

(i) $\forall S' \in \mathcal{E}: \{S \subset S'\} \Rightarrow \{S = S'\}$.
(ii) There exists eff, stable and maximal such that

$$\forall u \in L(A)^N: S(u) = C(\text{eff}, u). \quad (42)$$

Namely, take any $S \in \mathcal{E}$ such that (i) holds. By theorem 8 we have

$$S \subset C(\text{eff}_S, \cdot) \Rightarrow S = C(\text{eff}_S, \cdot).$$

Conversely, if eff is a stable and maximal e.f., then $C(\text{eff}, \cdot) \in \mathcal{E}$ (theorem 7). Moreover, if $S \in \mathcal{E}$ is such that

$$C(\text{eff}, \cdot) \subset S, \tag{43}$$

then by theorem 8 we have

$$C(\text{eff}, \cdot) \subset C(\text{eff}_S, \cdot).$$

We remark that the effectivity function associated with the s.c.c. $C(\text{eff}, \cdot)$ is eff itself (this is obvious by the maximality of eff and property (41)). Therefore the above inclusion yields:

$$T \text{eff}_S B \Rightarrow T \text{eff} B, \quad \text{all } T \text{ and } B.$$

By the maximality of eff_S this implies $\text{eff}_S = \text{eff}$ so that inclusion (43) actually is an equality.

There are strongly implementable s.c.c.s that are strictly contained in the core correspondence of their associated e.f.

Example. We suppose $A = \{a, b, c\}$ $N = \{1, 2, 3, 4\}$. We set

$$X_i = \{(\xi, \eta) \in A \times A / \xi \neq \eta\},$$

and for $x_i = (\xi_i, \eta_i)$, $i = 1, \ldots, 4$, we choose $\pi(x)$ such that

- if at least three of $\eta_1, \ldots, \eta_4$ coincide, then $\pi(x)$ is the common outcome;
- if $\xi_i = \xi_j = \alpha$ for some $i \neq j$, then $\pi(x) \neq \alpha$ (all $\alpha \in A$);
- if $\{\xi_1, \xi_2, \xi_3, \xi_4\}$ contains a whereas at most two of $\eta_1, \ldots, \eta_4$ are a, then $\pi(x) \neq a$

We let the reader check that these requirements are not contradictory.

In the message $x_i = (\xi_i, \eta_i)$, η_i represents a proposal to elect outcome η_i: if any two other agents make the same proposal, it becomes effective. On the other hand, ξ_i is a proposal to *veto* outcome ξ_i: if at least one other agent proposes to veto the same outcome, this veto becomes effective.

Any of our game forms yields the proportional veto function:

- any three agents' coalition is dictatorial: $v(T) = 2$;
- any two agents' coalition can veto any one outcome: $v(T) = 1$;
- any single individual has no veto power at all: $v(T) = 0$.

We claim that any of our game forms has at least one strong equilibrium for every profile u. To prove this claim, we note that given any three agents' coalition $T = \{i, j, k\}$ and any two outcomes, α and β, the following strategy x_T of T,

$$x_i = x_j = x_k = (\beta, \alpha),$$

is such that

$$\begin{cases} \pi(x_T, y_{T^c}) = \alpha, & \text{for all } y_{T^c}, \\ \pi(x_i, x_j, y_{\{i,j\}^c}) \neq \beta, & \text{for all } y_{\{i,j\}^c}. \end{cases}$$

Therefore, for any x_{T^c} the strategy 4-tuple (x_T, x_{T^c}) is a strong equilibrium for any profile u such that

α is on top of u_i and u_j, and

(α is on top of u_k) (44)

or

(β is on top of u_k and α is ranked second by u_k).

For most of the profiles u, there exists a three-agents' coalition $\{i, j, k\}$ and a pair $\{\alpha, \beta\}$ such that (44) holds true. The only counterexamples are the following:

(i)

u_1	u_2	u_3	u_4
α	α	β	β
γ	γ	γ	γ
β	β	α	α

and all profiles obtained by permuting the agents;

(ii)

u_1	u_2	u_3	u_4
α	α	γ	β
γ	γ	β	γ
β	β	α	α

and all profiles obtained by permuting the agents;

(iii)

	u_1	u_2	u_3	u_4
	α	α	γ	β
	β	γ	β	γ
	γ	β	α	α

and all profiles obtained by permuting the agents.

In cases (i) and (ii) the following strategy 4-tuple is a strong equilibrium:

$$x_1 = x_2 = (\beta, \gamma); \quad x_3 = x_4 = (\alpha, \gamma).$$

In case (iii) only, the slight bias that our game form embodies against outcome a will play a role. For a profile u of type (iii) the proportional veto core is $\{\beta, \gamma\}$. Next, a strategy 4-tuple $x = (x_1, x_2, x_3, x_4)$ is a strong equilibrium such that $\pi(x) = \beta$ if and only if

$$\pi(x_1, y_2, x_3, x_4) = \beta, \quad \text{all } y_2 \in X_2,$$
$$\pi(y_1, y_2, x_3, x_4) \neq \alpha, \quad \text{all } (y_1, y_2) \in X_1 \times X_2,$$
$$\pi(x_1, y_2, y_3, x_4) \neq \gamma, \quad \text{all } (y_2, y_3) \in X_2 \times X_3.$$

Such an x exists if $\beta \neq a$. Suppose, for instance, $\alpha = a$; then the following x does the job:

$$x_1 = x_4 = (\gamma, \beta); \quad x_3 = (a, \beta); \quad x_2 \text{ arbitrary.}$$

On the other hand, if $\beta = a$ there exists no x satisfying (45). Namely, the definition of π implies

$$[\forall (y_1, y_2) \in X_1 \times X_2 : \pi(y_1, y_2, x_3, x_4) \neq b] \Rightarrow [\xi_3 = \xi_4 = b],$$

and a similar statement holds for c.

Since in profile (iii) outcomes β and γ play symmetrical roles, we can conclude:

if $\{\beta, \gamma\} = \{b, c\}$, then $\pi[SE(g, u)] = \{b, c\}$;

if $\{\beta, \gamma\} = \{a, \gamma\}$, then $\pi[SE(g, u)] = \{\gamma\}$.

This in turn proves that the game form g strongly implements a (non-empty valued) s.c.c. that is strictly contained in the core correspondence of its associated e.f.

Since s.c. correspondences are collective arbitration methods, the smaller they are the more deterministic is the collective choice that they achieve. From the above example we can expect to implement at least some s.c.c. strictly contained in the core correspondence of their e.f. The following result shows that we cannot go too far in that direction.

Theorem 9 (Maskin, 1979). Every strongly implementable s.c.c. is strongly monotonic as well.

Corollary 1. If A contains at least three outcomes, a social choice *function* satisfying citizen sovereignty is strongly implementable if and only if it is dictatorial.

Corollary 2. If there are only two agents ($n = 2$), a s.c.c. is strongly implementable if and only if there exists a stable and maximal effectivity function eff such that

$$\forall \boldsymbol{u} \in L(A)^2 : S(\boldsymbol{u}) = C(\text{eff}, \boldsymbol{u}).$$

Proof. Let A and N, a game form g and a s.c.c. S be given. We suppose that g strongly implements S, and we prove that S satisfies the strong positive association property (Chapter 3, relation (6)). By lemma 3, Chapter 3 this will conclude the proof of theorem 9.

Choose $a \in A$, $\boldsymbol{u}$, $\boldsymbol{v} \in L(A)^N$ and suppose that for some strategy N-tuple x:

$$a = \pi(x).$$

Suppose, moreover, that the position of a is preserved from $\boldsymbol{u}$ to $\boldsymbol{v}$. This can be written as

$$\forall T \subset N : \Pr(T, a, \boldsymbol{v}) \subset \Pr(T, a, \boldsymbol{u}).$$

Therefore, if x is a strong equilibrium of g at $\boldsymbol{u}$ we have, for all T, $y_T \in X_T$:

$$\pi(y_T, x_{T^c}) \notin \Pr(T, a, \boldsymbol{u}) \Rightarrow \pi(y_T, x_{T^c}) \notin \Pr(T, a, \boldsymbol{v}).$$

Henceforth x is a strong equilibrium of g at $\boldsymbol{v}$ as well. Thus,

$$a \in \pi(\text{SE}(g, \boldsymbol{u})) = S(\boldsymbol{u}) \Rightarrow a \in \pi(\text{SE}(g, \boldsymbol{v})) = S(\boldsymbol{v}),$$

which was to be proved.

Corollary 1 now follows from the Muller–Satterthwaite theorem (theorem 1, Chapter 3).

To prove corollary 2 we show that for any stable and maximal e.f. eff the core correspondence C(eff, ·) is inclusion minimal strongly monotonic. Since it is strongly monotonic (by theorems 7 and 9) it is enough (by problem 7, Chapter 3) to prove the following. Choose any $u \in L(A)^2$ and $a \in C(\text{eff}, u)$. Then there exists $v \in L(A)^2$ such that

$$\forall i = 1, 2: \{b \in A / u_i(b) \leq u_i(a)\} = \{b \in A / v_i(b) \leq v_i(a)\}$$

and $C(\text{eff}, v) = \{a\}$.

From $a \in C(\text{eff}, u)$ we deduce that $\{i\}$ is *not* effective for $B_i = \Pr(\{i\}, a, u)$, $i = 1, 2$. By the maximality of eff it follows that j is effective for B_j^c, $\{i, j\} = \{1, 2\}$. We now choose a profile v such that

$$\left. \begin{array}{l} B_i = \Pr(\{i\}, a, v) \\ B_j^c \text{ is on top of } u_i \end{array} \right\}, \quad \text{all } \{i, j\} = \{1, 2\}.$$

This choice is possible because $B_i \subset B_j^c$ (from the Pareto optimality of a).

Since the s.c.c. C(eff, ·) is strongly implementable (theorem 7) it satisfies (41). Therefore

$$\{i\}\text{eff } B_j^c \Rightarrow C(\text{eff}, v) \subset B_j^c, \quad \text{all } \{i, j\} = \{1, 2\}.$$

Thus, for all $b \in C(\text{eff}, v)$ we have

$$u_j(b) \leq u_j(a) \Rightarrow v_j(b) \leq v_j(a), \quad j = 1, 2.$$

Since C(eff, ·) is efficient, we conclude that

$$C(\text{eff}, v) = \{a\},$$

which was to be proved. ∎

Corollary 1 is similar to the Gibbard–Satterthwaite theorem. If the cooperative behaviour of the agents is in order, then unless we are ready to promote a dictator some indeterminacy must result in the collective choice set. (Notice that other less-demanding cooperative equilibrium concepts will result in the same impossibility result: see problem 25 below.)

Corollary 2 essentially states that when $n = 2$ the core correspondence of a maximal (hence stable, see problem 23, question 2) e.f. is inclusion minimal strongly monotonic (problem 7, Chapter 3). Henceforth by theorem 9 every strongly implementable s.c.c. that has to be contained in one of these core correspondences (theorem 8) must coincide with it. This property extends to any strongly implementable s.c.c. of which the associated core correspondence is inclusion minimal strongly monotonic.

Lemma 5. Let λ and μ be some integer valued vectors satisfying (11) and such that moreover

$$\{\lambda_a = 1, \text{ all } a \in A\} \text{ and/or } \{\mu_i = 1, \text{ all } i \in N\}. \tag{46}$$

Then the core correspondence of $\text{eff}_{\lambda,\mu}$ is inclusion minimal strongly monotonic.

The proof is left as an exercise for the reader: if $\lambda_a = 1$, all $a \in A$, we have indeed the effectivity functions of the voting by integer veto methods and we can use theorem 4, section 5, Chapter 6. If $\mu_i = 1$, all $i \in N$, a similar argument develops, using theorem 4-bis, section 6, Chapter 6.

By paralleling the argument of problem 17, Chapter 6, we obtain another interesting property of the s.c.c. $S_{\lambda,\mu} = C(\text{eff}_{\lambda,\mu}, \cdot)$ when (46) holds: every single valued selection of it, viewed as a game form, strongly implements $S_{\lambda,\mu}$.

This means that any s.c. *function* S which is a selection of $S_{\lambda,\mu}$ has the following property. For all profiles $\boldsymbol{u}$: $S(\text{SE}(S, \boldsymbol{u})) = S_{\lambda,\mu}(\boldsymbol{u})$, where $a \in S(\text{SE}(S, \boldsymbol{u}))$ stands for

$$\exists v \quad a = S(v) \quad \text{and} \quad \forall T, \forall w_T \in L(A)^T : S(w_T, v_{T^c}) \notin \Pr(T, a, \boldsymbol{u}).$$

In particular, every s.c.f. selection of $S_{\lambda,\mu}$ shares the following property, called *exact and strong consistency*:

for all $\boldsymbol{u}$: $S(\boldsymbol{u}) \in S(\text{SE}(s, \boldsymbol{u}))$.

It says that for all profile $\boldsymbol{u}$ another profile exists which is a strong equilibrium with respect to $\boldsymbol{u}$ and selects the same outcome as $\boldsymbol{u}$.

At least three families of game forms are therefore available to strongly implement $S_{\lambda,\mu}$: the voting by veto game forms $g_{\sigma,\lambda}$ (see theorems 3 and

3-bis, Chapter 6), the universal game forms (see theorem 7 above), and the s.c.f. contained in $S_{\lambda,\mu}$. The latter are more appealing because there the message consists simply on announcing a preference ordering. On the other hand, the game forms $g_{\sigma,\lambda}$ share very nice non-cooperative properties (theorems 4 and 4-bis, Chapter 6) which do not seem to have a counterpart in the other game forms mentioned.

We remark, finally, that example 1 above together with theorem 9 show that the proportional veto core is not in general inclusion minimal strongly monotonic.

Theorems 7–9 say a lot about strong implementation, but they do not answer all questions that it raises, except in the case $n = 2$ (corollary 2 of theorem 2).

Given a s.c.c. S, a bundle of necessary conditions emerge for it to be strongly implementable:

S is strongly monotonic,

S is tight and satisfies property (41),

the effectivity function of S is stable and maximal, (47)

S is contained in the core correspondence of its effectivity function.

Whether conditions (47) are *sufficient* to ensure strong implementability of S is an open question.

In problem 23 below we explore the redundancies of conditions (47).

Two other stimulating open questions are the following.

(1) Is every inclusion minimal strongly monotonic s.c.c. strongly implementable? Since I.M.S.M. s.c.c. are known to satisfy conditions (47) (see lemma 6 below), this question makes sense. If the answer is yes, this would at least characterize the inclusion minimal strongly implementable s.c.c.

(2) Since an anonymous and neutral s.c.c. yields anonymous and neutral e.f., we know from the corollary of theorem 4 and theorem 8 that no anonymous, neutral and strongly implementable s.c.c. exists when $n = |N|$ is not relatively prime with respect to $p = |A|$. Conversely, suppose n *is* relatively prime with respect to p. Is the proportional veto core correspondence the only anonymous, neutral and strongly implementable s.c.c.?

Problem 23: The necessary conditions for strong implementability. All the s.c.c. considered are assumed to satisfy strong citizen sovereignty. Given A, N and a s.c.c. S we consider the five following properties:
1. S is strongly monotonic;
2. $\alpha\text{-eff}_S$ is a maximal e.f.;
3. $\alpha\text{-eff}_S$ is a stable e.f. and $S \subset C(\alpha\text{-eff}_S, \cdot)$;
2'. S is tight; and
3'. S satisfies (41)

(1) Prove that the following implications are always true:

$$2 \Rightarrow 2'$$
$$3 \Rightarrow 3' \quad \text{and} \quad 1 + 3' \Rightarrow 3.$$

(2) Prove that among properties 1, 2 and 3 no one is implied by the other two. More precisely, show that

$$2 + 3 \not\Rightarrow 1,$$

$$1 + 3 + 2' \not\Rightarrow 2,$$

$$1 + 2 \not\Rightarrow 3,$$

$$2 + 3' \not\Rightarrow 3.$$

Hint: To prove $1 + 2 \not\Rightarrow 3$, when $n = p - 1$, use the following s.c.c.:

$$S(u) = \{a / \forall i \in N, a \text{ is not ranked last by } i\}.$$

Then generalize to n and p arbitrary. Using this s.c.c. one shows in fact that

$$1 + 2 \not\Rightarrow S \text{ efficient}$$

(whereas S efficient is a consequence of 3').

6. Implementation by Nash equilibrium

All s.c.c. (resp. g.f.) are assumed to satisfy strong citizen sovereignty (resp. citizen sovereignty).

Definition 10. Given A and N, a game form $g = (X_i, i \in N, \pi)$ and a profile $u \in L(A)^N$, we say that an N-tuple $x \in X_N$ is a *Nash equilibrium* of g

at u if we have

$$\forall i \in N, \forall y_i \in X_i : \pi(y_i, x_{N\setminus\{i\}}) \notin \Pr(\{i\}, \pi(x), u).$$

We denote by $\mathrm{NE}(g, u) \subset X_N$ the (possibly empty) set of strong equilibriums of g at u.

Given a social choice correspondence S, we say that g *Nash implements* S if we have

$$\forall u \in L(A)^N : S(u) = \pi(\mathrm{NE}(g, u)).$$

We say that S is Nash implementable if there exists a game form g that Nash implements S.

Behavioural justifications of the Nash equilibrium are not easy to provide. Traditional game theory views it both as a non-cooperative stability notion – when individual agents are myopic, i.e. ignore the possible reactions by the other players to their own moves – and a cooperative concept – a Nash equilibrium outcome is an agreement self-enforced by mutual secrecy. Here we adopt the second cooperative viewpoint: one first a priori reason for doing so is that non-cooperative behaviour is more accurately described by the sophisticated equilibrium. Sophisticated equilibria are in particular Nash equilibria and for dominance-solvable games they yield a unique equilibrium outcome. On the contrary, Nash equilibrium outcomes can *never* be unique for all profiles (see theorem 10 below). One could object to this argument that sophisticated behaviour requires complete information for the agents. But, as will be apparent from the game forms constructed in the proof of theorems 11 and 12, the *same* complete information assumption is needed to justify the Nash equilibrium behaviour of the agents involved in these game forms. This behaviour, moreover, will be seen to be cooperative in essence: this is our second, a posteriori, argument that will come to full clarity only after the proof of theorem 11.

We remark first that strong monotonicity is a necessary condition for Nash implementability.

Theorem 10 (Maskin, 1977). A Nash implementable s.c.c. is strongly monotonic.

Corollary. If A contains at least three outcomes, a social choice *function* satisfying strong citizen sovereignty is Nash implementable if and only if it is dictatorial.

The proof of theorem 10 exactly parallels that of theorem 9 and therefore will be omitted.

Definition 11. We shall say that the s.c.c. S is *closed* if the following three conditions hold:
 (i) S is strongly monotonic;
 (ii) $\alpha\text{-eff}_S$ is maximal; and
 (iii) S satisfies (41).

We have seen in section 5 above that all strongly implementable s.c.c. are closed. In fact (see problem 24) conditions (i), (ii) and (iii) together imply that S is tight and contained in the core of its associated (hence stable) effectivity function.

Theorem 11. A closed s.c.c. is Nash implementable.

Corollary. An inclusion minimal strongly monotonic s.c.c. is Nash implementable.

Theorem 11 implies in particular that a strongly implementable s.c.c. is Nash implementable as well (a moment's reflection will convince the reader that this statement is by no means obvious). The converse statement is not true: see problem 24 below.

Theorems 10 and 11 characterize the inclusion minimal Nash implementable s.c.c. as being simply the inclusion minimal strongly monotonic s.c.c. (in short I.M.S.M.). Thus, we know the more deterministic s.c.c. that can be Nash implemented. If it is true that I.M.S.M. s.c.c. are *strongly* implementable as well, then Nash implementation lacks its ultimate appeal, since its less demanding equilibrium requirements do not achieve a more deterministic s.c.c. than strong implementation.

Proof of theorem 11. We fix a closed s.c.c. S and construct a game form g that Nash implements S. There the messages will take the following form:

$$x = (a, Z(j), j \in N), \quad \text{where } a \in A \text{ and for all } j, a \in Z(j) \subset A.$$

A message is said to be feasible with respect to S if there exists a profile $u \in L(A)^N$ such that

$$a \in S(u): Z(j) = \{b \in A / u_j(b) \leq u_j(a)\}, \quad \text{all } j \in N.$$

From the S.P.A. property ((6) Chapter 3) this is equivalent to saying:

for all $\boldsymbol{u} \in L(A)^N : (\forall j \in N, Z(j) \subset \{b \in A / u_j(b) \leq u_j(a)\})$

$$\Rightarrow (a \in S(\boldsymbol{u})). \qquad (48)$$

In the game form that Nash implements S the strategy set of every agent is the set of feasible messages with respect to S. Hence, a strategy $x_i = (a_i, Z_i(j); j \in N)$ amounts to a proposed outcome a_i and a profile $\boldsymbol{u}$ such that $a_i \in S(\boldsymbol{u})$. Since S satisfies the S.P.A. property, the fact that $a_i \in S(\boldsymbol{u})$ depends only on the sets $Z_i(j) = \{b \in A / u_j(b) \leq u_j(a)\}$, therefore the only relevant information is the $Z_i(j)$ for all $j \in N$.

We now construct a game form $g = (X_i, i \in N; \pi)$ in the following way. Endow A with some associative addition rule denoted "+" having the following property:

$$\forall a \in A : b \to a + b \text{ is onto } A \qquad (49)$$

(for instance, one can order A arbitrarily and identify it with Z/pZ; see section 2 above).

Next, for every non-empty subset B of A we choose a mapping σ_B from A onto B. Then the decision rule π is defined by

if $x_i = x_j$, all $i, j \in N$, then $\pi(x) = a_i$,

if for some i_0, $x_{i_0} \neq x_i = x_{i'}$, all $i, i' \in N \setminus \{i_0\}$,

then $\pi(x) = \sigma_{Z_i(i_0)}(a_{i_0} + a_i)$, all $i \in N \setminus \{i_0\}$, $\qquad (50)$

if no more than $(n-2)x_i$ coincide, then $\pi(x) = \sum_{i \in N} a_i$.

This game form adopts the proposal made by unanimous agents. Given a unanimous strategy N-tuple, individual i can manipulate the outcome within the set $Z(i)$ on which all other agents agree. Moreover, for all i, if the agents of $N \setminus \{i\}$ are not unanimous, then agent i can manipulate at will the outcome (this last claim is proved below).

Let us fix a profile $\boldsymbol{u} \in L(A)^N$ and choose an outcome $a \in S(\boldsymbol{u})$. Denoting

$Z(j) = \{b \in A / u_j(b) \leq u_j(a)\},$

we claim that the unanimous strategy N-tuple

$$x_i = (a, Z(j); j \in N), \quad \text{all } i \in N,$$

is a Nash equilibrium of g at $\boldsymbol{u}$. Namely, from (49) it follows that

$$\forall y_i \in X_i: \pi(y_i, x_{\hat{\imath}}) \in Z(i) = \Pr(\{i\}, a, \boldsymbol{u})^c.$$

Since $\pi(x) = a$ we conclude

$$S(\boldsymbol{u}) \subset \pi(\text{NE}(g, \boldsymbol{u})), \quad \text{all } \boldsymbol{u} \in L(A)^N.$$

We prove now the converse inclusion. Let x be a Nash equilibrium of g at $\boldsymbol{u}$. Three cases may arise.

Case 1: x is a unanimous strategy N-tuple

$$x_i = (a, Z(j); j \in N), \quad \text{all } i \in N.$$

By (49), (50) and the fact that $\sigma_{Z(i_0)}$ is onto $Z(i_0)$, we deduce that for all $b \in Z(i_0)$ there exists an outcome a' such that

$$\sigma_{Z(i_0)}(a' + a) = b.$$

Let x'_{i_0} be a feasible message of agent i_0,

$$x'_{i_0} = (a', Z'(j), j \in N),$$

that differs from x_i. Then by (50)

$$\pi(x'_{i_0}, x_{\hat{\imath}_0}) = b.$$

If $a' = a$ the existence of an x'_{i_0} different from x_i is proved in case 2. Hence, we have

$$\pi(X_{i_0} \times \{x_{\hat{\imath}_0}\}) = Z(i_0).$$

Hence, from the Nash equilibrium property of x we have

$$Z(i_0) \subset \Pr(\{i_0\}, a, \boldsymbol{u})^c = \{b \in A / u_{i_0}(b) \leq u_{i_0}(a)\}.$$

By (48) this yields $a \in S(\boldsymbol{u})$, the desired conclusion.

Case 2. At most $(n-2)$ among the x_i are equal. Then for all i there are some i_1 and i_2, both different from i, such that $x_{i_1} \neq x_{i_2}$. For all b there exists by (49) an outcome a such that

$$a + \sum_{i' \neq i} a_{i'} = b.$$

We claim the existence of a strategy $y_i = (a, Z(j), j \in N)$ such that at most $(n-2)$ strategies among $(y_i, x_{\hat{i}})$ coincide, and delay the proof of this claim for a moment.

Thus, $\pi(y_i, x_{\hat{i}}) = b$ and we have

$$\pi(X_i, x_{i\hat{i}}) = A, \quad \text{all } i \in N.$$

By the Nash equilibrium property of x this implies

$$\pi(x) = \text{top candidate of } u_i, \quad \text{all } i \in N.$$

Hence, $\pi(x) \in S(u)$ follows from the efficiency of S (a closed s.c.c. is efficient by the strong citizen sovereignty assumption).

It remains to prove the claim. Suppose first that $n \geq 4$. Given a, agent i is allowed to choose any feasible strategy of the form

$$(a, Z(j), j \in N).$$

Denote their set by $X(a)$. By efficiency of $S(a, A, j \in N)$ belongs to $X(a)$; henceforth $|X(a)| \geq 1$. If $|X(a)| \geq 2$ and at most one of x_{i_1} and x_{i_2} belongs to $X(a)$, then agent i can choose a strategy in $X(a)$ different from x_{i_1} and x_{i_2}, and the claim is proved.

If both x_{i_1} and x_{i_2} are in $X(a)$, our assumption $n \geq 4$ allows again agent i to choose $y_i \in X(a)$ in such a way that the claim holds true.

It remains to prove that $|X(a)| = 1$ is absurd. Namely, it implies that for all profiles u of the form

$$\begin{cases} u_j: b \text{ on top, } a \text{ second,} \\ u_i: a \text{ on top, all } i \neq j. \end{cases}$$

then indeed $S(u) = \{b\}$ (by the efficiency of S). By the SPA property of S this implies that every agent is effective for every singleton $\{b\}$, $b \neq a$. If

$p \geq 3$, this is clearly a contradiction. If $p = 2$, then S is the following s.c.c.:

$$S(u) = \{a\}, \quad \text{if } u_i(a) > u_i(b) \text{ for all } i,$$
$$= \{b\}, \quad \text{otherwise.}$$

In particular S is strategy-proof and Nash implemented by itself!

Suppose, finally, $n = 3$. Then if the claim fails we get $|X(a)| \leq 2$ which, by a similar argument, implies a contradiction when $p \geq 3$ and again yields a self-implementing s.c.c. when $p = 2$.

Case 3. Exactly $(n-1)$ among the x_i coincide, say

$$x_{i_0} \neq x_i = x_{i'} = (\bar{a}, Z(j); j \in N), \quad \text{all } i, i' \neq i_0.$$

The arguments developed in cases 1 and 2 yield

$$\pi(X_{i_0} \times \{x_{\hat{i}_0}\}) = Z(i_0),$$
$$\pi(X_i \times \{x_{\hat{i}}\}) = A, \quad \text{all } i \neq i_0.$$

Hence, by the Nash equilibrium property of x and denoting $a = \pi(x)$ (possibly different from $\bar{a}$), we have

$$a \in Z(i_0) \text{ and } u_{i_0}(b) \leq u_{i_0}(a), \quad \text{all } b \in Z_{i_0},$$
$$a = \text{top outcome of } u_i, \quad \text{all } i \neq i_0.$$

Suppose now $a \notin S(u)$, and consider a profile v such that

$$v_{i_0} = u_{i_0},$$
$$a = \text{top outcome of } v_i, \quad \text{all } i \neq i_0,$$
$$Z(i_0) \text{ is on top of } v_{N \setminus \{i_0\}}.$$

Then by SPA, $a \notin S(v)$. By the efficiency of S, this implies

$$S(v) \cap Z(i_0) = \emptyset.$$

Denote by eff the e.f. associated with S. Since S is closed eff satisfies (41). Hence, $N \setminus \{i_0\}$ eff $Z(i_0)$ would imply $S(v) \subset Z(i_0)$. Thus, $N \setminus \{i_0\}$ is not effective for $Z(i_0)$ and by the maximality of eff this implies

$$\{i_0\}\text{eff } B, \quad \text{where } B = Z(i_0)^c. \tag{51}$$

But $(\bar{a}, Z(j), j \in N)$ has to be a feasible message so that for some profile w

$$\bar{a} \in S(w)$$

and

$$Z(i_0) = \{b / w_{i_0}(b) \leq w_{i_0}(\bar{a})\}.$$

This last property implies that B is on top of w_{i_0}, which by (41) and (51) gives

$$S(w) \subset B,$$

a contradiction.

This concludes the proof of theorem 11.

The corollary of theorem 11 results from the following.

Lemma 6. *An inclusion minimal strongly monotonic s.c.c. is closed.*

Proof. Let S be an I.M.S.M. s.c.c. We have seen (problem 7, Chapter 3) that for every u and a such that $a \in S(u)$, we have

$$\exists v : S(v) = \{a\} \text{ and } \forall i \{b / u_i(b) < u_i(a)\} = \{b / v_i(b) < v_i(a)\}. \tag{52}$$

Let us prove first that S satisfies (41). Fix T and B both non-empty such that

$$T\alpha\text{-eff}_S B.$$

Choose u_T such that

$$\forall u_{T^c} S(u_T, u_{T^c}) \subset B.$$

Now consider the profile v_T for T defined by

B is on top of v_T,

u_T and v_T coincide on B and on B^c.

Since the operation from u to v will be used often in the sequel we name it "v_T is obtained by lifting B on top of u_T".
By the strong monotonicity of S we still have

$$\forall u_{T^c}: S(v_T, u_{T^c}) \subset B. \tag{53}$$

Now take any w_T with B on top. We must prove

$$\forall u_{T^c}: S(w_T, u_{T^c}) \subset B.$$

Suppose this fails: for some w_{T^c} and a we have

$$a \in B^c: a \in S(w_T, w_{T^c}). \tag{54}$$

By SPA we can choose w_T that preserves (54) and further satisfies

B is on top of w_T,

a is on top of B^c in w_T. $\tag{55}$

By (52) we can choose w_T such that, in addition to (55), we have

$$a \in B^c: \{a\} = S(w_T, w_{T^c}). \tag{56}$$

Now let us define $\bar{w}_T$ by

B is on top of $\bar{w}_T$,

$\bar{w}_T$ and w_T coincide on B,

$\bar{w}_T$ and v_T coincide on B^c.

Thus, we have

$\forall b \in B$: the position of b is preserved from $(\bar{w}_T, w_{T^c})$ to (w_T, w_{T^c}) implying by (56) $S(\bar{w}_T, w_{T^c}) \subset B^c$.

Moreover,

$\forall b \in B^c$: the position of b is preserved from $(\bar{w}_T, w_{T^c})$ to (v_T, w_{T^c}).

Therefore $S(\bar{w}_T, w_{T^c}) \subset S(v_T, w_{T^c})$, a contradiction of (53).

We now prove that the e.f. $\alpha\text{-eff}_S$ is maximal. Namely, choose T and B both non-empty, $T \neq N$ and $B \neq A$, and denote by $\mathcal{U}(T, B)$ the subset of profiles $\boldsymbol{u}$ such that

B is on top of u_T,

B^c is on top of u_{T^c}.

Suppose now that there exists two profiles, $\boldsymbol{u}$ and $\boldsymbol{v}$, such that

$$\boldsymbol{u}, \boldsymbol{v} \in \mathcal{U}(T, B) \text{ and } S(\boldsymbol{u}) \subset B : S(\boldsymbol{v}) \subset B^c. \tag{57}$$

Then consider the profile $w \in \mathcal{U}(T, B)$ defined by

w_T coincides with v_T on B,

with u_T on B^c;

w_{T^c} coincides with u_{T^c} on B^c,

with v_{T^c} on B.

For any $a \in B$ the position of a is preserved from w to v. Hence, by (57): $a \notin S(w)$. For any $a \in B^c$, the position of a is preserved from w to $\boldsymbol{u}$. Hence, by (57): $a \notin S(w)$.

Therefore (57) is not true. This implies that one of the three following situations arises:

$$\forall \boldsymbol{u} \in \mathcal{U}(T, B): S(\boldsymbol{u}) \subset B, \tag{58}$$

$$\forall \boldsymbol{v} \in \mathcal{U}(T, B): S(\boldsymbol{v}) \subset B^c, \tag{59}$$

$$\exists \boldsymbol{u} \in \mathcal{U}(T, B): S(\boldsymbol{u}) \cap B \neq \emptyset \neq S(\boldsymbol{u}) \cap B^c. \tag{60}$$

Condition (58) is equivalent, by the strong monotonicity of S, to T $\alpha\text{-eff}_S B$. Similarly, (59) means $T^c \alpha\text{-eff}_S B^c$. Thus, the corollary is proved if we only show that condition (60) yields a contradiction. We fix $\boldsymbol{u} \in \mathcal{U}(T, B)$ and a, b such that

$$a \in S(\boldsymbol{u}) \cap B^c; \quad b \in S(\boldsymbol{u}) \cap B.$$

Now let v be a profile such that

$v \in \mathcal{U}(T, B)$,
for all $a' \in B^c$: $v_i(a') \leqslant v_i(a)$,
for all $b' \in B$: $v_i(b') \leqslant v_i(b)$, all $i \in N$.

Since the position of a (resp. b) is preserved from u to v we have

$a, b \in S(v)$

Applying property (52) to a and v we get a profile w such that

B is on top of w_T,
for all $a' \in B^c$: $v_i(a') \leqslant v_i(a)$, all $i \in T$,
a is on top of w_{T^c},

and $S(w) = \{a\}$.

By lifting B^c on top of w_{T^c} we obtain a profile $w' \in \mathcal{U}(T, B)$. By strong monotonicity of S we will have $S(w') \subset B^c$. A symmetrical application of (52) to b and v yields the existence of a profile $w'' \in \mathcal{U}(T, B)$ such that $S(w'') \subset B$. Then we are back to the absurd property (57). ∎

The game form constructed above to implement any closed s.c.c. is essentially a coordination game where the Nash stability can be reached only if all agents, or at least $(n-1)$ agents, agree on their messages. This should make clear that the Nash equilibrium can be reached only be an intense exchange of information processes. In that context, however, coalitions are likely to form so that cooperative stability (as embodied in the strong equilibrium notion) is a more natural requirement.

The converse statement of theorem 10 yields an open question: Is any strongly monotonic s.c.c. Nash implementable?

Problem 24: Maskin's sufficient conditions for Nash implementability. Say that a social choice correspondence S gives no veto power to individual agents if

for all $i \in N$ and all $a \in A$: $N \setminus \{i\} \alpha\text{-eff}_S \{a\}$.

(1) Prove that a strongly monotonic s.c.c. that gives no veto power to individual agents is Nash implementable.
(2) Prove that a neutral strongly monotonic s.c.c. is Nash implementable.
(3) Give an example of a Nash implementable s.c.c. which is not closed.

Problem 25: On α-implementation.

(1) Let eff be a stable (not maximal) effectivity function. Prove the existence of at least one stable and maximal effectivity function eff_0 such that

$$T \text{eff } B \Rightarrow T \text{eff}_0 B, \quad \text{all } T \text{ and } B. \tag{61}$$

(2) Say that a s.c.c. S is α-implemented if the following holds true:

$$S(\boldsymbol{u}) = C(\alpha\text{-eff}_S, \boldsymbol{u}), \quad \text{all } \boldsymbol{u} \in L(A)^N.$$

Interpret this definition and compare it to the notion of strong implementability. Characterize the inclusion minimal α-implementable s.c.c.

(3) Let eff be the e.f. derived from a simple game (N, W) on A and suppose that

$$|A| < \nu,$$

where ν is the Nakamura number of (N, W).

Suppose (N, W) is not a weighted majority game. Then construct a non-additive effectivity function on A that is stable and maximal and, moreover,

$$T \in W \Rightarrow (T \text{eff}\{a\}, \quad \text{all } a \in A).$$

References

Abdou, J., 1981, Stabilité et maximalité des fonctions veto, Thèse, CEREMADE, Université Paris IX.
Maskin, E., 1977, "Nash equilibrium and welfare optimality", forthcoming in Mathematics of Operations Research.
Maskin, E., 1979, "Implementation and strong Nash equilibrium", in: J.J. Laffont, ed., Aggregation and Revelation of Preferences, North-Holland, Amsterdam.
Moulin, H., 1982, "Voting with proportional veto power", Econometrica, 50, 145–162.
Moulin, H. and B. Peleg, 1982, "Stability and implementation of effectivity functions", Journal of Mathematical Economics, 10, 115–145.
Nakamura, K., 1975, "The core of a simple game with ordinal preferences", International Journal of game theory 4, 95–104.
Peleg, B., 1982, Convex effectivity functions, Research memorandum no. 46, The Hebrew University of Jerusalem, Israel.

INDEX

additive effectivity function, 163–164, 173, 177, 187
agents, *18*
alternating veto, voting by, 141
anonymous
   social choice function or correspondence, *22*, 63
   veto function, 120
approval voting, 9
Arrow's theorem, 54
auction, Vickrey's, 12
auctioning the leadership, 12–13
average monotonicity, 86

battle of the sexes, 82
Bayesian equilibrium, 12
binary choices, voting by, 88–89, 91, 96
binary social choice function, 62–65
Black social choice correspondence, 38
Borda
   loser, 38
   scoring correspondence, *20*, 161, 169, 170
   scoring s.c.f., 112
   winner, 30

choice set, 19
citizen sovereignty, *48*, 65, 159
closed social choice correspondence, 202
coalitionally easy, social choice function, 106
coalitional manipulations, 70, 143–144, 188
committee, 1
Condorcet
   cycle, 30, 35, 67, 170
   paradox, 4–5, 27
   set, *30*
   type s.c.c., *46*, 67, 91, 160
   winner, 4–5, *26*, 30, 69, 91, 124–125
Coombs social choice
   correspondence, 38
   function, 24
Copeland social choice correspondence, 27–28, 35, 38, 67, 170

Core, 122
   veto, 142
   of an effectivity function, 176, 189, 190

demand revealing mechanism, 12
democracy, 3, 59
dictatorial social choice function, 48
divide and choose method, 12
domains of preferences, 8–9
   restriction of, 66, 68–75
dominance-solvable, game form, 10, *79*, 91, 93, 104, 108, 109, 174
dominated strategy, 79
dominating strategy, 61, 78

effectivity function, 11, *157*
   *-effectivity function, 169–170, 192
   α and β effectivity functions, 159, 160, 166, 172
efficient, social choice function, or correspondence, 20
elimination of dominated strategies, 79
equilibrium concept, 9–11
exact and strong consistency, 198

game form, *60*, 79
Gibbard-Satterthwaite theorem, 65

implementation, 3–4
   α-implementation, 211
improvement, of an outcome, 35
   elementary, 39
imputation, social choice correspondence, 47
incentive, economics of, 11–13
inclusion minimal strongly monotonic s.c.c., *47*, 148, 198, 202, 207
independence of irrelevant alternatives, 54
integer veto, voting by, 135–136

Kramer social choice correspondence, *28*, 35, 38, 67, 170

linear order, 18

213

majority principle, 4, 26, 69, 118–119
marriage lemma, 145
maximal effectivity functions, *171*–176
message space, 60
Miller's uncovered set, 31, 35, 170
minority principle, 5, 119–120
monotonic social choice
 correspondence, 35
 function, 36, 62, 97

Nakamura number, of a simple game, 184, 211
Nansen social choice correspondence, 38
Nash equilibrium, 200
 implementation by, 201
Nash implementable social choice correspondence, *201*–210
neutral, social choice function or correspondence, *23*, 63
non-cooperative agents, 61

outcome, 18

Pareto optimum, 20
 set, 20–21, 43
plurality
 correspondence, *19*, 80–82
 losers, 24
 with run-off, 34
preference profile, 18
Prisoner's dilemma, 61
proportional veto
 function, 121, 126–127, 179, 183
 core, 122–126

quota majority, 63
 games, 120

Rawlsian
 maximal candidates, 82–85
 social choice function, 82, 112
risk-averse implementation, 86, 101, 102

scoring
 method 4-correspondence, *19*, 30, 44, 67
 social choice function, 111–112
sequential elimination, voting by, 87, *90*, 97, 101
simple games, 157, 184
single peaked preference
 on a tree, 73
 ordering, 70
social choice
 correspondence, 18
 function, 18

social welfare functions, 52
sophisticated
 implementation, *80*, 91
 social choice functions, 102, 106, 114, 174
 voting, 10, 101, 138, 150
stable
 effectivity functions, *176*–185
 veto function, 122
strategic voting, 7–11, 78
strategy set, 60
strategy-proof
 game form, *61*, 74
 social choice correspondence, 67
 social choice function, 61–65, 68
strong equilibrium, 142–143, 148
 implementation by, 188
strong positive association, 41
strongly implementable, social choice correspondence, *188*–200
strongly monotonic social choice
 correspondence, 11, *39*, 41, 43–47, 67, 196, 201, 210
 function, 48
subadditive effectivity functions, 180–181
successive amendments, voting by, *90*, 96, 101
superadditive effectivity functions, 157, 166, 172, 174

tight, game form or social choice correspondence, 160, 172, 174, 190, 199
transitive majority domain, 71

unanimity
 property, 6, 21, 48
 with status quo, 158
unanimous approval, voting by, 105
uncovered set, 31, 35
universal game form, 166–167, 175, 189

veto
 anonymous voting by, 151
 core, 142, 151
 function, 120, 158, 169
 general voting by, 149, 164
 voting by, 5, 83
 voting by alternating, 141
 voting by integer, 135–136
 voting by successive, 78, 105
voting method, 2, 4–5

weakly strategy-proof s.c.c., 67
winning coalitions, 64, 120

zero veto power, social choice function with, 170

DATE DUE

MAY 23 1986			

DEMCO 38-297